to Ruth:–
  to quote (loosely)
Richard Eder: "A memoir
has the urgency of a
quest; it represents
something the author
has _lost_ — "

Refugees from Hollywood

Best,
Jean Rouverol

REFUGEES
from Hollywood

A Journal of the Blacklist Years

JEAN ROUVEROL

University of New Mexico Press

Albuquerque

Library of Congress Cataloging-in-Publication Data

Rouverol, Jean.
Refugees from Hollywood : a journal of the blacklist years / Jean Rouverol.
— 1st ed.
p. cm.
ISBN 0-8263-2266-2 (alk. paper)
1. Rouverol, Jean. 2. Butler, Hugo, 1914–1968. 3. Screenwriters—United
States—Biography. 4. Blacklisting of authors—United States. I. Title.
PN1998.2 .R74 2000
812' .5409—dc21
00-009135

To

Ramona

in memoriam

and to

her country, which took us in

when we needed

a home

Prologue

"Estas son las mañanitas
Que cantaba el rey David
A las muchachas bonitas
Se las cantaban así . . ."

IT WAS A COOL, DARK predawn, and the singers' voices, five or six of them, all male, drifted in the windows and reached with sudden and startling clarity into my sleep. I struggled to the surface and for a moment or two, confused, tried to think where I was and what was happening.

Ensenada. We were in Ensenada. . . .

The singing, curious, disembodied, was coming from outside our landlords' bungalow, across the yard from our garage apartment. The rest of the town was altogether silent, and the cool air smelled just faintly of the ocean, half a mile or so away.

"Despierta, mi bien, despierta,
Mira que ya amaneció.
Ya los pajaritos cantan,
La luna ya se metió . . ."

The singers were singing in perfect harmony and were obviously cold sober. So what in the world, I wondered, were they doing out there before it was even daylight?

I felt Hugo stirring beside me; he was awake now too. For a few minutes we both lay listening, silent, neither of us wanting to dispel the strangeness and enchantment of the music. There was no sound from the living room next to us, where the children were scattered about on their various cots and couches—and one folding lawn chair that our littlest, Emily, used as a bed. They went on sleeping.

> *"El día en que tu naciste,*
> *Nacieron todas las flores,*
> *Y en la pila de tu bautismo*
> *Cantarón los ruiseñores . . ."*

We didn't understand a word, of course; we'd both had high school French but no Spanish. We just lay there in the darkness, almost afraid to move for fear the song might end. And then it did, and the magic vanished. We heard Mr. and Mrs. Gonzales at their back door, laughing and applauding. There was a murmur of conversation, and the singers disappeared, on invitation, I suppose, into the house. A door closed, and there was silence again.

After a while a faint pale glimmer of daylight began to form in the square of our windows, but Hugo and I still lay there—both of us, I guess, overwhelmed once again by the strangeness of the place we'd come to, and the reason we'd come.

Actually, we were ducking a subpoena.

PART ONE

. . . We few, we happy few, we band of brothers;
For he to-day that sheds his blood with me
Shall be my brother . . .

(Henry V, Act IV, Sc. iii)

Chapter One

THE YEAR WAS 1951. Our troubles had begun a few months before, in January. No, that's not quite true. The seeds of our troubles had really begun in the midforties, when the country's wartime alliance with the Soviet Union had fallen apart and the Cold War had taken its place.

It was a curious time in American history. Politicians of both parties had quickly learned they could build whole careers on the single issue of anti-Communism. By the end of the decade a hard-drinking freshman senator named Joseph McCarthy was accusing the State Department of harboring Communists, and—of more immediate concern to us—the House of Representatives' Un-American Activities Committee (HUAC) had been garnering banner headlines with their investigations of left-wingers in Hollywood. They were also interested, of course, in discrediting the infant labor movement in the film industry and grilled each witness on his union affiliation as though this too were an ominous symptom of disloyalty. But their primary question was the now famous, "Are you now or have you ever been a member of the Communist Party?"

This query had a distinct "Have you stopped beating your wife lately?" quality to it, and several of the witnesses had insisted on answering in their own words, which the committee was not disposed to allow. So a number of shouting matches had ensued. But our friend Ring Lardner Jr.—good-looking, Oscar-winning son of a famous writer father—had been unflappable. "I could answer that question, Mr. Chairman," he had said. "But if I did, I'd hate myself in the morning."

Irony had availed him nothing, however, nor had the anger or eloquence of his fellows. Our other close friend Dalton Trumbo, enjoined to answer the committee's questions with only a yes or a no, had averred that many questions could be so answered "only by a moron or a slave," and the committee didn't like that either. In any event, the hearings ended with the "Hollywood Ten" cited for contempt of Congress, and after fruitless appeals, they had flown east the end of May 1950 to be sentenced. Two of them would receive six-month sentences, and Dalton, Ring, and the others, facing a harsher judge, would be given a year.

We heard later that Ring and his fellow writer Lester Cole, lodged initially in a Washington jail, were told they could serve their time in Connecticut since both had mothers living there, and, bound for Danbury, they had departed their temporary quarters handcuffed to federal marshals. But partway en route they'd had to change trains, and the marshals, with no idea where to find their connection, got lost in the station. So Ring, handcuffed to them, obligingly showed them the way.

Almost coincidentally with the start of the Ten's sentences, the Korean War had broken out. By the following January, Cold War passions were riding hotter than ever—when out on the West Coast rumors raced through Hollywood that a new sweep had begun.

Hugo and I at that point were working on a little domestic comedy at Columbia Studios. One evening late in the month we heard that several more of our fellow writers—including Waldo Salt, who had not only introduced me to Hugo, back in my acting days, but later had also invited us to join the party—had just received their billets-doux from HUAC's marshals, and Hugo, dressing for work the next morning, decided that he'd better not come home that night just in case. "I've tried the army," he said. "And I *know* I wouldn't like jail."

So he had elected to have dinner at a restaurant with his agent and a couple of our non-Red friends and perhaps to sleep away from home. Which is why I, in turn, was eating alone with the children in the dining room that night when we heard the doorbell ring.

I knew with absolute certainty who was outside.

And sure enough, when I looked through the peephole in the door, I saw what I was afraid of: two men with hats, standing under the porch light.

Now, as anyone who's ever lived in Los Angeles knows, no southern Californian ever wears a hat unless it's raining. Those two men might as well have been wearing placards. They didn't identify themselves, however; they merely asked for Hugo Butler.

I said he wasn't in. They asked when he would be. I said I didn't know. They asked where he could be reached. I said I had no idea.

Things seemed to require some sort of amplification. "We've had a little disagreement," I said, improvising wildly and frightened to the point of tears, "and I don't know where he's gone or *when* he'll be back."

The two men looked at each other, clearly unconvinced. Then they shrugged, said they'd be back, and left.

I closed the peephole window and tried to think what to do. If they had our address, they must have our phone number too, and our phone might be tapped. So I couldn't phone an alert to Hugo, at least not from here.

I went back to the dinner table. Not to eat—I couldn't, my heart was pounding too hard—but merely to give the visitors time to leave the neighborhood. I asked our housekeeper, Sarah, to put the children to bed, filled a couple of laundry bags (to legitimatize my departure in case anyone was still lurking outside), called a cab (they might know our license-plate number), and went to an all-night Laundromat a few blocks away to drop off the laundry and call the restaurant from a pay phone.

I asked for Hugo, and in a moment he came on the line. "Honey," I said. "Get on your horse."

There was a pause. "No shit," he said.

The next few days had a curious, improvisational quality to them. I don't know why we had never quite accepted the likelihood that this would happen; perhaps, like death, it simply seemed too melodramatic to apply to *us*. But there we were, without even a change of clothing or our toothbrushes, moving each night to the house of a different friend while we tried to formulate a plan of action and cope with all the loose ends. For the moment, we could only hope there would be no publicity about the subpoena so we could keep on working for a while longer. The one thing we would certainly need, with our long-range livelihoods in the industry now at stake, was money enough to live on for the foreseeable future.

There were other problems. Our four children, for instance. Our lively, inquisitive ten-year-old son Mike; his elfin, deceptively gentle sister Susie; our kindergartner Mary; and our eighteen-month-old Emily were wonderful children and we adored them, but we were finding that they made it very hard to duck a subpoena.

We chose the obvious solution. Having spent the previous decade trying to convince our two mothers that we really could raise our children as competently as *they* could, we swallowed our pride and distributed the oldest two to Hugo's mother and stepfather, who lived in a tiny hillside bungalow in Hollywood near our elementary school, and our Dutch-bobbed Mary and her little sister to my mother, down in the respectable, white-bread part of town near the country club. But we'd still need some plausible story to explain to Hugo's father, who'd had a heart attack recently and shouldn't be upset, why we were taking this abrupt and unlikely vacation.

As for the laundry, it stayed at the Laundromat for a week till I screwed up the courage to go back and pick it up.

Most unnerving of all, however, was reporting for work each morning at Columbia Studios, our clothes rumpled from having been slept in all night and our hearts in our throats for fear we'd be met at the gate by a U.S. marshal. We convinced our producer to move our story conferences to Palm Springs, where, in Hugo's mother's name, we rented a cottage on the outskirts of the village—and where we found we couldn't set foot outdoors without bumping into someone else in full flight. When Hugo went to the local barbershop for a haircut, the man in the next chair whose face was covered by a hot towel turned out, when the towel was removed, to be our friend Mickey Uris, another left-wing screenwriter on the run.

At this rate it was inevitable that the two men in hats would soon figure out where we were.

So we wrote at a feverish pace to finish our little Bob Cummings–Barbara Hale comedy, turned in our pages, said good-bye to Palm

Springs, and hit the road again. We were still paying rent on our house in Hollywood, with all our worldly goods inside, but it stood locked up and tenantless. We were afraid to go back even to pack up and move out. In any event, where to? We still had no long-range plans. . . .

With our ever-present need for survival money in mind, Hugo had arranged to start work immediately on a screenplay, *The Big Night,* with his director friend Joseph Losey, who had his own reasons for wanting to avoid Los Angeles. As a student, Joe had gone to the Soviet Union to study Russian theater—innocent enough when one's in college, but from a Cold War perspective, something that might look very suspicious indeed. So now, packing a portable typewriter, piles of yellow pads, and a minimum of baggage, the two men set out to move from one obscure motel to another through central and northern California, planning their script on the run and staying well out of the way of U.S. marshals.

As for me: I had no writing job now, but I did have a little radio job, the only relic of my acting days. For a dozen years or so I'd had a part on a long-running radio serial called *One Man's Family*—a rambling, lovable piece of Americana that whole families, all over the United States, had grown up listening to. I had developed a strong feeling of fellowship with the other cast members, but they knew little of my political life and nothing whatever of our current troubles. Now, turning up once or twice a week for taping sessions at the broadcasting station and confiding nothing to these nice people made me feel as though I were in disguise.

I was staying by now at my mother's with our two youngest, who seemed to be adapting comfortably to their change of abode, though small Emily had taken on occasion to waking up and crying inconsolably in the middle of the night. And sometimes on weekends I drove north to join Hugo in unlikely places like Walnut Creek or Castroville, the artichoke capital of the world, for a brief, anxiety-ridden reunion.

But in fact, we were treading water. What were we going to do with our lives from now on? When the not-very-impressive money we were presently earning or the modest sum we had managed to save was spent—how would we earn more?

Then in spring we heard that Dalton Trumbo had earned two months off his sentence for good behavior and was out of jail. Accordingly, I rendezvoused with Hugo, and we set out for the Ridge Route, in the Tehachapi Mountains, to drive to the Trumbos' ranch.

The Lazy T, a rambling Xanadu of a place, had started life as a scraggly little farmhouse on property worked by a cantankerous Trumbo uncle. The acreage, a few thousand feet above sea level, was covered with brush and scrub pine, with a brook running through it. It was land no crop could grow on, and any horse put out there to forage would surely starve. But Trumbo, his wife, Cleo, and their three children loved it, and during Trumbo's half-dozen prosperous years before the congressional hearings, they had remodeled, expanded, and refurbished till the house was transformed, with picture windows, marble fireplaces, oil paintings, and more silver bric-a-brac than I'd ever seen—all out in the middle of nowhere. Trumbo's father had died young, leaving the family in near poverty, and even after Trumbo had begun to sell his writing, he had supported his mother and sisters by working nights in a bakery. Reason enough, I guess, for him to become (as Ring would observe in a sixties magazine article) inexorably devoted to conspicuous consumption.

In past years we'd spent holidays there, our children and theirs melding into one large and happy gang. We'd also gone up often to keep Cleo company during Trumbo's jail sentence. Now, leaving the highway for the bumpy little road that would take us past all human habitation, and driving along stretches of high desert and patches of stunted pinewood to reach the familiar scrub-lined lake (created when Trumbo had dammed up the brook), and winding finally up the last little scrub-lined hill to get to his house, we couldn't help wondering how jail had affected him. He was, after all, the first person we'd ever known who'd served time.

We needn't have worried. Apart from his jailhouse pallor, he had settled back into his customary sybaritism without missing a beat. That evening, over Scotch and a good dinner, with firelight glinting on silver, he and Hugo considered the alternatives that faced us all and by midnight had decided, in a general way, on Mexico. Cleo and I, idolatrous wives that we were, agreed without a moment's hesitation.

Why Mexico?

For one thing, Trumbo had learned there was a good American school in Mexico City. For another, Hugo and I had never been abroad, so we'd never bothered to apply for passports. One didn't need a pass-port for Canada, of course, but Hugo had grown up there and the climate depressed him. Also, he had recently finished a screenplay of Defoe's *Robinson Crusoe,* and one of our friends already self-exiled in Mexico thought he could raise financing for a Mexican production.

Trumbo too was anxious to get away. The Hollywood Ten—or rather, the Hollywood Nine, since one of their number, director Edward Dmytryk, had turned friendly witness on his release from jail—were all worried that their recent imprisonment was only a prelude; they were afraid they might be resubpoenaed, asked the same question as before ("Are you now or have you ever been . . . ?"), and indicted on a brand-new charge of contempt, which could not really be construed as double jeopardy.

It was a worrisome possibility. The Hollywoodians, scattered about the South and East in various "houses of correction" (the government's euphemism for penitentiary), had tried to make the best of their incar-ceration. Ring had organized an ongoing jailhouse bridge tournament. Novelist Sam Ornitz had set up a group counseling program for his fellow prisoners, and to this day a plaque in the prison hospital com-memorates his service. Writer-producer Adrian Scott, a gentle, quiet man interned with Trumbo at Ashland, Kentucky, had become the Scheherezade of Cell Block Seven, endlessly spinning old movie plots for the entertainment of the other jailbirds. Nonetheless, for all of them, it had been a nightmare confrontation with a real and ugly world. Trumbo himself, since he could type, had been given the not-too-onerous job of warden's secretary and had struck up a few color-ful friendships (with men serving time for bootlegging, mostly), so the experience hadn't been pure hell. But he certainly had no wish to repeat it.

Even more serious was the threat of "relocation camps."

Another euphemism. The preceding year, Congress had passed the McCarran Act, authorizing the attorney general to intern "potential spies or saboteurs" in time of "war or insurrection." We knew the definitions could be loosely applied, and in view of the increasing un-popularity of the Korean War and the administration's fear of mass protests, there was a good chance they might be applied to people like us. A rumor persisted, in our circles, that the camps at Manzanar—vast acres of plywood dormitories, row on row, surrounded by barbed wire, where coastal residents of Japanese ancestry (even U.S. citizens) had been summarily interned during World War II—were being readied for pacifists and left-wingers. We didn't know if the rumor was true (we learned years later that it was, although since protests against the Korean War had never materialized, the arrests never took place). But in the current political climate, anything was possible, and we should probably leave the country as soon as we could.

But neither family, at the moment, was quite ready. After ten months in jail Trumbo was well-nigh penniless and would have to sell the ranch before he could make the trip. And Hugo and I had still not scraped together enough money to feel secure. We tried to reassure ourselves that if Hugo continued the Joe Losey job in out-of-the-way places and we both kept a low profile, we might be safe for a while longer . . .

Or would we?

It must have been late April or early May. I was driving up the coast from Carlsbad after a visit with Hugo's stepmother, who was still under the impression that Hugo and I were on "a sort of vacation," and in all honesty, I guess I had begun to find our precarious, spit-and-baling-wire life tolerable or even exciting. It was early twilight; the little beach towns were disappearing behind me, and now and then I had a few minutes' view of the ocean and the curve of the coastline. I was listening without much attention to the news on the car radio—when the newscaster read a bulletin from HUAC about the Hollywood figures they'd been unable to serve with subpoenas.

Highway, coastline, ocean vanished. I kept on driving, but blindly, as I listened to the names he read off: Paul Jarrico, who had won an Oscar nomination for his original screenplay of *Tom, Dick and Harry*. Fred Rinaldo, husband of my oldest friend and cowriter of a stream of *Three Stooges* and *Abbott and Costello* comedies. His collaborator, Robert Lees. A few more names I don't remember now.

And Hugo Butler.

As always in a crisis, my mind went into a sort of overdrive, functioning quite on its own. First, what to do about Hugo's father, with his heart condition? I pulled into the first gas station and phoned Hugo's stepsister to forewarn her and to suggest that she break the news to him gently. Then, back on the road again, I tried to figure out the best, quickest, safest thing for Hugo to do. . . .

Baja. The Mexican side of the border was completely unregulated. Mexico was too eager for tourist dollars to fret about any of the daily thousands crowding *into* Baja, and in all likelihood, I figured, the Americans would only question people coming *back*. . . .

It was evening by the time I caught up with Hugo in his current hideout, a little vacation rental cottage in Newport Beach, and found that friends had already phoned him about the broadcast and offered to drive him to Tijuana. While he was throwing his things in a bag, we tried distractedly to figure out our moves. He would look for a place south of Tijuana—Ensenada, maybe—for the summer. I would join him with the children as soon as the school term ended. We could try it there as a sort of foot-in-the-Mexican-water; it wasn't too far from home if we found we didn't like it. But if all went well, we could relocate to Mexico City at summer's end.

So I drove back to Los Angeles for the troubled interim, and Hugo headed south.

But not for Ensenada yet. At the airport just the other side of the border, he caught a flight for Mexico City, where a small band of Hollywood refugees had already begun to gather.

* * * * *

By now the HUAC hearings had reconvened—in Los Angeles this time, and with another difference. Having learned that the First Amendment didn't keep one out of jail, a number of witnesses were now claiming the protection of the Fifth, the right not to be forced to incriminate themselves. Most would have been quite willing to declare their own political beliefs, but if they did, they'd have had to answer all the committee's questions about their friends or be cited for contempt. So the Fifth Amendment seemed the only honorable course open to them.

Their silence on the stand, however, was viewed by the press, the public, and the film industry as a tacit admission of guilt, and they were instantly drummed out of their jobs. True, the Fifth had kept them out of jail—but they were now out of work too.

There was also a steady parade of "friendly" witnesses—writers, actors, and directors winning exoneration from the committee by publicly naming anyone they'd ever seen at a Communist meeting. Paul Jarrico's former collaborator Richard Collins appeared that spring and named twenty-three of his former friends, including Paul. And a screen-writer-playwright named Martin Berkeley, with whom Hugo had carpooled to MGM during the gas shortage early in World War II, named a hundred and sixty. Quite a lot of the friendly witnesses named Hugo. (By the time the dust had settled a few years later, only one had named me, and then only under my married name. I should have been grateful, I suppose, but in fact I felt vaguely insulted.)

For our parents, that spring was a harrowing time. Less perhaps for Hugo's mother, who was so staunchly loyal to her only child that anyone who disagreed with him had by definition to be wrong. But my mother, a playwright who had created the Hardy family (memorialized by MGM, Lewis Stone, and Mickey Rooney as middle America's quintessential view of itself), was torn between "I told you so!" and a frantic worry for our welfare.

And now that Hugo's father, once an actor and now a successful screenwriter and sometime executive at Paramount, had learned of our problem, he was beside himself. Attractive, well groomed, upwardly mobile, and a dedicated Republican, Frank found his son's political sympathies incomprehensible. In the midst of HUAC hysteria and the *Los Angeles Times*'s biggest, blackest headlines, he phoned me almost in tears of anger and frustration. " . . . All Hugo's talent, all his success, gone to waste! His whole career destroyed . . . !"

At the time, I suppose, that's how it looked. And would look for a long time to come.

But there were compensations.

In Mexico City, Hugo had encountered playwright John Wexley (*The Last Mile, City for Conquest*) and his wife, and the three of them had flown together to Acapulco. For Hugo, this initial glimpse of the tropics was love at first sight. Early in their stay, he and John had gone out on a sportfishing boat, and by day's end, John had hooked a swordfish. It had been a glorious battle, and afterward, with the swordfish's head, sword, and fins en route to Tampico to be preserved and mounted, the two men, sunburned and salty, had come back to the hotel in triumph. After a shower, Hugo had rejoined the Wexleys on their balcony overlooking the bay, and over long cold drinks, as the sun set in a blaze of red out on the Pacific and bongo drums set up a steady beat in the nightclub downstairs, Hugo thought of those two voluble "friendly witnesses" who between them had named almost two hundred names.

"Just think," he said. "Dick Collins and Martin Berkeley could have had all this!"

* * * * *

Meanwhile, back in Los Angeles, I was hovering uneasily at my mother's, trying for the children's sake to maintain the fiction that nothing was wrong. Daddy simply happened to be away on a writing job, that was all. And I was having to nerve myself for surreptitious forays to our silent, curtained house to dispose, one way or another, of our belongings—keeping one ear peeled for the doorbell, which might herald another visit from a U.S. marshal. On Hugo's written instructions, I sorted through fourteen years of domestic accumulation (like my white linen-lace wedding dress, for instance), deciding what to send to storage against an uncertain future and what we would need to take with us, as though Mexico were a desert island we were about to be cast away on. As much clothing, of course, as could be stuffed into our parachute bag . . . (*Not* my wedding dress, then.) Two typewriters. My guitar, which Hugo had given me the Christmas he was in the army but which I'd never learned to play. Our son's trumpet. One toy per child. A dictionary, a thesaurus, *Bartlett's Quotations,* Dr. Spock, and a cookbook . . .

And finally, when the children's school term ended, our Siamese cat, who'd been staying at my mother's with the two youngest girls and me. By now the storage people had come and gone, and our parachute bags, typewriters, etc., were fitted, along with the children and cat, into the twelve-year-old Cadillac limousine we'd bought just before the crisis, a tall, black, stately vehicle complete with holders for bud vases. It was early afternoon. I made sure the children's doors were locked, and at last, feeling for all the world like my Mormon grandmother setting out for the wilds with a handcart expedition, I revved the motor, hit the accelerator, and we were off.

Ten minutes after we left, the brakes failed, of course, so it was nightfall before we crossed the border and almost midnight when we caught up with Hugo at the Ensenada motel where we had agreed to meet.

But we were, miraculously, in one piece, and it was there, in Hussong's El Morro Motel on a rocky proclivity overlooking the dark waters of the Pacific, that our lives as expatriates actually began.

Chapter Two

OUR FIRST FEW months in Baja were a strange, almost dreamlike jumble of events. Hugo had found and rented the Gonzales's garage apartment with its decor of chrome, linoleum, and plastic, which he tried to ameliorate with beach combings of conch shells, anemones, and fishnet floats, and we settled in. Bit by bit, we began to get the feel of our new surroundings. We learned, for instance, that the shrill whistle we heard early most mornings was a signal from the fish canneries down on the waterfront that there'd been a good catch last night, and the cannery workers were being summoned to work. (Even without the whistle we could usually tell, if the wind was right, when the canneries were in operation.) And we began to expand our boundaries. We learned about Santo Tomás, a half hour's drive south of town, where vineyards and a winery nestled in nopal-dotted hills and where, in a restaurant at one end of a little grocery-and-curio store, we could sample a wonderful black bean soup flavored with lobster or quail or whatever the cook had caught that day. We also learned that on a hot day you could drink your red wine chilled and it tasted glorious.

The best discovery, though, was the lagoon.

With instructions from Señor Gonzales, we found our way beyond town to a sort of salt marsh and cow pasture, where we unhooked a gate in a fence, wound through salt flats to a great quiet lagoon sheltered from the sea by sandbars, and parked amid the scrub. We unpacked our towels and brown-bag lunches on the narrow banks, sending armies of sand crabs scuttling for cover, and with the children waded past the eelgrass to laze for hours in the warm shallows.

Ensenada in those days was a drowsy place, dust dry in summer in spite of the whole Pacific lapping at its shores. Actually, since the northern half of Baja California had only recently become a state, the village seemed much like a western frontier town. It had a jerry-built, anarchic look, with a (to us) wonderful sense of freedom. Only a few of its streets were paved, and I suppose there must have been a few policemen, but I don't remember ever seeing any. There were also a lot of lame dogs, which puzzled us till Hugo figured out that with cars still such an infrequent phenomenon there, the local animals had never really come to anticipate them and so had never given up the habit of lying in the streets. With the inevitable result.

In any event, with our satisfactions limited, we learned to take enormous pleasure in the ones we found. Good coffee, wonderful beer—and a bakery called La Guadalupana, where long loaves of French bread came out of the ovens at seven-thirty every morning and one could bring back a still-hot loaf for breakfast . . .

Three meals a day, however, were another matter.

I was beginning to find it hard to keep turning out American-style dinners for a husband and four children when there were no American-style grocery stores. The local poultry, naturally, was fed the cheapest and most available feed—fish meal—so eggs had an unmistakably fishy flavor, as did their parent hens. Beef and lamb, range fed, were scrawny and muscular, and the cuts in our neighborhood meat stalls looked like nothing I'd ever met before. Cooking, moreover, had never been one of my strong skills; I'd usually earned enough money to hire someone to do it for me. But Hugo, who loved hearth, home, and (most especially) a good table, had never really understood my adversarial relationship with the kitchen, so one month into our Ensenada stay he was showing signs of great impatience at mealtimes, and I was feeling browbeaten, child ridden, frazzled, and incompetent.

And then Ramona came into our lives.

It was by purest accident. Rosa, the young woman who came at unpredictable intervals to do our laundry, happened to ask us if we wanted to hire a cook. Rosa's mother, a toothless crone who sold tamales out of a bucket nightly at Hussong's Bar, had met a señora recently arrived from Guadalajara who was looking for work. Did we want to meet her? We did.

And so, one sun-drenched morning soon after our Fourth of July beach picnic, Hugo and I found ourselves at the foot of our kitchen steps in the Gonzales's backyard, talking (or trying to; she spoke no English and the few Spanish lessons we'd had hadn't helped much) to a short, stout, homely woman of about fifty who was explaining, as nearly as we could make out, that she'd come to Baja with a vacationing family she'd decided she didn't want to remain with. Her dark skin and wide cheekbones were pure Indian, and it was hard to imagine her turning out any culinary masterpieces, but she said she'd been working as a short-order cook in a Chinese restaurant in Guadalajara and before that had cooked for years for someone she merely described as "Señora Josefina," whose surname we never did learn.

But there was something sturdy and competent about her, and Hugo and I both knew that my domestic ineptitude demanded action of some sort. So that afternoon, with our blessing, she went off to market with a woven basket over her arm, and by evening we sat down at the kitchen table to a meal I only remember as heavenly. I've forgotten whether it was *enchiladas suizas,* with sour cream, or angry-red lamb chops *adobadas,* or chicken *veracruzano* with plantains and pineapple and chiles and tomatoes—she introduced them all to us in subsequent weeks—but at first bite we knew our troubles were over.

We learned more about her as the summer went on. She had been born and brought up in a mining town in Jalisco and told us of standing in her doorway as a little girl during the revolution, watching tracer bullets arc across the street as *Villistas* and *federales* shot at each other. She'd had a fourth-grade education, going to work as a domestic when she was twelve years old. And she said she had to have Friday nights and Saturdays off.

Oh? Why not Sunday?

It seemed she belonged to something called "The Church of God of the Seventh Day," which was, apparently, a combination of Mormonism, Seventh-Day Adventism, and Judaism, whose founding fathers, she said, were one of the lost tribes of Israel—something Hugo and I could never figure out either ethnically or geographically. She kept the Jewish food laws, altered somewhat in translation; sang a Spanish version of "Rock of Ages"; had a drawing of the Star of David over her bed; and wasn't allowed to drink, smoke, read novels, or go to bullfights. Given a recipe, there was nothing she couldn't cook, up to and including piroshki, pizza, gulyás, and cheese blintzes. She was also the wisest woman I have ever known and became the hub of our lives for twenty-two years, until her death. She was as much a mother to our children as I was, and they remember her with love.

She also helped teach us Spanish. It was she, in fact, who explained the serenade we'd heard that dawn early in our stay. The *"Mañanitas,"* she said, was traditionally sung just at daybreak outside a child's (or sometimes an adult's) window to waken him on his birthday or saint's day, and it came to mean, for me, Mexico itself.

Since Ramona's church had a large congregation in Mexico City, she approved heartily of our plan to move there when our amigos (the Trumbos) were ready to join us for the trip. But so far, no buyers had turned up for that idiosyncratic ranch of theirs, so we were all becalmed. Summer was fading into autumn now, it was too cool to swim in the lagoon anymore, and since school was now back in session stateside, the family groups who had been coming down from Los Angeles to visit us tapered off. I tried to stifle my concern that our children were missing a semester of school, but they, of course, were exultant.

The first rains came, turning the Ensenada roads to mud and ending all local excursions. Hugo did a little desultory writing, I spent most of my time reading to the children, but essentially we were killing time and beginning to sense our isolation when, late in September, our writer friend Eddie Huebsch wrote us that he and his wife, Bea, would be down for a weekend.

It was lovely news. Diminutive, feisty, and articulate, Eddie was the gadfly of the Left, but he and Hugo were deeply fond of each other. However, our pleasure at the reunion became dismay when, almost on the moment of their arrival, we realized the reason they had come. Eddie, his face flushed with fervor, his voice almost choking with moral indignation, announced that in his opinion we had no right to flee our friends or our country in time of trouble. We should come back to Los Angeles, he said, and "keep fighting."

Go back home? We were appalled at the idea. How could we live? The hearings had continued, we knew, and those of our friends who had chosen to stay and ride out the blacklist were finding it hard to get any kind of work. One couldn't even get a job at the post office without signing disclaimers and loyalty oaths. And the costs . . . ! Our meager savings, which would keep us for a couple of years in Mexico, would be spent in no time on lawyers' fees if Hugo had to face HUAC. Not to mention the rumor of those relocation camps . . .

Altogether, it was a miserable weekend. We spent it, the four of us, wandering about the bleak, autumnal little town, looking vainly for distraction and settling finally for the raffish gaiety of Hussong's cantina, where the argument raged on.

To my infinite relief, Hugo refused to be swayed by Eddie's eloquence, and our two guests left the following day, their cause lost. The next we heard of them, several months later, was that just ahead of a subpoena Eddie and Bea had piled their children and possessions in their car and headed east to lose themselves in the anonymity of New York City. The Left, it seemed, had decided it "didn't need any more martyrs."

So much for guilt.

And at last, in October, Trumbo wrote us that the ranch had been bought, was coming out of escrow, and they would meet us the first of November in San Diego, where we would regroup and proceed to Mexico City.

Why San Diego?

Since the Baja California peninsula was separated almost completely from Mexico's mainland by the Gulf of California, we would have to travel through the States' southwest to reach the Pan-American Highway. There was no practical alternative.

So bowing to necessity, we packed our bags once more; filled our stately black car to the gunwales; put Ramona on the bus for Guadalajara, where we would rejoin her en route to Mexico's capital; and with the children fairly bursting with a thirst for adventure and our cat taking it all with exemplary calm, we gave the apartment keys back to the Gonzaleses, gassed up, said good-bye to the lame dogs of Ensenada, and set out for the border.

Chapter Three

THE LAST FEW months we had made a few nervous forays into San Diego to get typhoid shots—unnecessary, perhaps, but we were covering all the bases. This of course required several border crossings, which to our surprise proved quite cursory. In that granddaddy of all traffic jams, the border guards usually had time to ask only, "Where were you born?" and, "Did you buy anything of value in Mexico?" So the occasional reentry into the States of one more carload of gringos set off no alarms.

Nonetheless, throughout this period, the local papers had been full of stories about the hearings, and Hugo's name had come up with uncomfortable frequency, so these trips were not made without a certain amount of apprehension, and we'd felt relieved and safe each time we'd gotten "home" again to Ensenada. Now, as our tall car trundled with its load into the parking lot of the San Diego motel where we were to meet the Trumbos, we had all the old misgivings: What name should we register under? And were we just being paranoid, or were They still looking for us? My one wish, that day in early November, was to get this trip-planning business over with and hit the highway as quickly as possible.

But as usual, if anything can go wrong, it will. The Trumbos had arrived and were waiting for us, but their oldest child, thirteen-year-old Nikola, had a sore throat and a fever. They would have to call a doctor.

It was, it turned out, a strep throat. So our one-night stopover in San Diego turned into three, which the men spent poring over road maps.

They decided we would limit each day's journey to no more than two or three hundred miles so the children wouldn't get too tired or restless. Each stop must be arranged for well in advance, and since the Trumbos' family group included their sheepdog, as ours included our cat (fortunately, they ignored each other), we would have to find motels that could accommodate four adults, seven children, and two animals simultaneously.

While the men worked out travel plans and Cleo nursed Nikola through the strep, I shepherded the six younger children to the zoo and the museum, where, naturally, all six ignored the more instructional exhibits and spent hours in the bat cave, where the press of a button brought hordes of stuffed bats squeaking and flittering about their heads. We also found a wonderful used-book store and laid on a supply of Howard Pyle, a *Scottish Chiefs* with Wyeth illustrations, and some Lucy Fitch Perkins "twin" books for the younger set. And hoping to compensate for the school they were missing, I bought a few first-grade readers for the two five-year-olds, our Mary and the Trumbos' Melissa ("Mitzi"), and we did, in fact, teach both girls to read on the journey.

At last, when Nikola's temperature was normal, we set out in tandem: we in our tall, ancient Cadillac; Cleo and her three children in their relatively new Packard; and Trumbo—with the sheepdog, which unhappily proved prey to car sickness—in a jeep pulling a teardrop trailer filled with his books. At first we drove, in our three cars, past countless ugly little desert towns, and then the terrain changed and we reached the wonderful high desert of the Southwest, ending our first day's run at Gila Bend, Arizona—to find that Mitzi, the Trumbos' youngest, had come down with strep throat. So it was another doctor, more antibiotics, and a three-day layover in Gila Bend.

Though we were anxious to get safely, once and for all, over the border, we felt we owed it to the children (and ourselves) to do a little sightseeing along the way. So, on the next leg of our journey, we detoured to Casas Grandes to wander among tumbleweed and saguaro cactus and explore the silent, ghostly Indian ruins that stood out there in splendid isolation. Then on to Lordsburg, New Mexico (where the travelers in *Stagecoach* were going, we reminded ourselves), to find that our next-youngest, Mary, had caught the strep.

By now, as in any newly formed society, the various members of our entourage had each carved out his particular function. By virtue of age, experience, and general panache, Trumbo had assumed the position of tribal leader, and Hugo, who within his own family structure was absolute monarch, fell comfortably into place as his second in command. He and Trumbo made all substantive decisions, which Cleo and I never questioned: they were the cartographers, planning the stops and the side trips and seeing to the general care and upkeep of the cars. Cleo, who over the last few years had become a skilled photographer, took pictures at each stop: fine, deep-focus stills. And whenever the wandering strep had felled another child and we were becalmed in another motel, I read aloud. At each long, long stop the still healthy children would gather around the new invalid's bed while I read *The Cave Twins* or *The Indian Twins* to the younger two, and then, as the little ones moved sleepily to the outskirts of the group or off to bed, I read *Robin Hood* or *King Arthur* or *Scottish Chiefs* to the older ones. The only child too young to be read to was our now not quite two-and-a-half-year-old Emily, who fell asleep each night to the sound of the other children's stories. It's no accident she grew up to become a librarian.

When Mary's fever was gone and she had become her own jolly, sturdy self again, we set out for El Paso, where we planned to pick up the Pan-American Highway and cross over into mainland Mexico. But just outside El Paso, Emily vomited all over the backseat of the car and said her throat hurt. So we checked into yet one more motel, asked the manager for the name of a good doctor, and settled down for still another three days' wait.

Why, one may wonder at this point, were we putting ourselves, and our children, through all this? How had we made such a political choice in the first place, and having made it, why did we cling to it with such determination?

To answer requires a little back story—to Hugo's childhood, in fact, or even before. To Canada, where his parents had migrated from Oxford a couple of years before the outbreak of World War I.

Hugo's father, who prior to the war had worked for the Canadian-Pacific Railroad (while he dreamed of finer things), had enlisted early in the Princess Pats, risen rapidly in the army's hierarchy, and by war's end was assistant provost marshal of London. After demobilization, his ambition whetted, he had come back from England on a troop ship and, in the process, had fallen in love with an entertainer on board who was singing to the troops.

He'd returned to Hugo's mother in British Columbia to ask for a divorce, then gone on down to Hollywood to join his shipboard lady and to seek his fortune in motion pictures. It was a blow Hugo's mother, Margaret, never quite recovered from, though in due time she did re-marry. Hugo was five years old at the time of his father's defection, and each night for a year when he said his prayers, he ended them with: "And dear God, please let my mother and my father get together again in three hundred and sixty-five days . . ." (reducing this number by one, of course, each night). By the time his ultimatum to God had only a few days left to run, it was clear He wasn't going to oblige. Frank had married the shipboard lady, and there was no possibility of a reunion with Hugo's mother. So Hugo decided that either God didn't listen to one's prayers or He hadn't answered because He didn't exist. In either case, he decided, religious faith was a waste of time. There must be something better to believe in.

He and his mother remained in Canada, and in due time she met and married another recently demobbed vet, Freddie. Good-looking, gre-garious Freddie had gone into the army before he had ever learned a trade and spent four years in the trenches. Once more a civilian, he had gone to work as a clerk in the United Cigar stores for thirty-four dol-lars a week. In the Great Depression, by which time his salary had dropped to fourteen dollars, he was fired, to be replaced by a college boy who would do the same job for ten. There were times during this period when Margaret—gently born and bred in Oxford and step-daughter of the dean of St. Mary's—went to work as a housekeeper to make ends meet.

When Hugo was in his early teens, his father divorced his second wife and married a third, so Margaret, having no ill feeling toward this new replacement, let Hugo come down to Hollywood for a visit, and Hugo discovered for the first time what it was like to live in affluence. During the intervening years, Frank had prospered, first as an actor (playing silly Englishmen, including Agnes Ayres's brother in Valentino's *Son of the Sheik*), then as a writer, and finally, until the heart attack, as a studio executive. There was a pleasant house in the Hollywood Hills, a cook, a butler/chauffeur, a handsome car. Hugo's new stepmother dressed expensively. She did her best to make Hugo feel welcome, but for an adolescent boy, comparisons were inevitable. He couldn't help thinking about his mother and those housekeeping jobs, and Freddie and the United Cigar stores.

As for me: I'd been brought up in a good Republican (albeit feminist) household, safely middle-class; my first real glimpse of poverty had been during the truncated run of a play my mother had written for me, which had opened on Broadway in November 1933 (and closed, alas, three weeks later). Walking from the subway en route to the theater and back on those chilly November nights, I'd been astonished to see gaunt men in threadbare coats, sheltering in doorways against the weather. The newspapers had been carrying stories about soup kitchens and unemployment marchers, of course, but it was another matter altogether to see with one's own eyes homeless human beings huddled in doorways.

So, for a few months, I'd had a brief flirtation with a left-wing "study group." But I had abandoned it because it was taking up all my reading time, and I knew if I was ever to achieve my real goal—being a writer—I'd do better spending my time with Dickens and Tolstoy than struggling through the Little Lenin Library.

For the next two or three years, then, during intermittent stretches as an English major at Stanford, interspersed with half a dozen movie parts in Hollywood (ingenue leads in low-budget pictures and character parts in big ones)—and another embarrassingly short Broadway run—I paid little or no attention to politics. And the December day I'd accepted my old friend Waldo Salt's invitation to lunch at the MGM commissary and met his fellow junior-writer Hugo Butler, the class struggle was as far from my mind as from theirs. We were too busy, all three of us, with our own professional concerns. Hugo was fascinated by film as a visual way of telling stories. Waldo was trying to write like Noel Coward. And I was trying to square an acting career with writing attempts and the ongoing task of self-education.

Actually, that day, I was quite dazzled by Hugo. He was twenty-two (to my twenty), and he had, I thought, a lovely wit. He also had brown eyes that missed nothing; a light sprinkle of freckles; a fresh, almost English complexion and pleasant, even features; reddish brown hair and a sturdy body (well, maybe the tiniest bit overweight), which seemed to me to house a delightful high school boy who was still growing up. In a tweed sports jacket, argyle socks, and square-toed brogues and with a faint scent of aftershave, he even *dressed* enchantingly, I thought. And when he phoned me later, offering to drive me to a party we'd all been invited to, in order to "obviate" my having to find my own way there, I was convinced. Any young man who used the word *obviate* in casual conversation was the man for me.

In any event, as I spoke of my brief fling with the Left at the table that day in the busy commissary, it was regarded by all of us as an amusing vagary, merely a distraction from the more serious business of getting on with our lives.

Not for long, though.

By the time we had courted, married, and were living in our own tiny Hollywood apartment—and oh, how wonderful it was to be grown-up, working, free of one's mother, and utterly, wildly in love with one's husband!—the post-Depression years and the rise of Fascism in Europe had the film industry in a ferment. Stirred by Steinbeck's *Grapes of Wrath,* we had become interested in the plight of California's migrant workers, which local left-wingers (among others) were trying to alleviate. There was indignation now too over Japan's ravaging of China; my friends and I protested by boycotting Japanese Christmas tree ornaments and wearing baggy lisle stockings instead of silk hose. And almost alone, it seemed to us, the Communists recognized that Hitler and Mussolini were using Spain as a proving ground for their troops and weapons, while the democracies imposed embargoes on arms aid to Spain's duly elected republican government. As armed aggression intensified abroad, anti-Fascist organizations in California mushroomed.

Then Germany marched into the Polish Corridor, and World War II began.

With singularly poor timing, Hugo and I had decided nine months earlier that we were ready to start our family, so I spent the first night of World War II timing my contractions and listening to radio broadcasts about Germany's torpedoing of a British passenger liner in the North Sea. (The baby that I subsequently delivered was one I would never see. She died of birth injuries three days after she was born.)

By 1941 France had fallen and Hitler had invaded Russia, and by December, Pearl Harbor had been bombed and the United States was at war. Hugo, newly naturalized, had applied for a commission in the navy and been rejected—perhaps for political reasons; we never learned. So now he decided he'd wait to be drafted. Meanwhile we were also busy having babies to make up for the loss of our first one. Increasingly it was beginning to seem that every obstetrical event of my life coincided with a major military or naval event overseas.

But we were both living as normal a life as people can in wartime, working, watching our children become delightful, idiosyncratic human beings—when Waldo Salt dropped by one afternoon with his invitation to join the party. And before the next day was out, Hugo had said to me, almost casually, "Honey? I thought I'd give Waldo the nod. Okay?"

And that's how we joined.

It wasn't a difficult decision. The political climate encouraged it; the Russians were our gallant allies, suffering terrible casualties but stopping the Germans at Stalingrad. Here at home, the Communist Party was legal; its candidates were on the ballot, and its primary spokesperson was Earl Browder, a gradualist who was saying that perhaps revolution was not inevitable after all, that a peaceful transition to socialism might be possible . . .

But perhaps the most telling reason was that most of our friends were already members.

For me, a joiner by nature, those once- or twice-a-month meetings at someone's house, with eight or ten friends sitting about a living room, fueled by coffee and Danish and discussing dialectical materialism, were an intriguing experience. It wasn't just a political commitment we'd made, I found; we had also committed ourselves to a fellowship, to a group of people we loved and respected. (I remember an old-time member, an aging character actress, telling me: "You always love your first group.")

In spite of my deep affection for my "group," however—a motley assortment of publicists, screen-story analysts, character actors, a teacher or two, a sprinkling of not terribly prosperous doctors and dentists, and an assortment of left-wing wives either with or without careers of their own—I was sharply aware that the group Hugo had been assigned to, almost entirely male and made up of fairly prominent screenwriters, with a sprinkling of producers and a couple of directors, which met in Beverly Hills, was in career terms a far more prestigious one. I wondered who made these assignments and on what basis. Was there a certain amount of career snobbery involved here? And—just possibly—could the party's position on women's equality be more lip service than performance?

The question soon became academic. By early 1945, Hugo's MGM contract came up for renewal, and a new one was presented him with the promise that "this will keep you out of the army." Offended, Hugo had refused to sign it, and within weeks the draft board had reclassified him 1-A. By early spring he had received his "greetings" to report for induction.

Party officials immediately, and routinely, placed him on honorable withdrawal, a status that was automatically extended to me, too. It seems that the party, in its total support of the war effort, wanted to make sure that left-wing soldiers would feel no division of loyalty whatsoever between their politics and the army. Winning the war was all that mattered.

So Hugo had gone off to his induction with a feeling of exhilaration: he was part of an honorable war; he felt it was a "people's army" he was joining. Being a slightly overage, slightly overweight buck private on KP at Camp Roberts for a monthly pay of $35 quickly disabused him of *that* illusion, however; within six weeks, all he wanted was to get out of uniform and come home.

(And here, an aside from the home front. Liberated once again, as I had been once before in my teens, from having to educate myself in Marxism, I turned during Hugo's absence to writing my first novella. The high point of my life came the evening I phoned him at the recreation hall at Fort Ord, where he'd been transferred, and told him it had just sold to *McCall's* magazine for $5,000.)

The birth of our daughter Mary (probably conceived in a bosky fringe of the abandoned parade ground at Fort Ord, when Hugo had gone AWOL from another KP assignment to meet me on one of my visits up there) made him eligible for discharge. Altogether he had served a year, most of it spent editing his rec hall newspaper. But army service, odious as he may have found it, had reduced his weight, lowered his blood pressure, cured his preulcer condition, tightened his muscles, tanned his skin, and altogether made him look like a very exciting stranger; I found his return an almost dizzying experience.

He'd also picked up his party membership almost immediately but had stated quite firmly his preference about mine: "With three children, the PTA, and your writing," he'd said, "Christ, I'd never see you!" And so I had not rejoined (justifying the decision by writing and selling three more *McCall's* novellas), though I eased my political conscience by keeping up with *People's World* and hewing as closely as possible to the party position on almost everything.

But that, alas, had been changing rapidly since the war's end. Half a year after Hugo had come home, Winston Churchill (who had been such a hero to us during the Blitz!) had made his "Iron Curtain" speech about the dangers of Soviet expansionism. Earl Browder had been removed as party chairman for "revisionism." And the Cold War was under way.

Within another year, the Hollywood Ten had been subpoenaed.

It was far harder by then, with Communism becoming the bogeyman of the Western world, to maintain one's faith, but we did, stubbornly. Hugo was going off to his meetings as though his year in the army had never happened. And if, as the years wore on, he found himself more and more miscast as an activist and less happy with groupthink, his fellow members in the party were still his best friends. And to save his own career by denouncing them before a congressional committee, simply because the political climate had reversed itself, was unthinkable. It was never even a choice.

That was why, finally, by mid-November of 1951, we were here in a motel in El Paso, waiting for our small, feverish Emily to get over her sore throat so we could get on with our flight.

And then at last, at long last, when she was well enough, our unwieldy group of refugees packed up once more, piled baggage, children, and animals into our three cars, traveled in tandem the last few miles to the border, and crossed over into Mexico.

* * * * *

Perhaps it was our imagination. But suddenly the very air seemed to change, to be fresher, more free. Anxieties fell away. We found we loved the very backwardness of the little towns we passed, and Cleo stopped her car to take a commemorative picture of the first honest-to-goodness adobe hut we saw, a tiny place huddled under tall cottonwood trees. In Ciudad Chihuahua, where we stopped for dinner and the night, we saw two tall, thin, barefoot Indians wearing only loincloths—Tarahumara Indians down from their villages farther up in the sierra. Awed at the sight, we were astonished that the local towns-people paid them no attention at all. (Later I would learn they came down into the city frequently to barter.)

Reassured, however, that we'd made one stop without some child getting sick, we drove on to Parral, an ancient mining town from the time of the Spaniards, where we checked into a motel and our nine-year-old Susie said her throat hurt.

That's where I discovered that a doctor making house calls in a small Mexican town uses a spirit lamp to boil up his syringe in its metal case before giving an injection. Less foolproof than an autoclave, perhaps, but cheap, portable, and practical. Later we would discover that every Mexican medical student, before receiving his license, must spend a prescribed period of time practicing in one of the country's doctorless areas; this is Mexico's equivalent of our internship and provides medical care to the poorest provinces.

In any event, when it seemed our wandering streptococcus had exhausted itself, we took up our travels again, to stop the next night in the city of Durango (all this had once been Pancho Villa country, but we didn't know it then) and again in Zacatecas, where the arches of an ancient Spanish aqueduct marched beside us along the highway. By this time the children had reshuffled themselves, the two five-year-old girls choosing to ride together and the two boys, our Mike and the Trumbos' Chris, ignoring the living history we were driving past and entertaining themselves instead by telling each other science fiction stories or inventing countless verses to a song the oldest, the Trumbos' Nikola, had taught them: " 'Leprosy, / My God, I've got leprosy, / There goes my eyeball / Into my highball, / There goes my chin / Into my gin . . . ' " and so on, for endless miles, as we drove. They didn't learn much about Mexico, but they had a fine time.

The farther south we drove, the more "Mexican" our surroundings became. The landscape changed too, becoming hilly and dotted with trees. We discovered that every town boasted at least one tree-shaded plaza, its *zócalo,* always with a lovely little wrought-iron bandstand, which seemed to serve as the town's nerve center or its heart. I remember being sent by our hotel clerk to the plaza in Aguascalientes one evening just at twilight to hear thousands of birds that swarmed in from all over the countryside, making such a to-do in the trees as they twittered and fought and settled down for the night that they drowned out every other sound. And I remember watching a Sunday *paseo* in another plaza in another town where, lit unevenly by streetlights shining among the trees, the young men circled in one direction and the young girls in the other, passing and repassing each other till they chose partners and dropped out of line. Many of the town's old married couples, we were told, had first met at the *paseo*.

And then on to a motel in Guadalajara, an attractive, bustling small city, where Ramona caught up with us and where Mike and Chris both came down with strep.

They were both quite sick, and while Cleo and I nursed them through it, Hugo and Trumbo decided to make use of their time by flying ahead to Mexico City to house hunt. Their plane, however, seemed to be a milk plane, making stops every few minutes in some farmer's pasture or cornfield, and it was in no way reassuring to see on the pilot's instrument panel a little votary light under a statuette of the Virgin of Guadalupe, along with a pair of bronzed baby shoes.

They reached Mexico City intact, however, and Hugo told me later of getting up at daybreak the morning after their arrival and looking out his hotel window at the lovely, tree-lined, rain-wet Paseo de la Reforma far below him, to see a shepherd herding a flock of sheep up the grassy island in the middle of the boulevard. Time hadn't exactly stood still in Mexico, he decided, but it hadn't moved very fast either.

Apparently he and Trumbo found an English-speaking realtor, because within a few days they had discovered and chosen a couple of houses not too distant from each other and were on their way back to rejoin us. And at last, by the end of November, our two ten-year-olds had recovered and we could set out on the last leg of our journey.

But not without one final detour. We'd heard about a newborn volcano, Paracutín, in the state of Michoacán.

Paracutín had been born a year or two before in a farmer's cornfield, where the farmer had taken to sleeping outdoors because the ground there was so agreeably warm. He must have been dismayed at the original eruption because it cost him not only his warm sleeping place but his whole cornfield. In fact, by the time we reached the general area, the whole village had gradually been buried, with only its church spires still visible in a sea of now hardened lava.

The side trip, we'd been told, could be made from Uruapan, which proved, when we reached it, to be a lovely little mountain town of narrow cobbled streets and unexpected glimpses, through filigree iron-work gates, of enclosed, flower-filled patios. The little one-story hotel we checked into had such a patio, riotous with flowering plants and tiled fountains and caged birds, each small, sparsely furnished room opening off it, and we were altogether enchanted.

Since we wanted to be back on the highway by midmorning the next day in order to reach Mexico City by nightfall, Trumbo, in charge of logistics as usual, arranged for a guide to take us to view the volcano at the pitch-black hour of 4 A.M. It seemed, when the time came, a dubious pleasure. Emily was sound asleep in my arms and the rest of us only half awake as we set out in two cars (plus guide) to travel a narrow, winding dirt road for an hour or so through utter darkness, to cross a seemingly bottomless crevasse on two planks and pull up on a promontory on the farther side, where the guide told us to stop. This, he indicated, was as far as cars could go.

Provided by a couple of enterprising concessionaires who lived some-where nearby in the dark wilderness about us, donkeys were produced, which would carry us by path to a lookout point another hour's distance away, where one could have a clear view of the volcano.

But Emily still slumbered on; an hour's donkey ride along a mountain path through the darkness didn't seem an awfully good idea for either one of us, so I chose to stay in the car with her while the others, now wearing ponchos the donkey owners had provided for warmth, set forth into the night with the guide.

Secure in the closed-up car, I must have dropped off, because I woke abruptly to the sound of two muffled explosions in the middle distance. The darkness was lifting, but from where the car was parked, nothing was visible except a mountainous bleak landscape; even the volcano's glow was hidden by a row of hills. What had those explosions been, and where were the watchers in relationship to them?

Emily slept on undisturbed, but I spent a bad hour, forming scenarios in my head of what might have happened. At last, however, the donkeys and their riders drifted back into view single file along the path. Tired but awed, Hugo and the others dismounted and reported on their long ride out, along the dark, narrow path edging the slopes where at one point the lava-covered ground was warm to the touch. At first, he said, there'd been little to see except bare, blackened tree trunks thrusting up out of the dark hillside, all that was left of a pinewoods that had once stood there. They had reached, finally, a guides' lean-to from which they could look out over the desolated, lava-covered valley toward Paracutín and see its glow. They'd been still huddled there watching when two explosions had abruptly bellied up from the crater and it belched out smoke, fire, and rocks with a terrible thunder. That's what I had heard, safe in the car miles away.

In the decade ahead of us, we would come to think of the valley of Mexico as almost synonymous with its two towering volcanoes Iztaccíhuatl (long dormant) and Popocatéptl (quiescent, but well behaved). But once in a while, one or another of us would have a memory of another volcano—a younger one, still small and obstreperous, rousing itself to rain fire and rocks over the Michoacán valley it had already destroyed.

* * * *

It wasn't yet much past dawn when we wound our way back to our hotel to have breakfast and pack up; the morning was still fresh when we reached the highway. We wondered, as we drove, at the difference between this lush, heavily wooded state and what we'd seen of the rest of Mexico, with its scant growth and paucity of arable land. We skirted the end of Lake Pátzcuaro, where the fishermen, in their canoes, use fishnets shaped like giant butterflies and where, we were told, we had missed by a month the colorful annual celebration of the Day of the Dead on the lake-island of Janitzio. And then, stopping for lunch at a restaurant in the mountain town of Morelia, we bumped straight into a reminder of the life we'd left behind us.

Eating with a camera crew at a nearby table was Norman Foster, with whom I had acted some fourteen years before in a low-budget murder mystery called *The Leavenworth Case* and with whose previous wife, Claudette Colbert, I'd worked (as patient to her psychiatrist) in *Private Worlds*. He was directing now, it seemed, and he and his crew had just finished a location shoot outside Mexico City.

Greetings were awkward; we didn't know how much he had read about the hearings, or whether he guessed why we were in Mexico or what he'd do about it if he did. Was he enough of an ideologue to mention this encounter to the FBI or to the American consulate here?

And if so, what then? I avoided introductions (he would certainly recognize Trumbo's name) and murmured something about our "coming down to try living here for a year," and Norman, all cordiality, assured me we'd love it.

So it was a hasty, rather nervous lunch, and we were glad to be on our way again. Up, up to the ridge of the mountains that ring the valley of Mexico and then down to the valley floor, itself more than seven thousand feet high, to enter Mexico City from the west instead of the north, which left me forever afterward hopelessly confused about directions.

By then it was almost evening. Maps outspread on laps, we found our way along the busy streets to Las Lomas, a neighborhood that looked for all the world like any prosperous American suburb. The Trumbos continued on to the chilly but imposing small marble edifice Trumbo had chosen for them, and we pulled up outside the pleasant but almost painfully conventional dwelling Hugo had rented for us. (It was owned by a vivacious young woman with—at that time—six children, whose husband, she told us later, was now only a *diputado*—a congressman—but who would someday be *presidente*. We all laughed politely at the joke. But twenty years later he did indeed become president; his name was Luís Echeverría.) As Hugo and I unloaded and carried in our bags, the children tumbled out of the car and scurried about the house like rabbits, exploring every corner. There was a tile solarium with a hammock, which each child tried to claim as his own, and a number of small, square rooms with an unconscionable amount of mahogany cabinetwork. We looked at it uncritically, glad that our troubles were over—over, at least for the next six months, when we would discover the house that would really become home to us.

Before we settled down for the night, however, Hugo drove downtown to pick up an English-language paper. That's how we discovered that of the dozen and a half first-run movies—Mexican, European, English, or American—that were showing in Mexico City that week, four had been written or cowritten by Hugo or me.

Sic transit.

PART TWO

When I was but thirteen or so
I went into a golden land,
Chimborazo, Cotopaxi
Took me by the hand . . .

—W. J. *Turner*

Chapter Four

MEXICO CITY in the early 1950s was a wondrous place, with Popocatéptl and Iztaccíhuatl ("White Sleeping Lady") to the east, soaring ten thousand feet above the valley floor. The air was almost piercingly clear, and at night there were more stars than I'd ever seen in my life. Lake Texcoco, which in the Aztecs' time had filled much of the floor of the valley, had been drained to a fraction of its former self, but there was still enough of it to hint at past glories. And the watery weirs of Xochimilco, the floating gardens, still survived to tell us what the settlements on the verges of the lake must once have been like. Almost our first excursion after settling in was to Xochimilco, where our two families struck a deal with a boatman and were poled in his flat-bottomed punt along the canals between lanes of poplars, while another dugout-load of mariachis followed us, playing Mexican folk music.

At first, until we learned our way around, our cicerones were George and Jeanette Pepper, a bright, knowledgeable couple down from Hollywood long enough to have picked up a certain amount of expertise about Mexico. Jeanette had been an economist and statistician, and George, initially a violinist with the Los Angeles Philharmonic, had later become executive director of one of Hollywood's anti-Fascist committees and then, under duress, a self-exile like us. It was George who, at the time of our arrival, was busy trying to package Hugo's screenplay of *Robinson Crusoe*.

Actually, this was a matter of some urgency to us. We had enough savings, we thought, to last just over a year, but after that we'd be badly in need of money, or at least the prospect of some. And simply going out and getting a job was impossible. Like most countries, Mexico had laws against foreigners working without a permit, and *inmigrado* papers (resident status with a working permit) were hard to come by.

We also learned from the Peppers that tourists here were required to leave the country to renew their *turista* cards every six months, a prospect we didn't relish, since we didn't know what we could expect on the Texas side of the border by then. And if our cars, which were also considered tourists, didn't leave with us, they—the cars—would be arrested and impounded. In fact, the more we learned about living in a foreign country, the more complicated it seemed.

For the moment, however, we were becoming acclimated. Our house, though painfully conventional in aspect, was comfortable enough; it seemed, actually, rather like an impersonal, very small hotel. As for our Spanish: we took a few lessons from an impecunious businessman, discovering in the process that tutoring was a frequent source of income for Mexico's tiny, struggling middle class. Our teacher and others like him also moonlighted by selling insurance on weekends; it sometimes took three jobs to support a family above the poverty level.

And we were learning that life with Ramona was a series of gustatory surprises: boiled tripe with chiles and garbanzos, I remember, and *mole poblano* (a fiery sauce of ground toasted sesame seeds, chocolate, and seven different kinds of chiles), and, one memorable day, a roast kid, which she had brought home raw from the market complete with head, hooves, and hide. It had given Mike a terrible turn when he'd gone prowling through the kitchen for a midmorning snack. "Mother!" he'd yelled. "There's an *animal* in the refrigerator!"

Ramona had also added to our, or perhaps her own, domestic felicity by bringing an assistant home one day from church—a young Otomí woman from the *mezquital,* the parched, desertlike country of north-central Mexico; her name was Isabel (or maybe Ysabel; we were never quite sure). Silent, shy, she wore under all circumstances an abashed smile, and her vocabulary consisted mostly of *"Mande ustéd?"* (roughly translated, "At your service?" or, more simply, "Yes, ma'am?"). Short of leg, wide of thigh, cheerfully homely, she performed without a murmur every task Ramona demanded of her. The children played with her, teased her, and came to love her second only to Ramona.

We had registered the children at the American School, which like its Mexican counterparts in the capital was now on its annual two-month vacation, and while they waited for classes to begin, we took them sight-seeing with us. Nearest at hand, of course, was Chapultepec Park, only minutes away from the house. *Chapultepec* in the Aztec language Nahuatl means "Hill of the Grasshopper," though I never saw any there. It was a thoroughly satisfactory park, with a tree-shaded little zoo encircled by a child-sized railroad, and a lake with rowboats for rent, and soft-drink kiosks, and a small midway complete with merry-go-round—of special delight to the smallest Butlers and Trumbos. Overaged and badly in need of paint, its horses still kept their magic, their wooden manes forever flying, eyes wild, teeth bared in mouths strained perpetually open in some sort of unacknowledged race with time, and as I stood watching the children ride by to the familiar strains of the calliope, I remember thinking that some things were the same the world over.

We also drove in two carloads out to Chapingo, where an hacienda expropriated during the 1910–1918 upheavals had been turned into a national agricultural school, its former chapel transformed by Diego Rivera's lovely, muted murals into a visual history of the revolution. And then on to Teotihuacán, the Pyramid to the Sun, where the children raced enthusiastically to the sacrificial top hundreds of feet up and I was seized by acrophobia at the fifth step and stayed there.

It was on this first trip to, or perhaps from, the pyramids, as we were driving down one of the narrow, cobbled side streets of the neighboring village, that we noticed signs scrawled on some of the doors we passed. Slowing, we read one of them. It said, *"Somos Católicos. No queremos la invasión protestante."* ("We are Catholics. We do not want the Protestant invasion.")

It gave us pause. Somehow we had not expected religious intolerance in this lovely, friendly country that had become our sanctuary. Still puzzling, we drove on, deciding finally that this was some sort of local aberration and choosing to forget it.

This was also the day, and the place, where Trumbo and Hugo became serious collectors.

Approached furtively by a local townsman who offered to sell them *"cabecitas,"* tiny, ancient stone heads unearthed by the hundreds from the soil thereabouts and peddled illegally to tourists, the two men showed the first symptoms of a new fever. From this innocent beginning, they would go on regular Sunday trips to the brick pits at Tlatilco where workmen, digging clay for bricks at the site of an ancient pre-Columbian burial ground, were continually coming upon pottery shards and tiny ceramic figures, in pieces or whole (*"enteros"*), which sold for fifty centavos each. From there, and after some homework on the subject, it was only a few steps to the clandestine acquisition from dealers of more impressive and more expensive trophies: lovely, potbellied dogs from Colima; or whimsical Mickey-Mouse-like Chupicuaro figures with lips, eyes, and hair superimposed in clay; or mysterious Olmec heads with their high, almost hydrocephalic foreheads. . . .

Cleo and I understood the addiction. With such a figure looking down from the mantelpiece, one could almost feel the presence of the ancient people who had made it. These pieces of ceramic weren't just an art form; to us, now, they became a continuous living glimpse into Mexico's long-ago past.

It was illegal, of course, to take "archeological treasures" out of Mexico, but that at the moment was the least of our worries. If the climate for dissent in the United States didn't improve, we might be here for a long, long time.

Then it was Christmas, our first Christmas in exile, with Chapultepec Castle and the whole *zócalo* downtown strung with lights, transforming the stained gray walls of the old buildings into a nighttime fairyland. I made a hasty Christmas, buying the children hand-crafted toys from the popular-arts stores downtown (which they greeted with polite dismay on Christmas morning, I'm afraid.) We trimmed a tree with painted tin made-in-Mexico ornaments, and, just in time for the holidays, our little band of brothers was enlarged by two more families, the Lardners and the Hunters.

The fraternity was complete again.

Their last few years together in Hollywood, Trumbo, Hugo, Ring, and their fellow writer Ian Hunter had become a close quadrumvirate, working together, playing together, drinking together, and spending their evenings philosophizing, arm wrestling, and trying to top each other's jokes. Like Trumbo, Ring had also been given two months off his jail sentence for good behavior. (His stay there, actually, had been much enlivened by the knowledge that one of his fellow inmates was former congressman and HUAC chairman J. Parnell Thomas, recently convicted of taking kickbacks from members of his office staff.)

Ring's present wife was actress Frances Chaney, the widow of his brother, who had been killed in wartime France. Ian's wife, Alice, had been a screen story analyst and then (like George Pepper) the executive of a progressive political-action committee. Ian himself—deliberate of speech, looking not unlike a slightly overweight Byron—was a gourmet cook and his wife a close second. And since none of the other three wives was, we anticipated correctly some memorable Hunter meals.

So there was another flurry of house hunting, netting the Lardners a house in the Lomas not far from ours and for the Hunters a truly lovely small Spanish colonial house on the grounds of the San Angel Inn, a seventeenth-century Carmelite monastery-turned-hostelry and then abandoned till modern investors had rediscovered it. There was more sight-seeing; we straggled, a now unwieldy group including three Lardner children and the Hunters' four-year-old son, Tim, through the museum at Chapultepec Castle, where I fell in love with a sweet-faced death mask of long-ago president Benito Juárez and the children gazed with bloodthirsty interest at the parapet where, in 1847, a handful of teenage cadets, the *"Niños héroes,"* had wrapped themselves in the Mexican flag and jumped to their deaths on the rocks below rather than surrender it to the advancing American troops.

And the four husbands settled down to pick up their friendship exactly where they'd left off two years ago, when the Hollywood Ten had gone to jail.

It was a friendship so close, so satisfying, that it almost superseded the four marriages. At least, that's how it had sometimes seemed to me in the Hollywood days and, to an extent, still did. Evenings, when the eight of us had eaten one of the Hunters' unforgettable meals (or, if we were at our house, one of Ramona's) and the men, fueled by liquor that was gratifyingly cheap in Mexico, got into another of their heated, witty, outrageous discussions, I lingered on the outskirts of the talk with the uneasy conviction (which I never told anyone, even Hugo) that we wives were not quite members of the club.

Or perhaps that was only my own private feeling, a throwback to my childhood when, a failed tomboy, I was always the last kid on the block recruited for kick the can or chosen for baseball, because all the boys in the neighborhood knew that no matter how hard I tried, I could neither hit nor catch.

Years later, when my consciousness had been raised, I could look back on those evenings with a different perspective. But at the time, I only felt a vague discomfort and wished that *someone* would let me on the team.

* * * *

By early February the Mexican school system's long vacation, held in winter because the summer rainy season turned most of central Mexico into a soggy mass, ended, and our children started classes.

The American School was a roomy, well-maintained group of buildings on a pleasant, grassy rise in Colonia Tacubaya, on the farther side of Chapultepec Park, with a student body of about a thousand, ranging from kindergarten through high school, roughly half of them American. Our children, like most of those educated in the public school system, considered school as neither bad nor good but merely inevitable and accepted this one without demur. Though initially most of their classes were in English, they spent an hour a day studying something called "Special Spanish," designed to mainstream them as quickly as possible into the regular half-English, half-Spanish curriculum. (All schools in Mexico, for accreditation, had to meet the national elementary-school requirements in all subjects.) The teachers, in both English and Spanish, were first-rate, the subject matter well ahead of the California system, and to those of my stateside peers who object on principle to bilingual education in the United States, I can only say that the system works. Our children got a wonderful education in both languages and are still comfortably bilingual. In fact, their foundation in Spanish made it wonderfully easy for them to learn French and Italian later on.

In any event, with all but the youngest children (our Emily and the Lardners' Jimmy) safely stowed away in classes during the day, we adults settled into something approaching a routine. In their marble mausoleum a few blocks from us, Cleo had turned one of the Trumbo bathrooms into a darkroom and was busy processing the photos she had taken on the journey down. Trumbo was at his typewriter, working on a real-life screenplay called *The Jean Field Story* (one of his few to be neither made nor sold, even under a pseudonym). Ring was at work on a novel about a latter-day Candide, later published as *The Ecstasy of Owen Muir,* his wife busying herself with domestic tasks but chafing to be back in New York, looking for acting jobs. The Hunters were prowling about the city and its environs getting acquainted with Mexico's popular arts, which were easy to fall in love with. I was researching and writing a short story laid in a Quaker service camp in Mexico (which didn't sell either), and Hugo, to our infinite relief, had begun to work with Spanish refugee director Luis Buñuel on rewrites of Hugo's *Robinson Crusoe* script for a local two-language production.

Buñuel was a fascinating figure. A not very tall man with simian arms and shoulders, balding head, and exophthalmic eyes, he was married to a tall, blond, handsome Frenchwoman he'd met during his early filmmaking days in Paris, and as he and Hugo became more immersed in preparations for *Crusoe,* we went often to Sunday afternoon *comidas* in their backyard, where Jeanne Buñuel cooked paella over an outdoor stove for her husband, her two sons, and assorted bright, voluble Spanish-intellectual friends.

Jeanne's paellas were things of beauty. A medley of chunks of fish and whole clams and shrimps and bright red *langostinos* (crawfish) in their shells, with baby artichokes and pieces of chicken and Mexican sausage buried in a saffron-golden rice, they were served up steaming from a wide, shallow iron cooking pot, and together with baskets of hot French bread and bowls of salad and glasses of red wine (Buñuel sometimes took his in a long, thin stream from the spout of a wineskin) and eaten at rough wood picnic tables, they were an altogether new experience for us. By our second or third Buñuel Sunday, we were beginning to think of our eating habits back in California as painfully pallid and provincial. In fact, our journey down into this country and our first few months here were making us think of our whole lives as pallid and provincial, political problems notwithstanding.

Buñuel was also a renegade Catholic, so wildly irreverent that Hugo and I, agnostics both, used nonetheless to wonder when the lightning would strike. It never ceased to astonish us that this gentle, courteous—almost courtly—man could have created the landmark *Le Chien Andalou* (cowritten with his boyhood friend Salvador Dalí before the Spanish Civil War), which contained, in the slashed-eyeball image, perhaps the most savage single shot in film history. As for his subsequent *L'Age d'Or*, he told us with great satisfaction that it had so inflamed the Parisian audience at its premier that they had torn up their theater seats and thrown paint at the screen.

There were more contradictions. Though his favorite sport was skeet shooting, he couldn't bear to cause the death of any living thing; when he came on a housefly or a spider in his house, he escorted it outdoors and set it free. And of the early months of the Spanish war, he would admit later in his memoir: "I, who had been such an ardent subversive, who had so desired the overthrow of the established order, now found myself in the middle of a volcano, and I was afraid."

As his country had fallen in the path of the Fascists, Buñuel had gone from Spain to France and, finally, to the United States, finding work as film archivist for New York's Museum of Modern Art. But his old friend Dalí, who had become a supporter of the Fascists in Spain, had denounced him in his newly published autobiography as an atheist, creating such a wave of negative publicity for the museum that Buñuel felt he had no choice but to offer his resignation. Eventually he brought his family to Mexico City, where his recent *Los Olvidados* (retitled, in the States, *The Young and the Damned*) won for Mexico its first award at the Cannes Film Festival.

But he seemed content with his Mexican exile. *"Es mi cementerio encantado"* ("It's my enchanted cemetery"), he said. And his commitment to *Crusoe* at this point was helping George Pepper raise more of the financing.

Altogether, the preparations for *Crusoe* were giving us a touch of cautious confidence these days; we could think now of a longer stay here. On the children's weeklong May vacation, we bundled ourselves into our tall, stately car again and drove to the Texas border to renew our tourist cards (having serious overheating problems en route because we had driven through a field of—of all things—monarch butterflies, which had died by the thousands plastered against our engine grille). And on our return, we began to think about finding a house with a longer lease and, we hoped, a more Mexican ambiance.

We found it.

Serendipitously, as it happened. I'd met a young American woman, Jeanne Heller, whose husband was in Mexico producing a Mexican version of *Howdy Doody*, and we had agreed to get my almost three-year-old Emily and her not quite five-year-old son Kent together to see if there was any basis for friendship between them. And so, one early afternoon not long after, Emily and I navigated the busy Avenida de los Insurgentes across town to the lovely Spanish colonial suburb of San Angel Inn, parked the car along Jeannie's pepper-tree-and-jacaranda-shaded street, and rang the bell at a pair of blue metal gates punctuating a long brick wall.

Jeannie and her little boy admitted us. We found ourselves in a small garden enclosed on two sides by that same wall and on the third by a row of organo cactus and honeysuckle, with tropical trees and shrubs edging the grass between. Facing us, across a modest patch of lawn, was a small, square, dusty-rose modern house with a freestanding cement staircase curving down from a cantilevered upper floor to the overhung veranda in front, where the tangled tentacles of an elephant-ear plant grew crazily all over the shaded facade.

I looked at it all, the house, the garden, and unaccountably began to tremble.

The children were introduced and were persuaded to go off to play with Kent's new wagon while my hostess—with an almost casual mention that the neighboring house overlooking this one, of similar architecture, was the studio of Diego Rivera—took me indoors for coffee. Oh, yes. There was a small, almost austere fireplace built flush into one wall, with built-in bookshelves on either side; one whole wall of glass doors and windows looking out into a small back garden as lushly planted as the front; and on the wall of the dining L at the end of the living room, a *mural,* which managed, like so many of the Mexican murals we'd seen, to be both socially significant and beautiful at the same time. The whole house was small, simple, functional, and wonderful. By now I knew why I was trembling. I felt exactly as I had the day I'd met Hugo that first time at the MGM commissary: a sense of meeting my fate, or a big part of it, face-to-face.

"Let me know," I said to Jeannie, trying to sound casual, "if you ever want to leave this place."

She called me two months later and said they were leaving.

* * * * *

Just before we moved, a story appeared in the Mexican papers that Jeannie, bilingual enough to translate, reported to me.

A young Mexican father, it seemed, had taken his four-year-old son to the merry-go-round in Chapultepec Park the previous weekend and stood by watching (as I had, when I'd taken our own small children there) while his little boy had ridden round and round on his horse, waving to him as he passed. When he dismounted, however, the child told his father the horse had bitten him.

The father dismissed the story, of course, and they'd gone home.

Within hours, the child was dead.

Doctors diagnosed snakebite. So public-health officials had gone back to the park, where the distraught father identified the horse his child had ridden. The officials dismantled the horse and cracked it open.

They found a nest of young coral snakes in its head.

The father and his child were strangers to us, but the story gave me nightmares for a long time afterward. Even when I thought I had put it out of mind, it hovered there in my subconscious like those worrisome anti-Protestant signs on the doors at Teotihuacán, adding a strange, anxious subtext, as though there might always be something unknown, unexpected, hiding behind the cheerfulest day, the bluest sky. Serpents in the carousel.

Chapter Five

"HOUSES," says E. M. Forster's heroine in *Howard's End*, "are alive ..."

It was true. Moving our family and still sparse possessions into our new dwelling—unpacking into the built-in cupboards and shelves and onto those bits of our landlord's minimalist furniture already in place—we were too busy to realize it, but here we were, exiled, living in a country not our own, and we had stumbled onto the house we would come to love more than any we had ever lived in. It's been half a century since that first summer in San Angel, but when I close my eyes I can still see, through the windows that walled our living room on the east, the maguey and the nopal outside, the banana palm and the loquat tree and the pepper and the castorberry tree that helped enclose our tiny yard, and indoors, almost at my feet, the early sunlight slicing in, setting the dark red tile floor ablaze and lighting up the L of the dinette and the muted colors of the mural: factories and oil wells and a capitalist skeleton in top hat and high-button shoes on one side of it and fecund Mexican countryside and Aztec ruins on the other, and my heart aches to be there again.

The mural's painter, our landlord, Juan O'Gorman, had studied architecture under LeCorbusier in Paris and had designed this house like a small battleship, without an inch of waste space. Its blue metal door frames were so narrow that I, who tended to move hastily about with arms akimbo, was constantly thwacking my elbows. There was a dark little kitchen, S shaped and narrow, which anyone but Ramona would have despaired of, and our hallway stairs, with their cement steps not carpeted but painted, had as balustrade lengths of painted iron pipe (well—why not?). And the cluster of bedrooms upstairs were almost cell-like in their simplicity, but each had a roomwide bank of windows across one whole wall, looking out.

O'Gorman had also designed (in much the same style) Diego Rivera's studio next door, separated from us by a stretch of brick wall and a stand of organo cactus; the maestro's studio, all windows, peered down over our front garden like a kindly, nonjudgmental uncle. In later months, during our children's various birthday parties when everyone had spilled out onto the front lawn for a rowdy game of musical chairs, we could sometimes see Don Diego himself watching down from his windows, his round, froglike face wreathed in smiles.

The lower panes of his windowed wall were opaque, giving him at least a little privacy, but through the upper panes we could make out, strung from his ceiling, great, giant Judases: colored papier-mâché demon figures crawling with sculpted lizards and scorpions and strung with firecrackers, like those smaller figures set off by Mexican children on the *Sábado de Gloria* (the Saturday before Easter), which the maestro apparently collected. Our Mike, however, who had been much impressed with the Rivera murals we'd seen out at Chapingo, had more curiosity—and a better view. The glass wall of his bedroom upstairs faced Rivera's across only those few feet of garden, and at night when his lights were out, he used to lie in bed and, through his binoculars, watch the maestro painting at his easel in the lighted room beyond, amid the dangling Judases.

For myself, though, the moments I came to treasure most were the early mornings: waking well before the rest of the family, coming downstairs in my bathrobe to get a cup of *café con leche* from Ramona in the kitchen, and taking it outside to the veranda, where the air was moist now and sweet smelling after a night's rain. Sitting there on a deck chair to read the English-language paper, with the fresh smell of honeysuckle on the air and, if I glanced up, a glimpse above our front wall of the San Angel Inn's seventeenth-century Carmelite-mission rooftop across the street, outlined against a washed-blue sky . . . This was my own time, before the day's responsibilities began, and I loved it.

But for the family as a whole, the most wonderful part of our new dwelling was the great empty lot adjoining us on the farther side, closed off from the street by the same brick wall that enclosed the whole block and separated from our yard by little more than a few cactus and a stand of honeysuckle. Hip deep in weeds, it was a huge area, big enough for at least three or four houses. No one seemed to know whom it belonged to, and no owner ever turned up to claim it—but our baseball-enthusiast friend Ian Hunter knew in a moment what use it must be put to.

That's how our Saturday morning interfamily, intergenerational baseball games were born.

They were an instant success. With players ranging in age from nine to fifty, skills varied, of course. Of all our four families, the truest athlete was probably Cleo Trumbo, who, lean, lithe, shy, and utterly herself, often seemed more like a wild deer than the wife of a Hollywood screenwriter. And our Mike, always wonderfully coordinated, made his reputation early on with a double play. Hugo was an enthusiast, but as a boy, he'd been too chubby for many sports and in college had even had to quit crew because of a heart murmur. So now, though he played with zeal and competence out on our own diamond, he earned more recognition for his wit than for his skill.

But in general, age, sex, size, or skill made no difference. Dew wet to the knees, the players bunted, hit pop flies, or struck out, yelling or cheering or moaning in dismay while I, no athlete, hovered in the yard, looking after my small Emily and any other child too young to wield a bat or stayed busy in the kitchen (since Saturdays were Ramona's day off), showing our six-year-old Mary how to make lemonade.

And while our four Hollywood families formed the nucleus of the group, we were soon joined by others. Earliest recruits were the two older Kilian boys, friends of Mike's from the American School; their mother (a teacher there); and their father, who, like Bob Heller, had been working on the Mexican version of *Howdy Doody*. Their youngest boy, too little for baseball, spent his time unsuccessfully trying to teach our small, puzzled Emily how to play mumblety-peg, but she never got the hang of it.

Our neighbors the Druckers, who lived near the Hunters in one of the houses on the Inn grounds, joined us too. David, somewhat older than the rest of us, whose general enthusiasm for life we all found infectious, had been a New York attorney. One of his client companies back home had been a Russian trade organization, which under recent law would have required him to register as a "foreign agent," so he, knowing perfectly well that he was no such thing, had chosen to avoid this Hobson's choice by moving with his family to Mexico instead.

Another volunteer was a classmate of Mike and Chris's, a lean, dark-haired, dark-eyed girl named Linda Oppen, whose father was a carpenter/cabinetmaker; the family lived over the San Angel post office, not far away, and seemed to know everyone we knew, so we assumed they were probably radicals, though we hadn't gotten very well acquainted with them yet.

And there was a psychologist from Berkeley named Hans Hoffman, a big, bluff, good-looking man who, with his wife, Anne, had been among a group of Berkeley radicals called before a local grand jury investigating a physicist referred to in the press only as "Scientist X"—who turned out to be someone the Hoffmans barely knew. But the publicity alone had been enough to end Hans's academic career and had brought *that* family to Mexico.

Our Saturdays were falling into a pattern now. When the players had worn themselves out, they would drift back, damp and disheveled, to our front yard to eat their brown-bag lunches on our veranda while Hugo and I put out beer, lemonade, coffee, and sometimes, if Mary and I had been very ambitious, potato salad. Often during the rainy season clouds would gather during the morning, and then by midday the rain came, pummeling down suddenly on all sides of us while we sat safe and dry under the veranda's overhang, just out of its reach.

Afterward, sated, we would move inside to lounge about our little living room as the rain went on beating against the back windows and listen to David Drucker's wife, Esther, whose hobby was folk music, accompany herself on the guitar; we joined her or not, as the spirit moved us, in "Sixteen Tons," "John Henry," "Buttermilk Hill," "Greensleeves," and "Barb'ry Allen" (and later, as we became more acclimated, songs like Mexico's "*La Llorona*"). There were times those Saturdays when it seemed in spite of everything to be the best of all possible worlds.

But while we were enjoying it all, the baseball, the picnic lunches, the music, and above all the fellowship, it didn't occur to us (how could it?) that not everyone viewed these gatherings with the same eyes. Years later, when the blacklist and the Cold War had ended and most of us had returned to the States, several of us (out of morbid curiosity, I suppose) sent to Washington under the Freedom of Information Act for copies of our FBI files. And that's how we discovered, shuffling through pages ninety percent blacked out (for "security" purposes!), that the FBI had been regularly reporting our ball game Saturdays those years as a cover for "Communist meetings."

Blissfully unaware of this surveillance, however, we were settling in. The children went off each morning to catch the school bus at the corner. Hugo was increasingly busy with Buñuel on rewrites and preproduction of *Robinson Crusoe,* but we began, when we could, to get acquainted with our new environs.

We were one house down from Avenida Alta Vista, which, lined in spring by purple jacaranda trees, began its meandering climb a mile or so beyond, up the nearby slopes to a widespread *panteón* (cemetery) that looked down over this part of the valley of Mexico and where many of Mexico's famous were buried. Climbing farther (as we did one Sunday, two carloads of assorted Butlers, Trumbos, Lardners, and Hunters), one reached the heavier brush and then the sudden darkness of a pinewoods and ultimately, a spot called the Desierto de los Leones.

This was truly a misnomer, since it was certainly no desert and there were no lions. It was instead another ruined monastery, in much worse repair than our own San Angel Inn. Heavily shaded by woods and the surrounding mountains, it was an unsettling relic of Spain's dark history here during the Inquisition. Its dank cellars were still studded by alcoves where, centuries ago, heretics had been chained for the water-drip torture. Naturally the alcoves, their rusted chains still embedded in the walls—together with the ominous history of the place—absolutely enchanted the children, who fingered the chains with awe, and shuddered happily, and hoped against all hope that a lion might turn up too.

But if one traveled south from our house instead of west, one reached Cuernavaca.

Close enough to Mexico City to make a good day's outing and several thousand feet lower than the 7,300-foot-high capital, it would become our close-to-home vacation spot and a reminder that we were nearer the tropics than we realized.

A toll road was being built (for those who could afford it), but in the meantime, one drove the winding old road up and over the intervening mountain range (another seven thousand feet high), trying not to run down the odd cow, or herd of goats, or stray bicyclist, or even the occasional deer that might be just beyond the next curve. It was on our first trip over this road and, as I remember, not far from the summit, when the children spotted a group of white-painted wooden crosses, perhaps a half dozen of them, set back from the road and partially screened by trees and brush. What, we wondered, had happened here? Later we would learn that the crosses marked the graves of a group of *Cristeros,* militant Catholics who, in the 1920s, had been part of a plot to overthrow Mexico's anticlerical government. But they'd been betrayed, intercepted here en route to Mexico City, and shot on the spot.

For the moment, however, we merely puzzled at it all and drove on: over the crest and down, down toward the valley below and the lush outskirts of Cuernavaca, where we had arranged to visit the Maltz family.

As the road began to level off, it wasn't just the greenness, the rich tropical growth that struck us, but the odors too: of moisture, and rotting undergrowth, and charcoal fires, and roasting tortillas all mingled with the fainter smell of farm animals. This valley had been an agricultural center long before it had become the country's playground, and now, as we drove into the town itself, we found it a haphazard but agreeable mix of market stalls and curio shops, churches, hotels, verdant little parks with their bandstands, a few public buildings left from colonial days, dwellings with handsome gardens half hidden behind walls, and a general air of lushness and decay—a sort of sensory overload captured brilliantly, we would find when we discovered the book, in Malcolm Lowry's *Under the Volcano.*

And as we made our way through the unfamiliar streets toward the Maltzes' address, we wondered what impact all this seductive chaos would have on anyone who actually lived here. . . .

For whatever reason, we had never struck up a real friendship with the Maltzes, though of course we had infinite respect for Albert's achievements as a playwright with New York's Group Theater and as a writer of short stories and screenplays. Like Trumbo and Ring, Albert was one of the Hollywood Ten who'd received a full one-year sentence, but unlike them, he had found no way to adapt to prison life. He had come down with infectious hepatitis early in his stay, prison food made him even sicker than he already was, and he had faced the last months of his sentence in real fear of rearrest and another jailing—which, he was convinced, would kill him.

So, according to his wife Margaret's telling of it, when he was due for release, he had arranged for her to meet him with the family car loaded for immediate emigration; she'd met him at the prison gates, and they had driven all night, not stopping till they were across the border. Unlike most of the blacklistees, however, he had no need to live close to the local film industry, because, I gathered, he had an independent income and could afford to write what he pleased. So he, Margaret, and their two adopted children were able to settle here, in a residential suburb of Mexico's lotus land, in a pleasant house with a pool.

They welcomed us cordially; we'd stay for *comida*, wouldn't we? Sorry their children weren't here, but come in, come in, would we like a swim? . . . Albert will just get the barbecue going. . . .

Curiously, I remember almost no details of our visit with them that day; I know only that then, as always in stateside encounters in previous years, there seemed to be a solemnity, a reverence about Albert's position in both the world and the household, and Margaret, a good, conscientious, intelligent woman some dozen years older than Albert, seemed more like his acolyte than his wife. And as the day wore on, I had a fleeting sense that I had somehow stumbled into a church I wasn't a member of, with a deity I found it hard to accept.

As for *comida*, that didn't come off as planned either. Albert had put a good-sized T-bone on the coals and ushered us indoors to make us drinks—but a stray dog got under the gate, grabbed the steak off the barbecue, and made off with it. We saw him just as he was disappearing with the steak in his jaws.

There were other trips to Cuernavaca, during which we checked out the local pyramid (a small one, as pyramids go), and a side trip to Palo Bolero, where we walked a rope-suspended footbridge across a chasm to reach a small lake fed by a waterfall with a wonderful aqueous cave behind it. And once there was an evening trip down without the children, to a grown-up party of which I remember only a slightly drunken lady photographer who insisted to our fiercely embarrassed friend Ian that she "wanted to walk barefoot through his hair." The festivities broke up too late for us to drive back over the mountain, and Hugo and I were directed to a local hotel just off the main plaza, which might have room for us at this late hour.

And I remember as we were checking in my almost guilty feeling of pleasure, of being either on an assignation with Hugo or a honeymoon—which always heightened my enjoyment of our trips away from home. . . .

Our discovery of the real tropics, though, happened almost by accident. At least for me.

During one of the long school holidays—probably the *"dieciséis"* (the September 16 celebrations of Mexico's *Independencia*)—our Mary, then in second grade, had been invited by the family of one of her school friends to Acapulco, and stifling my ferocious tendency to overprotect, I had let her go. A few days later, an early returning member of the group stopped by to give me an update. Mary was getting along marvelously, it appeared; she was already as brown as a berry and hadn't a shred of fear. She'd been paddling on her little plastic life preserver all the way out to the buoys where the boats were anchored in Acapulco Bay. . . .

I was swept by panic. Mary couldn't swim!

The moment the visitor left, I began to throw clothes into a suitcase. Three-year-old Emily, seeing me pack, burst into tears: "I want to go too. I've never *been* to Apulcoco!"

I didn't even wait for Hugo to come home. Within an hour Emily and I were at the airport, en route to save Mary before she drowned.

When we reached Acapulco and the house where Mary and her host family were staying, we found her in no danger of drowning whatsoever. She was rosy, happy, and having a wonderful time.

But on our way into town from the airport, Emily and I had seen real, honest-to-goodness jungle edging the tarmac and the road into town. We'd seen palm trees lining every seascape, and the hotels and houses of Acapulco clinging to the green hills that cupped the bay, and a different view of the bay or the ocean at every turn, and we didn't want to go home. I telephoned Hugo to come down and join us and checked us all into a lovely, small hillside hotel looking out over the bay. Each bedroom had a little screened sleeping porch, with palm fronds rustling gently at the screens, and by the time Hugo arrived, the girls and I wanted the September holidays to last forever.

But they didn't. And home again in Mexico City and the real world, Hugo and I took a good look at our savings and realized that they were, not surprisingly, in steep decline.

While we'd never been extravagant in our previous lives, we'd never learned to live strictly within our income either. Why should we? From the moment each of us had become a wage-earning adult, we'd been able to find employment in our chosen profession. Even now, with all our troubles, small sums had come drifting in. Early in our stay, Bob Aldrich, always a loyal and generous friend, had written, asking Hugo to write something he called a "sand and tits" picture, and Hugo had obliged, finishing in something under a week. Bob, who at that time was just struggling to establish himself as a director, had paid him two or three thousand dollars. (Later the picture had been released pseudonymously as *World for Ransom* and to my relief proved not raunchy at all but just a well-put-together adventure picture.) And sometime during our second year in Mexico, modest sums had begun to arrive in my name for a picture I'd written on spec (speculatively) a couple of years earlier with our director friend Bernard Vorhaus. Bernie had titled it *So Young, So Bad;* it dealt with a group of teenagers at a home for delinquent girls, starred Paul Henreid as a psychiatrist, and launched the careers of a whole group of talented teenage actresses: Anne Francis, Anne Jackson, and Rita Moreno. And since the whole production had been shot more or less on the cuff, I'd been paid with a percent of the gross. The returns couldn't support us, of course, but they helped.

But *Crusoe,* to which Hugo was now devoting himself full-time, was still only a labor of love. Shooting and postproduction work still lay ahead, and a distribution deal, which would finally bring in a little money, had yet to be arranged.

So we were beginning to wonder with some anxiety which would come first, returns from *Crusoe* or an empty bank account—

—When I discovered I was pregnant.

Where had it happened? Cuernavaca, that night we'd had to stay over unexpectedly? Or Acapulco, another unplanned-for holiday? (I remembered the palm fronds rustling on our screens in the night breeze off the bay . . .) Or here at home? There were, after all, those ceramic storks, one on each side of our bed, which the Hellers had left behind them as a gift when they moved out . . .

My dismay was not at being pregnant, which always brought me a fierce, almost Darwinian sense of joy and fulfillment, but at the timing. Another baby now, with our professional futures so much in doubt and no assurance we would ever be able to return to our own country? How could I even break the news to Hugo?

I knew well enough what it would mean to him: another child to support, to worry about, to educate—and to preoccupy me at a time when he (still really an only child, and so a bit spoiled) wanted more, not less, of my time and attention. And since my own earnings were sporadic at the best of times, the bulk of the financial responsibility for this new addition would of course fall on him. . . .

Oddly, though I remember my own worries about his reaction to the news, I have no recollection of what he actually *said* when I told him. None at all. My fears about his response may have proved groundless. I wish I could remember.

But I have a very sharp memory of Ramona's reaction when I told her. Trying to allay my anxieties about being able to afford another baby, she told me that in Mexico there was a saying: *"Cada niño llega con su propio pan"* ("Every baby arrives with its own loaf of bread"). Later I would learn that in Spain they say that every baby arrives with its own shoes.

But shoes or bread—our lives had just become a good deal more complicated. Especially for Hugo.

Chapter Six

I THINK there must be a god who looks after independent filmmakers.

The script of *Crusoe* was at last ready for production. Interiors would be shot on a sound stage at a Mexico City studio, Tepeyac. But the bulk of the picture, the exteriors, would be shot on location—many of them, when Crusoe was alone on the island, shot silent, for economy's sake; Crusoe's narration, in both Spanish and English, would be dubbed in later, along with other sound effects. The pirates would need live sound, naturally, as would Crusoe's scenes with Friday, but everything that could be done in postproduction would be. And for the location scenes, Buñuel and our friend George Pepper, who was the picture's coproducer, had chosen Manzanillo, a little seacoast town on the Pacific, surrounded by jungle and with a few still wild, photogenic beaches doubling as the island. It was imperative, of course, that location shooting (all of it outdoors) be completed before the next rainy season—but thus far, no actor had been found for the title role.

This was the state of affairs when Orson Welles's *Macbeth* came to town.

It was screening with Spanish subtitles at one of the local theaters, and Jeanette Nolan McIntire, a friend since my *One Man's Family* days, was playing Lady Macbeth. So one evening after I'd gotten the children to bed, Hugo and I drove downtown for a night at the movies.

And discovered Dan O'Herlihy, the Irish-English actor who played Macduff.

We had seen him in other pictures and had even met him briefly at a gathering at the McIntires' a few years ago. But in *Macbeth*, as the bluff, bereaved father ("What, all my pretty chickens and their dam /

At one fell swoop?"), he was splendid. He looked imposing in a beard, and he had a fine voice. Would he do for Crusoe?

He would indeed. Wheels were set in motion. George Pepper learned that O'Herlihy was not only available, he was enthusiastic. And Jaime Fernandez, a younger brother of Mexico's famous "El Indio" Emilio Fernandez, would play Friday.

It was urgent, of course, to avoid having either George's or Hugo's name linked to *Crusoe* in any way, since the investors hoped for an American distribution. Accordingly George, needed on the set in his role of coproducer, had become "George P. Werker." But Buñuel, putting art above commerce, insisted that his screenwriter too be on the set during shooting in case rewrites were needed, and Hugo was eager to oblige. So as soon as the company was settled in on location and ready to work, and figuring he'd solve the problem of his public identity as the need arose, Hugo packed his bag, bade us good-bye, and set off with his portable typewriter to join them.

He went by way of Guadalajara, where he caught the little one-class train that traveled to the west coast—discovering, in the process, that it was occupied about equally by people and their farm animals. It was also boarded at every stop, he told me later, by peddlers hawking soft drinks and snacks; they would ply their wares up and down the aisles till the train took off again, and then, as it began to pick up speed, swing down to the ground. Farther west, the train made its way through heavy jungle and across trestles that had Hugo holding his breath— but it reached the seacoast at last with everyone intact.

When he caught up with the company at the little hotel they had chosen as headquarters, he was introduced to the crew under his mother's maiden name and acquired an instant history. He became "Mr. Addis," a wealthy Canadian wheat rancher who had struck oil on his Alberta ranch and had invested some of his new fortune in the picture. It was a nice cover, but he had one worry: would O'Herlihy remember their previous meeting?

Fortunately, he didn't. Hugo took care, however, to do his rewrites at night with the curtains drawn. And his daytime role as "investor," he found, netted him far more respect from the company than is ever accorded the screenwriter.

Actually, there was another slight problem. The preceding year, a number of Manzanillo residents, several of them doctors unable to reach the hospital for antivenom serum in time, had died of scorpion stings. This news gave O'Herlihy serious qualms, since most of Crusoe's action took place barefoot on the beach. Hugo didn't tell me how the problem was resolved—handmade moccasins, maybe—but it did give him the germ of an idea for a haunting little film story he wrote later, called *Alacrán!* (Scorpion!), which was made in Mexico in 1968 as *Figuras de Arena* (Sand Sculptures). This would be the last of his stories ever to be bought, the offer reaching me by phone in Hollywood at the very moment Hugo was in hospital with what proved a fatal heart attack.

The *Crusoe* footage being shot in Manzanillo, and to a lesser extent on the Mexico sound stage later, was proving almost as much Buñuel as Defoe, and Hugo himself was so fascinated by Buñuel's own special vision that he did not question this approach to the material. In the finished picture, for instance, when Friday comes upon the flotsam salvaged from the shipwreck and out of simple curiosity puts on a woman's dress, it evokes a furious overreaction from Crusoe—raising an odd resonance about the castaway's frustrated sexuality during his years on the island. And during Crusoe's illness, he has a fevered dream image of scrubbing a pig, while his hallucinatory father (in dialogue transposed from the book's much earlier father-son scene prior to Crusoe's sea voyage) lectures him on the advisability of hewing to "the middle station of life." Both pure Buñuel, but moments that linger indelibly in one's memory of the picture.

As the screenplay finally evolved, it was a story of solitude, of man's need for and dependence on his fellow man. The most moving scene of all, I think, was conceived not by Defoe at all, but by Hugo and Buñuel: the scene when Crusoe, driven almost mad by loneliness, goes to the island's valley of echoes and, desperate to hear a human voice even if it's only his own, shouts out the Twenty-third Psalm as, line by line, his voice echoes back to him: "The Lord . . . is my shepherd; I shall not want . . . He maketh me . . . to lie down in green pastures: he leadeth me . . . beside the still waters . . . He restoreth my soul . . ."

* * * * *

Meanwhile the makeup of our little circle of friends in Mexico City was changing.

A reverse migration had begun. The Lardners, with Frances impatient to get back to the theater, had left for New York when their six months' lease was up. Their departure was followed another six months later by the Hunters, who were finding it fairly urgent to get employment. In years to come, Ian and Ring would establish a highly successful, albeit pseudonymous collaboration in television in New York and England, but at the time, as each family left, we felt increasingly bereft. The Trumbos were still in Mexico and of course the Peppers (with George still heavily involved in *Crusoe*), but in the main, the Hollywood coloration of our group was fading fast.

However, there were still the families from other parts of the country who had preceded us down, and with these we were beginning to form closer friendships. As in a stateside suburb, these relationships tended to be on a whole-family basis, children and parents together. While we were getting to know and enjoy the Hoffmans, their oldest child, Erika, just the age of our Susie and like Susie slender, pigtailed, thoughtful, and studious, was quickly becoming her best friend. Mary would miss having her playmate Timmy Hunter in the neighborhood, but her favorite friend by far was still the Trumbos' youngest, Mitzi. And when the Hellers returned to Mexico from their brief sojourn in the States, their young son, Kent, and our small Emily became, by instant agreement, Mickey Mouse and Pluto. It wasn't exactly that they became the *incarnations* of these two characters, though when they were together, they would answer to no other names. Their relationship to their alter egos was more complex. They had an unnerving habit of conducting their every conversation as though it were being read aloud from the printed page. For instance, Kent would say to Emily: " 'I know,' said Mickey, 'let's play fire engines.' " And Emily would say to Kent: " 'Okay,' said Pluto. 'Let's!' "

As for our Mike: At school and on our baseball field, he and the Kilians' older boys—Crawford, passionately devoted to science fiction, and Lincoln, inevitably a Civil War buff—had become, along with Chris Trumbo, an inseparable foursome, with Linda Oppen (whose major enthusiasm was horses) making an occasional tomboy fifth.

But we still had only a passing acquaintance with Linda's parents. Finally, though, on one of Hugo's early trips home from Manzanillo, the senior Oppens invited us over for dinner.

There's no special reason that it should have seemed such a strange

and wonderful evening, but it was. For all our radical politics, Hugo
and I were both astonishingly conventional when it came to living arrangements. George and Mary Oppen, on the other hand, were true
bohemians, perhaps the first we had ever met. Their apartment, off a
stairway next to the San Angel post office, was a rambling series of
rooms that may once have been separate dwellings but were now strung
together one flight up from a small back courtyard where one of the
neighbors kept chickens, I remember. Their front door, off the landing,
opened into George's woodworking shop, a confusion of worktables
and a lathe and tools and bits of raw lumber and, since George was
studying wood carving at a Mexican arts center (on money from the
GI Bill of Rights), several half-finished portrait carvings of his friends
in bas-relief, looking down at us from the walls, or, here and there, a
bust on a pedestal amid the clutter. Mary also had work space, though
this tended to be in whichever room could currently accommodate her
easel and painting supplies and elderly sewing machine and photography equipment.

There were, apparently, two or three bedrooms off at the farther end
of the apartment, but here, closer to hand, one went through a kitchen
that was fairly primitive even by local standards to reach a living-dining room where, that first evening, Mary served us by candlelight a
quite good Mexican meal with a bottle of Mexican red wine. When
dinner ended, she simply covered the table—empty wine bottle, dirty
dishes, fragments of food, and all—with a tablecloth, to be dealt with
tomorrow, and, now able to ignore the meal's wreckage, we moved a
few feet away to more comfortable chairs to settle down for the
evening's real conversation.

George seemed to have some sort of tiny income (from a family
inheritance, we assumed), but he and Mary had early on decided to
spend as little of it as possible on lifestyle so they'd have something left
for things that really mattered. Radicals from their early years, they
seemed also to have lived for a while in France in the 1930s, on their
tiny budget, and told of sometimes having to catch fish from the Seine
for their dinner. They'd also spent time in New York, which Mary
hated, and during the war, George, who had enlisted early, had been
an infantryman in the Battle of the Bulge. He and two fellow soldiers
had been trapped in a foxhole under heavy enemy fire; George was the

only survivor, but it had taken him the better part of a year in the hospital to recover.

After the war they'd wandered about the States in a trailer, stopping only when or where they felt like it, with George doing an occasional odd job or bit of house building when the spirit moved him or the family economy demanded. They had just settled down on their own bit of land in California when the Cold War broke out and the FBI began their worrisome visits. Before long, George and Mary had packed up Linda; their dog, Kinch; a few books; George's tools; and Mary's camera and sewing machine and, with another refugee friend in tow, set out for Mexico.

As we swapped personal odysseys, Linda sat off to one side with her arm around their handsome Doberman, Kinch, listening; as it grew late she grew very sleepy, and her eyelids drooped, but Hugo and I hated to see the evening end. We were entranced by our hosts' stories of their vagabond years, and we also found them wonderful to look at: George's lean, Old World face, with his dark eyes and his shaggy mustache and high thin forehead and aquiline nose, looked almost hawklike in the candlelight; and Mary was his antithesis, as fair as he was dark, with clear blue eyes, blond hair done up in a careless bun, an apron pinned over her housedress. I had a fleeting feeling that when I grew up I wanted to look just like her, if it could somehow be arranged.

Altogether, in that wonderful, cockamamie apartment, with Mary's canvases hung frameless on the walls, and George's wood carvings, and here and there the odd tool, or tube of paint, with the abandoned dinner table now just a bunch of curious shapes under the shrouding tablecloth, off to one side of the room—and from below, the night sounds of San Angel's main street drifting up to us—it had been a magical evening.

And when I asked about the dog (who seemed perfectly content now to have Linda using him as a pillow), I learned something else about these people. His name, Kinch, I asked: did it have any particular meaning?

"It's from Joyce," said George. *"Ulysses."*

I felt abashed. I'd read *Portrait of the Artist* and *Dubliners,* which I'd loved, but each time I'd tried *Ulysses,* which I'd done twice, I'd stalled at page 140, and I don't think Hugo had even gotten that far. Had there been a "Kinch" mentioned in those pages? They had left me so confused that I had no idea. Now, clearly, I had to face the fact that carpenter by trade though he might be, George was probably more literate than either Hugo or I. On the way home I vowed to myself (again) that someday I'd read *Ulysses*—carefully—and *finish* it.

But it didn't occur to us, as we drove home, that there might be some central fact about themselves that our hosts had not included in the family tales we'd just been listening to. We only knew we had two new friends now, to make up for the ones who were leaving, and we found them altogether spellbinding.

Hugo, though still involved with *Crusoe,* was once again home on leave from Manzanillo on November 2 when the Oppens took us, along with another couple, in their rattletrap old panel truck to see our first *Día de los Muertos* (Day of the Dead) at Nativitas, a drought-ridden little village on the lava flow a few miles beyond Mexico City. To the church, this was All Souls' Day, but since Mexico's early people boasted their own rich folklore before the Spaniards ever arrived, the holiday had become, over the years, an engaging mix of the two wildly different cultures.

It was already evening when George pulled the panel truck up just outside the ironwork fence that enclosed the village's ancient burial ground, and as we disembarked we were almost deafened by mariachi music blasting from speakers nearby. Here at hand we could make out figures, almost life sized, poised in a midair leap over the iron fence: grinning papier-mâché skeletons and a hooded, grinning figure of Death on a pale horse. Beyond, inside the enclosure, there seemed to be a good many people clustered about, but our view of them was clouded by some sort of smoky haze, with a faint orange-tinted glow thrown upward from below. As we made our way inside we saw that whole families were gathered here in groups about the burial places of their departed; they had strewn marigold petals in an almost solid carpet over the graves (which gave the place its eerie orange cast); at each grave site, stubs of candles burned, sheltered from the breeze by torn bits of newspaper, which muted the glow, and smoke drifted up from an incense burner on every grave, making the whole scene dreamlike and unreal.

And as we made our way along the path that wound toward the

little church in the background, we passed something that stopped us: an enormous pile of blackened human skulls, hundreds of them, clearly relics of the Aztec burial ground that had occupied this space for centuries before the Spanish invasion.

All the living celebrants around us, though, were having a wonderful time, clustered about their family plots as though for a party—picnicking, drinking, chatting convivially, and scattering *pan de muerto* for the dead to eat later when everyone had gone home. (For "dead" read, more accurately, "rats.") This keeping in touch with the dead, we realized, was clearly an occasion for joy. As the Oppens moved on ahead of us, another of our group paused at an especially festive grouping to chat with one of the celebrants, commenting (in far better Spanish than either Hugo or I could yet manage) with enthusiasm about the event. And the townsperson answered with sober courtesy, in the words used in Mexico to welcome any newcomer to one's home, *"Esta es su casa, señor"* (roughly, "My house is your house," or, more literally, "This is your house, señor").

And now came other holidays, in season. There was a co-op Thanksgiving dinner at the Hoffmans', with each family cooking and bringing part of the provender, and labor songs sung afterward to someone's guitar (probably Esther Drucker's). The Oppens were there too, and a few other families we'd gotten to know, and altogether we had a lovely sense of belonging. Evenings like this, along with our Saturday-morning ball games, and assorted picnics and excursions, were beginning to give us a close-knit feeling, as though we and our children were part of a very large family or a very small town.

And then of course came Christmas. Having bought the children all the wrong presents (local folk-art toys) last year, I vowed to do better this year. I discovered a music store and, our declining bank account notwithstanding, bought the children a number of rhythm instruments and assorted music makers, among other items. We had a pleasant, ordinary Christmas Eve, with stockings hung (or rather Scotch taped to the wall above the fireplace, since we had no mantelpiece), parcels in their wrappings piled under the tree, and, as always, *A Christmas Carol* read aloud. When the children had gone to bed, we filled their stockings and, when we were sure they were asleep, left each child's stocking at the foot of his/her bed (to keep them all busy for perhaps an extra half hour tomorrow morning, we hoped). Then, exhausted, we went to bed too.

Just at midnight, from every churchyard in San Angel and nearby Guadalupe Inn (our neighboring *colonia*), church bells began to chime. Rockets went off. Even firecrackers. (Firecrackers, for heaven's sake?)

This pandemonium went on for hours. And just at dawn, as Hugo and I were finally dropping off, the children woke up and discovered their harmonicas, tambourines, and xylophones.

Every Christmas was a discovery of what not to get them.

Then it was the new year. The *Crusoe* company had finished shooting, and the film was in postproduction. By now, though, the whole company was holding its collective breath: Hugo's friend and agent Ingo Preminger, up in the States, was negotiating a distribution deal with United Artists studio.

Hugo's name, of course, could be nowhere mentioned. H. B. Addis, that convenient invention for use during shooting, would not do for a writing credit, nor would any other fictitious name; studios and financiers were well aware by now that any unfamiliar name could be shielding a blacklistee. As writer, the film would need the name of a live body that could be produced on demand, preferably someone credible from the entertainment industry.

George Pepper's producing partner solved the problem by contacting a friend, an executive at a New York radio station, to ask if Hugo could borrow *his* name. So, for the next four-odd decades (until a more enlightened time in history), the putative writing credit of the *Crusoe* screenplay bore the name of a nice, generous New York radio producer we had never met named Philip Ansel Roll.

There was one narrow escape, though.

Sometime that winter, Hugo and I, perhaps to celebrate some milestone in Ingo's negotiations for the picture's distribution, had gotten dressed up and gone to a restaurant in the city's fashionable Zona Rosa for one last splurge before we became too broke even to contemplate eating out. We had been seated at a velvet banquette along the wall and were settling down comfortably to our drinks when abruptly I felt Hugo stiffen, and he indicated to me the man who'd just been seated at the table just beyond us, on the same banquette.

I sneaked a look. It was Leo Townsend, a screenwriter and friendly witness who had named thirty-seven friends before the committee. He was with a woman we didn't recognize, and from the way he kept his face carefully turned away it was clear he recognized us.

He and his dinner partner ordered drinks, and for a time he and Hugo managed to ignore each other. But just as our dinner had been served, the maitre d' caught sight of Hugo and came rushing over. "Señor Addis!" he said excitedly—and asked if the picture had finished shooting. (Hugo told me sotto voce later that this man had played the pirate captain who had come ashore on Crusoe's island, but apparently, like actors the world over, he worked in a restaurant for a living.)

Hugo kept his answers as elliptical as possible, but we were terrified that when we finished dinner and got up to leave, Townsend would corner the maitre d' and ask him what picture he and Hugo had been talking about. Clearly we didn't dare leave before Townsend did.

So there we sat, taking an eternity to finish our meal, eating desserts we didn't want and certainly couldn't afford, and drinking cup after cup of coffee.

So did Townsend. Whether we had guessed his intentions correctly, I've no idea, but he and his dinner partner and Hugo and I sat there almost side by side, each couple pointedly ignoring the other but each trying to outwait the other till the restaurant closed. Except for the staff, we were the last four people to leave.

By now, we were well into January. I was seven months pregnant, and we still didn't know when our first *Crusoe* money would come in.

Chapter Seven

I'M IN THE MIDST of a nightmare. A tiger is chasing me up a long, narrowing cave. I'm hugging to my bosom a bag of groceries as I run. The tiger is gaining on me. Ahead, the cave is narrowing to a dead end. And now, with nowhere left to go, I turn to face him, trying vainly to shield myself with the groceries. But the tiger crouches for a spring and easily overleaps the pitiful barrier—when I wake up, frightened and out of breath. It takes a moment or two for my heart to stop pounding, and I know, almost without thinking, what the dream was really all about.

In those early months of 1953, I had a lot of anxiety nightmares.

I was well into my last trimester. It had been an easy pregnancy; that was not the problem. As a rule, my customary optimism increased enormously whenever I was pregnant; something inside me seemed to tell me I was fulfilling my biological imperative and all was right with the world.

On the other hand, I was also the family accountant: the one who wrote the checks, paid the bills, and supplied Ramona with grocery money on a daily basis—so long as Hugo (with an occasional contribution from me) provided the money to make it all possible. That, of course, was the tiger.

Checks for my *So Young, So Bad* were still coming in, but in diminishing amounts now. They paid our rent, but not much else, and we had no idea how long they would continue. *Crusoe,* however, was still the great unknown. Ingo had arranged a distribution deal for it with United Artists, but we couldn't expect any returns from it for at least a couple of months; the coffers would be empty before the baby arrived.

Hugo sought out Trumbo one day to discuss the situation with him. "I'd always heard about the poverty in Mexico," he said ruefully. "But I never realized it was contagious."

Trumbo confessed that he and Cleo were in much the same shape as we were. However, he had a proposal: what about the Monte de Piedad—the national pawnshop, occupying a vast colonial building that formed one side of the city's great *zócalo* downtown—as a temporary solution? He had a few items he could pawn to meet their immediate needs (like Cleo's jewelry, which he'd given her in better days); he could take those downtown, together with whatever items Hugo wanted to put up, to see how much he could get for them. And, he pointed out, he should be the one to negotiate, since he'd had a lot of experience with pawnshops at various points in his career.

And so next morning Hugo drove across town to the small marble palace in the Lomas, which the Trumbos were still renting, and delivered to him all our family valuables: our portable radio, his (Hugo's) Leica, both our wristwatches, my first-anniversary ring (an antique, with a flawed, purple-red stone we'd always assumed was a ruby), and the amethyst brooch (also antique) that he'd given me when he'd come home from the army. And Trumbo, armed with these family treasures and his own, set out for the Monte.

I don't remember how much each family realized from this adventure, but whatever it was, we knew that at best it would only feed us for a few weeks. And after that, what?

Nor did we know for sure what Trumbo's fallback source of funds would be when they had spent their own pawn money, but we knew there wasn't much need for worry there. Trumbo was endlessly resourceful. He always seemed able to float a loan from one or another of the independent producers he'd worked for "under the table" during the lean days after his HUAC appearance—pledging, perhaps, to pay it off with another rewrite or another screenplay, written fast. And he always delivered.

But except for Bob Aldrich, who was still struggling to build his career, Hugo had no such contacts; most of his work in Hollywood had been for the major studios, where he was now anathema. He wrestled with the problem for a few days and then, knowing there was no alternative, did what his pride had kept him from doing long before: sat down at his typewriter and wrote letters to my mother, his father, and a few nonblacklisted friends, asking for a modest loan and offering as security a percentage of his interest in *Crusoe*.

The most painful letter to write, the one he found the most humiliating, was the one to his father.

Then, with the letters sent off, we settled down to watch the mails for the responses.

More than a fortnight went by. Not a word. By the third week, we telephoned Hugo's mother, whom Hugo had detailed to collect and forward any checks that were forthcoming. And she, bewildered, said she'd airmailed several checks to us at least two weeks ago.

I phoned my mother and got the same answer.

By now we'd gone through the money from the Monte and had nothing else of value to pawn. The morning came when we had to ask Ramona to buy the groceries with her own money, if she could.

Clearly the mails were being tinkered with, but on which side of the border? This side, certainly—but why? We'd leaned over backward to be apolitical, as all our friends here had advised us to be, in a country not our own. We'd been models of propriety. . . .

The only person we could think of to ask about it was our local mailman. So, when he sounded his distinctive little *pito* (whistle) at our gates later that morning, I was downstairs as fast as my awkward girth would let me go and outside the gates.

As always, Señor Flores, of the worried face, the scraggly mustache, and the perpetual five o'clock shadow, was leaning on his bicycle out on the street, his mailbag slung over his back. He handed me the day's mail, which I thumbed through quickly, finding nothing of importance, and, trying to phrase things so he wouldn't feel *he* was under suspicion, I told him about the missing letters from the States.

He looked painfully embarrassed. And muttered something about our mail being *"revisado."*

It was a word I didn't know. Trying to help me out, he added, vaguely, *"Algo politico . . ."*

Something political? Was he telling me that our mail was being censored?

I said I didn't care about our mail being read; it was the money *in* it that we needed. I tried to explain how badly we needed it. He suggested that I meet him at the post office that afternoon when he went off duty, and he would take me to his supervisor.

Without any real hope of tracking our handful of letters through the labyrinthine levels of Mexico's postal bureaucracy, I set out at the appointed hour, with small Emily (who as usual wanted to go too) in tow. We parked on a side street in San Angel, made our way to the teeming little post office (passing en route the stairway that led up to the Oppens' apartment) and on through to the rear entrance to a courtyard where, apparently, the mailmen tethered their bikes in good weather and where we met Señor Flores.

He steered us to a bleak little room that opened onto the courtyard, introduced me to his supervisor (whose air of almost timid courtesy convinced me he was probably just up from the ranks), and recounted our problem of the missing mail—explaining, again embarrassed, that *"la señora está enferma"* ("the señora is ill"), a polite reference to my advanced state of pregnancy.

In the best Spanish I could muster, I repeated the story of the checks we needed so badly and of having had to borrow money from Ramona that morning—and in the middle of the recital found myself so embarrassed and so desperate that I burst into tears.

Both men were dismayed. Even Emily (who had never seen me cry) eyed me in panic. I apologized as best I could. The supervisor said he'd see what could be done. . . .

Utterly discouraged, I thanked both men, and Emily and I made our way back to the car and home.

Hugo met us at the front door. I gave him a report of our visit and trudged upstairs to take a nap.

Within an hour, I heard Señor Flores's *pito* outside the gates again but was too disheartened to get up and answer it myself. In a moment, Hugo came upstairs and tossed a handful of airmail letters on the bed. All bore two-week-old postmarks.

"Never underestimate the power of a woman," he said.

It wasn't till I read a brief story in the inside pages of—of what? The English-language *Mexico City News*? The foreign edition of the *Chicago Tribune*? No matter. A story I read somewhere said that Donald Jackson of HUAC, in company with (as I remember) the committee's attorney, had arrived in Mexico for a brief visit earlier in the month and during his stay had conferred with the mayor of the Federal District (the administrative term for Mexico City). This was all in passing reference, with no elaboration of the bare facts, but I could only assume that the congressman's junket had resulted in the promise of some sort of local censorship of the blacklistees' mail.

But since this was Mexico and not the United States, no effort whatever was made to conceal or even implement the official interference; all the letters had simply been waylaid and left on a shelf somewhere, I guess, contents included. I doubt if anyone had ever given them a second thought until our friends at the local *correo* had intervened.

But now, at last, we had about three thousand dollars, which would see me through my delivery, pay the children's tuition at school and Ramona's and Isabel's salaries, and feed us, God willing, till the first *Crusoe* money came in.

The baby arrived late in March: a darling, round-cheeked, bald-headed (*pelona*) little girl whom we named Deborah. Actually, since the doctor, knowing I was given to long labors, had given me a shot of some sort of hormone, she was almost born in the hall en route to the delivery room. And it was here, in the city's Spanish hospital, that I discovered one of Mexico's primary charms. New mothers were not regimented as they were in hospitals in the States, nor were nursing babies rationed in the amount of time they were allowed with their mothers. If the baby slept or hiccuped through its nursing session, it was simply left there till it had satisfied itself. Hospital schedules in that blessed country were of far less importance than the mothers' and babies' happiness and comfort.

And by summer, Hugo had received his first check from *Crusoe*. Ten thousand dollars. He brought it upstairs to me where I was feeding Debbie and showed it to me.

"I could have wept," he said.

Chapter Eight

PRIMAVERA is the Spanish word for "springtime."

When I first learned it, I thought, with my limited Spanish, that its literal translation had to do with the phrase *"de veras,"* which is used in Mexico to insist that one is telling the absolute truth (much like our "honestly!" or "I swear!"). So the whole word, I reasoned, must translate to "first truth"—a notion I found captivating.

Etymologically, I may have been quite, quite wrong. Nonetheless, whatever its root meaning, I still think it's one of the most beautiful words in the Spanish language.

Springtime in the valley of Mexico, though, is another matter. And that year, 1953, had been no exception. It had been dry, essentially, since the previous autumn, and by now, on the cusp between spring and summer, all moisture seemed to have vanished from the atmosphere. All through March, April, May, we'd been struggling with cracked lips and eyes reddened from the dust that blew across the valley from the parched edges of Lake Texcoco. We had watched the *nubes esteriles,* the sterile clouds, pile up on the horizon and roll across the city and then disappear without giving us so much as a raindrop. Sometimes there'd be a distant roll of thunder, but it had always been a false promise; no rain.

There were hours during the day when the city's water pipes ran bone-dry. That's why almost every Mexican rooftop held a cistern, with or without a pump, and because sometimes even these ran dry, one learned the advisability of subscribing to a bottled-water service. This might or might not be *agua purificada* (purified water) as advertised, but at least it was wet.

And then, finally, the heavy clouds relented and paused over the valley long enough to give us our first light rain. It had come like a benediction.

By mid-June, gardens all over the city had taken on new life; ours had once again turned a variety of passionate shades of green. By now there was a downpour almost every afternoon and sometimes at night too, and when morning broke after a night's drenching, everything about us—the garden, the weeds in the lot next door, the inn's ancient rooftop visible across the street—looked newborn.

It was on one of these mornings that I'd gotten up early to change and feed Debbie, who was proving to be a delightful little creature with a lovely, sunny disposition; we'd played for a few minutes, quietly, so we wouldn't wake up her father or her siblings, and I'd put her back in her crib for her early-morning nap and gone downstairs for my first-of-the-day cup of Ramona's *café con leche,* which I took out to the veranda in front. There was perhaps a half hour of privacy before the rest of the family began to stir; I left my coffee near my deck chair, amid all that welcome moist freshness, and went on to the gates to retrieve the English-language *Mexico City News*—

In big, black headlines the paper said the Rosenbergs had been executed.

It was unbelievable.

It had been, of course, more than two years since they had been declared guilty of giving nuclear secrets to the Soviet Union. But since the appearance of the two gentlemen with hats on our doorstep that January evening in Los Angeles, we'd been too preoccupied with our own problems to pay much attention to any of the newspaper headlines—and anyway, we had felt that the Rosenbergs' conviction, which seemed so intensely political to us, would surely be overturned on appeal. Even these last few days, though we knew that Justice Douglas of the Supreme Court (perhaps their only hope for a stay of execution) was off mountain climbing in the Rockies, we were convinced that he'd be located and would grant a stay. Or someone would. However anti-Communist the States were at this moment in their history, we reasoned, they would never in the world execute these two people in peacetime. . . .

But it had happened. They were dead.

From its inception, as the story of the Rosenbergs had begun to unfold in the papers and on the radio, my own feeling had been one of unease. They were almost certainly innocent, I thought—but what if they weren't? Could they, either one of them, have been foolish enough, reckless enough, to have actually done what they were charged with?

That "what if?" nagged at me until I found it easier not to read about the trials at all. To this day, I know few of the details. Our own political troubles during that whole period were all I could cope with. It was bad enough to have one's opinions under fire; I couldn't face the possibility that a couple of dedicated Marxists could actually have tried to translate their philosophy into an act of espionage. If they had, I didn't want to know about it.

The radicals we had known had been, if anything, superpatriots, with an almost romantic devotion to the principles of the Founding Fathers. For all of us, socialism—economic justice—was simply an extension of the "inalienable rights" our forebears had posited. We all felt the current Cold War hysteria was as much a national aberration as the Alien and Sedition laws of long ago; the witch-hunting we had fled was deplorable, and we didn't know how long it would last, but it would pass. I didn't know of a single refugee, however devoted a party-liner, who didn't believe that someday, sooner or later, political sanity would return and we could all go home.

But this? This headline staring at me, with the lovely Mexican morning pushed back out of my consciousness? I didn't see how it could happen.

I took the paper upstairs and woke Hugo to show it to him. It was as incredible to him as to me.

How can I describe the pall that spread over our day, over our lives, that morning? What kind of holy war was our government conducting, to put to death two earnest people, parents of two young children?

Later, reading about the event in the international papers, I came on a story that may or may not have been apocryphal. In the care of sympathetic friends, and kept from the television set the last day or two so that if worst came to worst, they wouldn't be confronted with reports of the execution, the two young Rosenberg boys had chanced to turn on the family's radio and heard the news flash. And one of the little boys had said, "Good-bye."

It was more than a parent could bear.

Earlier we had put aside this evening to go to a Réné Clement picture, *Forbidden Games,* which was playing at a local movie theater; now, the thought of going to a movie, *any* movie, on such a night seemed out of the question.

But the critics had called it a small masterpiece, and we were afraid it might leave town before we could see it. So at day's end, though we were still badly distracted, we summoned up our forces, ate an early supper, gave the children a shorter-than-usual story time, got them into bed early, and, leaving Ramona in charge, drove off to see a French movie with Spanish subtitles.

The theater where the picture was playing was midway between our house and downtown. We made our way there through the early-evening traffic, parked, bought our tickets, and were taking our seats as the lights dimmed . . .

And then, silent, we watched.

Forbidden Games is the story of a small child savagely orphaned when a German plane strafes the refugees fleeing Paris during World War II. Her puppy, also a victim, dies convulsing in her arms. Lost, utterly alone, she is befriended by Michel, a little farm boy from the nearby countryside, and is given grudging shelter by his family. In the weeks that follow, the children turn death, which they struggle to comprehend, into a game, a ritual, by burying small dead birds and animals and decorating the graves with crosses they steal from the village cemetery. When the "game" is discovered, their elders are outraged, and the little girl is summarily turned over to the authorities. Our last view of her is at a train station, alone in a milling crowd, a ticket with her name and destination dangling from her sweater. Suddenly she hears someone in the crowd speak the name "Michel," and she thinks it's *her* Michel. She is shrieking his name, running about the crowded station, searching for him, calling and crying, as the picture ends.

As the screen went dark and the house lights went up, Hugo and I simply sat there—swept by the child's terrible sense of loss, of helplessness, of aloneness. The little girl crying, "Michel!" became two little boys learning of their parents' execution and one of them saying, "Good-bye."

Around us, the audience stirred, got to its feet, and moved toward the aisle and out toward the lobby. I guess we did too, though we were still under the spell of what we had seen. And it seems to me now, as I try to summon it up again, that the streets were wet as we came out; it had rained while we were in the theater. Or wasn't that the way it was? As I remember, we walked the wet sidewalk to our car without saying a word, and got in, and drove home along the dark, wet Avenida Insurgentes, too sick at heart to speak.

Chapter Nine

AN UNEXPECTED by-product of our Mexican exile was that Hugo had become a bullfight fan.

He'd done the reading. He knew the history and the mythology. And from his first trip to the Plaza Mexico, he was a confirmed aficionado. Sundays had become a ritual for him: the one day of the week he became thoroughly Mexican.

Ramona, quickly sensing the pattern, adapted to it. Sunday mornings we woke up to the smells of toasting sesame seeds and roasting chiles (preliminary to the making of a *mole*). By midmorning the house would be redolent with the rich smell of turkey or chicken simmering in broth as it waited for the addition of bitter Spanish chocolate, cloves, cinnamon, garlic, and six or seven different kinds of chiles—among other ingredients. By noon Hugo would have put a record of *paso dobles* or Spanish *zarzuelas* or Mexican folk music on the portable gramophone we'd bought with our first *Crusoe* money and would be sitting with a cigar and a glass of tequila, ready for the real action of the day to begin.

By the time we'd done justice to the *mole,* driven the few miles between San Angel and the Plaza Mexico, and parked and made our way to the wide terrace that circled the plaza, the area was already athrong with vendors selling beer from buckets of ice, or ears of corn roasted in their husks and kept hot in buckets of coals, or tacos assembled from makeshift braziers and dripping with salsa—a medley of odors to warm the soul. Small bands of mariachis had sprung up on all sides like mushrooms and were playing in noisy competition with each other, and loudspeakers boomed out *paso dobles* from the band inside the plaza, with noises of crowd, vendors, musicians, and loudspeakers blending in a kind of steadily mounting cacophony.

Inside the plaza, with the crowds pushing their way through the tunnels to emerge onto the sloping tiers of benches, the poorer fans in the cheap seats facing west (*sol,* meaning they'd have the setting sun in their eyes during the *corrida*) and those who could afford them filling the seats opposite on the *sombra* (shady) side—there was an air of even more boisterous expectancy. (Actually, legend had it that the busiest period of the year at the Monte de Piedad was during the bullfight season, when the poorest aficionados flocked downtown to pawn anything they could do without so they could buy tickets for the next bullfight.)

Then, just before four o'clock, there was a moment of hasty settling down, a sort of collective holding of breath—and at last a flourish of trumpets, and the *paseo* began: that glittering parade of *toreros* in their suits of lights, banderilleros, picadores on their horses, all beautifully costumed (even the horses), all circling the ring with the formality of a religious procession—a wonderful meld of show and symbolism.

Then of course began the highly ritualized process by which it becomes possible for one man (say, 160 pounds) to kill one bull (900-odd pounds), something well-nigh impossible unless certain steps are taken along the way: the whole group taking temporary refuge in the *callejón* (alleyway) behind the fence that circles the ring as the bull comes charging out. Everyone studies his behavior as he's being caped: Does he veer to one side or the other? Does he toss his head, and to which side? Even the *torero,* using a large, bicolored cape (the *capote*), tries a number of passes, ascertaining from the bull's responses what to expect further into the battle. . . .

Then there's the placing of the spears by the mounted picadores, aiming at a point between the bull's shoulder blades; this is designed to lower the bull's head and allow a point of entry for, eventually, the *torero's* sword. And then the placing of the gaily ribboned banderillas, partly for the same purpose and partly (in theory) to correct any tendency the bull may have to hook to either side. And now the *torero,* coming in with a muleta (a smaller cape) and a real sword (the first one, we learned, was wooden and just for show) to train the creature to his command. Out there in the ring, he must teach it to charge when he wants it to and to stop when he wants it to; passing it closer and ever closer to him in response to a flick of the cape, a sometimes breath-stopping demonstration—and always, measuring the bull's growing fatigue and the steady weakening of those neck muscles until he feels the time has come. Then he dares to pause, to take careful aim, and to go in over the horns, to plunge his sword in that one vulnerable spot between the shoulder blades (hoping the bull won't toss its head at just the wrong moment). And all this with a show of grace and fearlessness, knowing that the crowd's thirst for thrill must at all costs be satisfied . . .

Did all this derive, as legend had it, from the story of Theseus and the Minotaur? Or did its fascination for the crowds have even more primitive roots? On the other hand, we'd heard that the Russian ambassador of that period never missed a bullfight during his tour of duty here. "It's the only place in Mexico," he'd been quoted as saying, "where one can see good ballet."

Neither myth nor ballet had much to do with Hugo's fascination with the sport; he simply found it a spellbinding spectacle. Unfortunately, though, the Trumbos didn't agree.

Soon after our arrival in Mexico, they had gone with us to a bullfight, and one of the kills had been clumsy; the *torero,* going in for the kill, had sent his sword into the bull's lung, and the poor animal had staggered about the bullring vomiting blood while the audience, to a man, booed the bullfighter. The Trumbos, who had kept a cow and several horses on their ranch that they'd been quite fond of, were pro-bull from the outset and came away from the plaza white-faced and outraged.

Except for the rare "bad kill," however, Hugo saw little difference between slaughtering an animal for beef and killing it in a bullring, except that in the bullring it has a chance to revenge itself on its attacker and even a chance, however infrequent, of winning the *indulto*—fighting such a brave fight that the crowd waves its handkerchiefs in a sea of white to ask that its life be spared. Bulls that win the *indulto* are sent back to the ranch to live out their lives happily siring dozens of calves (on the theory, treasured by bull breeders, that their courage is an inheritable characteristic). Whereas bulls sent to the slaughterhouse, Hugo pointed out in his subsequent, ongoing argument with Trumbo, have no chance at all for either survival or revenge.

"And anyway," he insisted during one of these discussions, "if that's how you feel, why aren't you a vegetarian?"

However fervent, though, these verbal fencing matches were friendly, even philosophical. Continued one evening over *panuchos* at our favorite Yucatecan restaurant, one somehow found its way several weeks later into both Walter Winchell and a gossip column in the *Hollywood Reporter,* transmogrified by gossip into a shouting match, expulsion from the restaurant, and a public fistfight. We were so outraged by the allegation that we wrote off to a stateside attorney about the possibility of suing for libel. And the attorney responded, reasonably, that it might be rather difficult, considering our current situation, to prove that our careers had been substantially damaged by the story.

At any event, sometime during the bullfight season of 1953–54, Hugo had gone alone to see a *corrida* featuring a good-looking, once popular, but now slightly over-the-hill (age thirty-seven) *torero* named Luis Procuna.

Bullfighting, like boxing, requires the nimbleness, the quickness of reflex, of a younger man. Maybe even Procuna himself was beginning to think he was overage for such a hazardous sport; perhaps that's why he chose, that particular Sunday, to play it safe by killing his second bull too quickly. (Each of a bullfight's three *toreros* fights two bulls in an afternoon.) The crowd, cheated of its show, was furious; they pelted Procuna, down in the bullring, with seat cushions and torrents of abuse, and the bullring's judge (the reigning dignitary) indicated by a hand gesture to the crowd that he was levying a stiff fine on the hapless *torero.* The crowd roared its approval.

Chagrined, Procuna conferred with one of the attendants nearby and learned, apparently, that there was another bull outside in the bull pen (as there often was, to serve as understudy in case of mishaps). Now, with hand gestures that all aficionados are familiar with, he indicated to the audience that he was buying an extra bull for them. As quick to forgive as they were to condemn, the audience cheered.

And as the gift bull came charging into the ring, Procuna, ever the showman, marched to the space below the dignitaries' box, removed his cap, and with great formality and a straight face dedicated the bull to the judge who had fined him.

The crowd loved it.

As it happened, Polvorito was a magnificent animal and Procuna in an "I'll show you" mood. He put on the bullfight of his life, with a dazzling display of passes: passes *al pecho,* and on his knees, and standing on the *estribo* (the strip of wood that ran along the base of the wooden fence of the bullring, where the bull could easily pin him against the fence), and passing the bull and then turning his back on it with a flick of the cape and arrogantly walking away, knowing he had the bull so conditioned by now that it would not charge unless he ordered it to. The crowd went wild. And when he went in for the kill, he did it expertly, and the bull dropped on the spot.

Procuna was awarded ears and tail, a rare event. The audience swarmed down into the bullring and took him up on their shoulders, shouting, *"Torer-o! Torer-o!"* And as Hugo, high up on the bleachers, was finding his way to the aisle, down to the tunnels and out, the crowd below was carrying their newly minted hero out of the ring, still shouting at the top of their lungs the same rhythmic incantation—bent, apparently, on carrying him on their shoulders the whole way home.

Our Mike, who had been to an afternoon movie downtown with a friend's family and was being driven home afterward, found Avenida Insurgentes totally blocked by the hundreds or perhaps thousands of aficionados, still bearing the matador on their shoulders, still hysterically shouting, *"Torer-o! Torer-o!"* the entire length of the boulevard.

And Hugo, for his part, came home to report the afternoon's excitement and to telephone George Pepper with an idea for another film project.

In the meantime, Trumbo's earlier experience at the bullfights had given him an idea for a movie too.

It was the story of a young Mexican boy on a bull ranch whose pet calf (and only real friend) has been raised for the bullring and certain slaughter. The boy is unable to keep it from the bullring, but there, it fights such a magnificent fight that at the crowd's insistence it is granted the *indulto* and is allowed to return to its ranch with its young friend. Produced a year or two after the Trumbos' return to the States by a couple of Trumbo's independent-producer friends, the King brothers, it was released in 1956 under the title *The Brave One* and bore the name of one "Robert Rich" as its putative writer.

The screenplay was nominated for an Academy Award, to Trumbo's not-very-well-concealed delight. And on awards night 1957, when

"Robert Rich's" name was read off as winner of the Oscar for best screenplay and no screenwriter stepped forward to accept the statuette (the presenter offering a lame excuse for "Rich's" absence instead), the real authorship became the worst-kept secret in Hollywood—going far toward achieving Trumbo's professed aim those days of reducing the whole blacklist to ridicule.

(Still later, when saner heads and a sense of justice prevailed once more in Hollywood, the Motion Picture Academy revised its records and granted the Oscar to Trumbo under his own name. By then, though, Trumbo had little time left to enjoy his triumph; within fifteen months he would die of lung cancer.)

As for Hugo's approach to the same subject matter:

Ostensibly a recounting of the Sunday of Procuna's "Polvorito" fight, from early morning through his dressing for and finally the *corrida* itself, with its triumphal end, Hugo felt that the picture must also show the life of a *torero*, something of the history of bullfighting, something of the sociology (since so many bullfighters, like Procuna, had come from childhoods of excruciating poverty), and, using archival footage when available, it must show the tragic deaths of so many of Procuna's predecessors (including the legendary Manolete) to point up the terrible risks of the profession and the ever present anxieties of its practitioners.

Hugo had always felt that a too lavish budget ruined a picture, leading inevitably to overproduction, whereas a stringent budget forced the filmmaker to be more creative and to leave more to the imagination of the viewer—a must, he felt, in any entertainment medium. Also, inveterate novel reader that he was, he had always been intrigued by the uses of narration in film. In this case he could make a search of the available newsreel footage, use it wherever possible (with an actor, as Procuna, narrating overshot when needed), and stage and shoot only those scenes that were absolutely necessary to tell a valid and coherent story.

What he was actually doing was inventing a now accepted form called *docudrama,* at precisely the same time that other documentarists in other countries were doing the same thing, though of course he didn't know it then; the term hadn't even come into being yet. It just seemed to him a means of making an effective, and inexpensive, film in two languages.

Enthused about the project, George Pepper quickly struck a deal with a small studio that made newsreels and documentaries. Procuna agreed to do the film; a local director, Carlos Vela, was assigned, but Hugo undertook some of the directing himself (something he'd always wanted to do) and soon found himself traveling to bull ranches all over central Mexico with the crew, either watching Vela or shooting footage himself of *tientas,* mock bullfights where young bulls are caped to test their courage. And the film would be called *Torero!*

It didn't occur to me in those years, though it has since, to wonder what it was about bullfighting (apart from the color and excitement, of course) that appealed to Hugo so profoundly. The English/Canadian culture he'd grown up in found such a sport abhorrent. Why, then, the attraction?

It must have been, I suspect, the bravery, the dauntlessness of the *torero,* testing his own courage by challenging the bull to charge, yet not stepping aside an inch as it came thundering toward him.

By nature cautious—to the point of cowardice, he used to claim—he had all his life deliberately forced himself to do what he was most afraid of. Sailing his own small dinghy alone on Puget Sound as a boy, for instance. Standing up to a fraternity initiation at college and refusing to accept the hazing that freshmen pledges were subjected to. Joining four of his college mates to sail a sixty-foot sloop across the Pacific to Hawaii (and coming in thirteen minutes after the winner). And refusing to accept that contract from MGM because the story editor had said it would keep him out of the army, though it meant letting himself be drafted as a buck private instead.

And, of course, his political choices.

Manolete said, "It's easy to be courageous when you are more afraid of the crowd's ridicule than you are of the bull." There was no mocking crowd of onlookers in Hugo's sedentary, writer's life, but perhaps, all through his years of growing up and earning a living and being blacklisted, there was an onlooker inside him, judging him harshly, requiring him always to prove himself and face what he feared most. That, I think, was almost surely why he identified so profoundly with his picture's protagonist—the lone man down in the ring, facing the oncoming bull.

Chapter Ten

IT WAS SOMETIME during that year—1953—that Hugo took me downtown to Prendes for lunch and we had the argument about my name.

Or was it about my name?

We had eaten at Prendes before. It was one of our three or four favorite restaurants: a thriving, bustling, unadorned white-tile place in Mexico City's commercial district that served good martinis and fresh seafood. Popular with Mexican businessmen, it seemed part of the rhythm of the city, and I'm sure countless business deals were made over the tables here during the local equivalent of the three-martini lunch. I remember noticing, as we went in that day, a sign in the front window saying there was a separate dining room for ladies—but then, since women in Mexico didn't even get suffrage till that year, why should I have been surprised?

My spirits were high. Having Hugo take me out to lunch (even more than to dinner, which I also loved) seemed not only a lovely escape from reality, but also gave me a feeling of slightly guilty stolen pleasure, as though I were his mistress and his wife might find out about us, whereas at home I *was* his wife, who had to worry about the bills, the children's grades, and what groceries we'd need tomorrow.

In any event, there we were, being led to a table during the busy hour of *comida,* and I was feeling singularly lighthearted. We settled into our chairs, and Hugo ordered martinis for both of us, and when they came, straight up and very cold, we studied the menu.

It listed *criadillas.*

One of the things I'd learned, going to the bullfights those Sundays with Hugo, was that dead fighting bulls didn't escape the slaughter-house. After the *corrida,* their carcasses were butchered and the steaks and ribs and innards sent to the various good restaurants around town. Including the *criadillas,* which, in a culture like Mexico's, where ma-chismo was admired above all else, were very popular with Mexico City diners.

It followed. From earliest times, men have eaten parts of those ani-mals they wanted to emulate. The liver or heart of animals that were swift or strong, for instance. Why not the *criadillas* of a brave fighting bull?

That, however, didn't enter my thinking at the moment. I simply happen to like variety meat. Liver, kidney, brains, even tripe—I like them all. But *criadillas* I had never tried, and I was curious. So I or-dered them.

Hugo raised his eyebrows, but he didn't say anything—not then. He relayed my order to the waiter and ordered *huachinango* (red snapper) for himself. Then, as we sipped our martinis, he brought up the story I had just finished and was about to clean-type and send north to my agent. (Come to think of it, that was probably what we were celebrat-ing when we planned this outing.) What name, Hugo asked, was I going to use as author?

I shrugged. My own, I said. Why not? Just because there was a black-list in films, it didn't necessarily follow that there was one in the maga-zine market.

"Are you out of your mind?" he asked. "What makes you think there isn't?"

I was startled at his sudden ferocity. *Crusoe* was finally in release, bearing the name, as screenwriter, of that New Yorker we didn't even know—and getting very good reviews. And now busy with *Torero!,* Hugo had decided to credit the screenplay to "Hugo Mozo" (*mozo* is Spanish for houseboy or butler). I hadn't realized, though, that per-haps he was feeling especially bitter that day at being deprived of credit on *two* pictures he was very proud of. I simply shrugged off the ques-tion and pointed out that there wasn't a blacklist on the New York stage, for instance.

There wasn't? he said. In that case, why were so many of our left-wing actor friends working as bakers, or barbers, or salesmen? Why was our once highly successful character-actor friend Jeff Corey now back in college, taking a degree on the GI bill, at this late date?

The waiter arrived before I could answer, and my plate was put down in front of me. It bore two round balls, somewhat larger than golf balls, braised and served in a sort of browned-butter-and-Madeira sauce.

I picked up my knife and fork to slice into one of them and caught sight of the horrified look in Hugo's eyes. "What's the matter?" I asked.

"Nothing," he said. Then, "Are you really going to eat those?"

"I ordered them, didn't I?" I said. "Why?"

"I just wondered," he said. He busied himself with his *huachinango.* "How are they?" he asked after a moment.

His face was grim. I had suddenly become the enemy.

"Very good," I said. "Like sweetbreads, but firmer."

Abruptly he turned on me again. "Get this through your head," he said savagely. "You can't use your name on this story or any other. Not for magazines, not for plays, not for books. You are as blacklisted as I am. Nothing with your name on it is going to sell."

For a moment I resisted, trying not to believe it. That *his* name was banished, now and for a long time to come—perhaps for our lifetimes— I had somehow gotten used to. But that my own, my maiden name, the name I'd acted under and continued to use professionally in writing jobs and story sales after my marriage, the name that was my whole *identity*—the idea that this too was condemned to oblivion swept over me like a black wave. I felt as though I were losing an arm or a leg. I went on trying to eat and knew that in a moment I was going to cry, right here in public.

"I don't know what made you think you *could* use it," he said.

Tears rolled down my face and dropped into my *criadillas.* My name. I wanted to keep my name.

He watched me, unmoved. "Now you know how it feels," he said.

I wiped my eyes with my napkin, and we finished our meal in silence. Neither of us felt like ordering dessert; we had coffee, and paid our bill, and left.

I never did find out—for sure—whether the blacklist had reached the magazine market. My agent insisted it hadn't. I do know I didn't sell that story, or any other under my own name, until almost the end of the decade. After trying, and failing, to get a prose-writing friend to front for me, I stopped writing stories and novellas altogether for several years. The idea of inventing a new persona and trying to establish a reputation in magazines all over again seemed too overwhelming.

Or was it simply coincidental? Maybe I was so busy, those years, with the children and their lives and with the occasional odd film job I picked up (uncredited, of course) that there wasn't much else I wanted to write. I never asked myself.

Nor did I, in my blind devotion to Hugo, so much as wonder at his sudden rush of anger that day or find it out of character. Actually, it was an early-warning sign of possible future problems that I, in my ignorance, chose to ignore.

Chapter Eleven

AFTER THE INCIDENT at Prendes, however, fate—or perhaps even the law of averages—seemed to give us a period of respite. Thanks to an occasional check from *Crusoe,* our debts were paid. With the exception of Hugo's Leica, which he had not redeemed in time and so lost to some anonymous purchaser, our possessions were bailed out of the Monte. And Hugo was able to devote himself with a free mind to the completion of *Torero!*

And our children seemed to be adjusting well to our life as expatriates. Or at least, so it seemed—although once in a while Mike, as the oldest and therefore the most aware of our political situation, let drop a small hint of unease. . . .

This term his social studies teacher at school had asked her seventh-graders (who, like the rest of the student body, represented a wide ethnic mixture) to research and write a paper on the history of whatever ethnic group they were descended from. Mike, most of whose forebears came from the British Isles and western Europe, also knew he was one-sixteenth Jewish (Hugo's mother having discovered as an adult that her most illustrious grandparent was a Jew), and this was the portion of his ethnicity that he chose to look into. Along the way, he learned about *marranos* ("swine"), Spain's bitter term for Jews who, during the Inquisition, pretended conversion in order to avoid persecution but who continued to practice their own religion in secret. "Mom," he said wistfully one evening over his homework, "couldn't we just be *marranos* Communists?"

By and large, though, he kept his worries to himself, and we, completely unaware that ever since the Rosenbergs' execution he'd been having hideous nightmares that Hugo and I might share the same fate, pursued our (for us, by now) normal lives. Over the sixteenth of September holidays, we took the children to Oaxaca, a day's drive south in a high valley among the Sierras, where we were charmed by the city's lovely old colonial architecture, and, on a grass-grown hillside plateau overlooking the valley, fell in love with the timeless tranquillity of the ruins of Monte Albán.

And sometimes during those months, when Hugo's friend and agent Ingo Preminger came down to discuss some sort of business arrangement with Hugo and/or George Pepper, we took him (and the children) to Las Estacas, our favorite picnic spot near a long-abandoned sugar refinery south of Cuernavaca, where springs bubbled up to make a little river and one could rent an inner tube and float for half a mile downstream, with cane growing green and tall on either side and Indian laurel trees making a pattern of shade and sunlight all the way down. Ingo, drifting dreamily along on his inner tube and altogether enchanted, said, in his inimitable Viennese accent, "It's wonderful! It's like being in the middle of Technicolor!"

Altogether, then, this year of 1953 was proving an interesting and even moderately busy one for us. Our little Debbie did indeed seem to have "arrived with her own bread" because, as we moved into autumn, not only was Hugo working, but now I too had a screenwriting job, for Bob Aldrich.

Since the *World for Ransom* script Hugo had written for him early in our stay here, Bob, up in Hollywood, had been building a name for himself, picture by small picture. Now he'd been assigned a big-budget project, *Veracruz,* and came down to scout locations and rent a house for his wife and children for the duration of the shoot. Never one to concentrate on just one picture at a time, however, he told Hugo he was also looking for a small-cast, low-budget picture to film afterward. Hugo gave him the tear sheets of one of my *McCall's* novellas, and Bob thought it might be just what he needed.

It wouldn't net us much money, because the payment for both story and screenplay together (about fifty-five hundred dollars, as I remember) would be coming not from studio coffers but from Bob's own pocket, and from even that modest sum we'd be paying a fourth, the going rate for "fronts" in those days, to our old friend Jack Jevne. Jack was a gentle, quiet man in the sunset of his career who had long ago written silent pictures for Douglas Fairbanks. We would use his name on the screenplay, and if Bob needed to produce a living, breathing writer for story conferences up in Hollywood, Jack could be there as the "author."

So we forged ahead with the adaptation—or rather, I did. I'm sure Bob thought he was buying our joint endeavors, but Hugo by now was deep in his bullfight footage, working at a moviola in a rented cutting room alongside a nice young Mexican film cutter from whom he was learning the craft of film editing. However, evenings after I'd gotten the children to bed, he went over my day's work and made suggestions, and in fact our second draft was more nearly a real collaboration.

And we both liked Bob and wanted to please him. A husky, pink-cheeked man with a deceptively mild demeanor, he was stubborn, combative, and litigious toward producers, studio heads, and other parent figures but unswervingly loyal to the people who worked under him. After the screenplay left our hands, it underwent a few revisions, so our alter ego Jevne had perforce to share "his" writing credit. But after Bob had finished *Veracruz* he did indeed set up and make our picture, now titled *Autumn Leaves,* using Nat King Cole's version of the title song as theme music and casting Joan Crawford and a young Cliff Robertson as the lonely, mismatched leads. Based originally on a young man who had married into Hugo's father's family, it was the first film out of Hollywood to deal with a psychopathic liar, and it seems, in the year since it was made, to have acquired a modest "cult film" status.

It is also, at the still later date of this writing, one of the films the Writers Guild of America has requested corrected credits on in its effort to redress the injustices of the blacklist. So now, when new prints of the film are made, they will include our names.

Meanwhile, as the year marched toward its close, there were more changes in our community.

A number of the refugee families who had settled originally in Cuernavaca were, apparently, discovering a bitter truth about lotusland: you couldn't make a living there. And one by one, they were moving up to the Federal District, where, if you had a marketable skill, an occasional employer might help you get working papers.

First to move up were the van der Schellings. Bart was a great tall, reddish-haired Dutchman; in his youth a basso profundo in local opera, he had in time become a member of every left-wing political movement in Europe since World War I; he'd been serving as a general in Spain's International Brigade when a bullet in his neck ended his military career and almost his life. He spoke an almost unintelligible mix of Dutch, German, French, English, and Spanish; had a vast gusto for living and a vivid memory; occasionally still wore a dog-collar brace to support his damaged neck; and at parties held us all spellbound with stories of the Spanish war or, with his guitar, sang its songs—"*Los Cuatro Generales,*" "*Jarama Valley,*" or "*Die Thaelmann Colonne*" in his great, booming bass. When he'd first reached Mexico from Spain and the States, he'd taught singing; now, in his sixties, he was tuning pianos for a living, and his wife, Edna—under her maiden name, of course—was teaching music at the American School.

Already relocated were Max Lieber, a slightly built, crotchety but highly literate man who'd been Albert Maltz's literary agent in years past; his wife, Minna; and their two children. We'd known them only casually, but during my pregnancy we had swapped houses for a week, ourselves enjoying a few days of Cuernavaca living while the Liebers used our house as a base from which Minna could job hunt. Now she too would be at the American School, teaching fifth grade.

And the Maltzes had moved up.

Not for monetary reasons, but for something far more gothic: a time bomb had exploded on a Oaxaca-bound plane on which Margaret and her daughter were traveling.

The passengers had survived by a miracle: the pilot, with his instrument panel shattered and a large hole in the fuselage, had managed to bring the plane down through cloud cover to a small military field below. From here the injured passengers, including Margaret, could get medical help, and seven of the passengers who, it seemed, had jobs waiting for them in Oaxaca, could fly on. That, however, proved the unraveling point. When the seven reached Oaxaca, they found the jobs nonexistent. Casual conversation among them and a check with the authorities revealed that they'd all been "hired," given plane tickets (and privately been insured) by two scoundrels in Mexico City—who were now in jail and being tried, as each accused the other of masterminding the crime. Margaret, altogether fascinated and still limping from the shrapnel in her legs, was now taking a translator friend to every court hearing, collecting data for a book (later published as *Seven Shares in a Gold Mine*), and discovering in the process the intriguing differences between Mexican legal procedures and our own.

Having the Maltzes as neighbors, however, raised a few small private problems for Hugo and me. For while we were fond of Margaret, our feelings about Albert were still decidedly conflicted.

On the one hand, he had gone to jail for his principles, which we shared. And certainly no one could question his achievements as a writer: in plays, books, short stories, and film, he had been extraordinarily productive. Nor was there ever any doubt of his generosity with his time: he could always be counted on for a careful, thoughtful critique of a piece of writing if asked. But on the other hand . . .

Sometime after World War II, I remembered, I had read a book by Margaret Halsey titled *With Malice Toward Some,* about her experiences in wartime England. In it, Halsey described British shoes as looking as though they'd been designed by someone who had never actually seen a shoe but had heard one described. This, we used to think, was Albert—wanting, we felt, to live up to his conception of "a good man." He may never have really met anyone who answered that description, but he had a rough idea what he should be like and patterned his self-image accordingly. A well-to-do boy who'd run away to the circus in his teens, he was constantly striving to be "one of the guys"—with the end result an altogether self-fabricated persona with both spontaneity and humor left out. Poor man, he did try, but his labored attempts at jokes when he spoke to our children, for instance, had them looking at him as warily as though he had two heads.

In short, he could in no way replace the Hunters or the Lardners, whose return to the States had left a huge hole in our lives—a feeling that became acute late in 1953 when the Trumbos announced their decision to go back too.

Dalton and Cleo had never felt truly at home in Mexico, and with their money running ever lower, Trumbo thought it unwise to be so far from the job market. Also, he was a highly political animal; he hated being neutralized, as one had perforce to be in a foreign country—especially

Mexico, where an article in its constitution gave the president the right to deport any foreigner whose presence was considered "inexpedient" to Mexico.

That's right. No hearing, no trial; just a simple *"denuncia"* from any Mexican national, and the "denounced one" is over the border and out. Some of our acquaintances would discover in the next few years that this article could be invoked quite at random, whenever the government faced any inconvenient social unrest and found itself in need of scapegoats.

So, with witch-hunts in the States still continuing full blast and a return home thus not an option, most of our colony were careful not to jeopardize our asylum here in any way. Also—who knows? Perhaps we had all found financial survival so tenuous thus far that politics now seemed a luxury we could no longer afford. Perhaps the troubles we'd been through earlier back home had knocked some of the courage out of us; we may have learned, the hard way, the virtues of conformity.

But not Trumbo. He missed the smell of battle. He couldn't wait to get back home where he could protest, loud and clear and whatever the consequences, on any issue he felt strongly about (and in fact, on his return, he did rejoin the Communist Party for a brief time, simply because everyone else he knew was leaving it). He and Cleo set their family's departure date for early January of 1954.

This, Hugo decided, must be the occasion for a rousing good-bye party for them. We plunged into preparations, inviting the whole refugee community; we trimmed the house inside and out with those lovely colored-paper cutouts used in Mexico for decoration on holidays; and Ramona cooked for days. The evening of the party, for those guests crowded out of our little living room, Hugo set electric heaters on the veranda against the cold night air and lamps against the darkness of the yard. Beer was chilling on ice in all our laundry tubs, and mariachi records were stashed in readiness beside our valiant little record player. It would, we hoped, be a wonderful bash.

Which it was, at first. Partway through the evening, though, the Druckers received a phone call relayed to them from Oregon, telling them that their bright, talented older daughter had had "some sort of breakdown" at college and one of them should come up at once.

Frantically worried, both parents fled home to pack and leave as fast as they could get a flight. The party continued without them, but much subdued. At the back of all our minds, I suspect, was the thought: *What if this should happen, at this distance, to one of mine?*

One more anxiety for our colony of expatriates.

The colored-paper cutouts from the party were still in place four days afterward when our friend John Collier and his former secretary and bride-to-be Harriet Hess were married in our front yard.

John, at this point in his career, was already established both in his native England and to some extent in the States too as a writer of witty, literate, and gently demonic short stories. He was not a radical, but most of his friends were, which got him almost as blacklisted as they were. (Also, as he discovered later, his persecutors had managed to confuse him with another John Collier who'd been a U.S. Commissioner on Indian Affairs, which *really* muddied the waters.) His closest friend, screenwriter Gordon Kahn—as short as John and as witty but not yet in print—had driven up from Cuernavaca with his wife; he would be John's best man and, having lived in Mexico a bit longer than the rest of us, could function as expert-in-charge-of-Mexican-bureaucracy. Soon after his arrival, he and John made a hurried trip into San Angel and came back with a municipal judge to perform the ceremony: a cheerful man with a smile full of gold teeth, a two days' growth of beard, and, to everyone's dismay, a partially open fly. He was also a little drunk, though the day was still young.

The wedding was conducted in Spanish legalese, most of which we didn't understand. Names were signed in an enormous ledger the judge had brought with him, the judge's mild intoxication was increased slightly by a glass of the wedding champagne (a local brand, but efficacious), and at the wedding lunch provided by Ramona immediately following the ceremony, our Emily, now four and a half and entranced by the bride in her bouffant pale yellow wedding dress, climbed up into her lap and invited her to spend the night with us.

Trumbo's letter, addressed jointly to ourselves and the Peppers, arrived a few days later.

The family had departed, a day or two after the good-bye party, in two separate batches. Trumbo's sometime producers the King brothers had found them a house in the hills northwest of downtown Los

Angeles, and Cleo and Melissa, the least sturdy of the clan, had flown up ahead to start the settling-in process while Trumbo and the oldest two Trumbo children, Nikola and Chris, along with their sheepdog and the family cat, set out with their luggage in the hired car in which they were being driven to the border crossing between Matamoros and Brownsville. So far, so good.

Trumbo's goal in working out the logistics of the journey, however, had been to get his beloved collection of pre-Columbian sculpture out of Mexico, which, understandably, treasured its antiquities and forbade their unauthorized export. So, ever the Machiavelli, he had plotted a border crossing so wonderfully complicated that it *couldn't* fail.

It had taken a good deal of preparation.

First of all, there'd been his teardrop trailer, relic of his trip down into Mexico in the first place. This time he had packed it by hand and with great care, putting his beloved antique *figuras,* well wrapped, at the bottom, then above them a layer of *falsos* (imitations, sold to tourists by the thousands) as decoys, and above these, a gallimaufry of household items, clothing, and suchlike. This he had shipped in its entirety to a warehouse in Matamoros, the Mexican border point facing Brownsville, Texas, to await his arrival.

Brownsville was important because that was where Trumbo's jeep— the one that he'd driven down, pulling his teardrop trailer, during our initial migration—had been in storage for a year. When he'd gotten his Mexican residence papers last year, he hadn't been able to afford to nationalize it, and since under Mexican law a car had to have the same residence status as its owner, the jeep had had of necessity to spend the year beached, as it were, across the border. Now Trumbo figured that once he and the children reached Matamoros, on this side of the border, he would arrange to have the jeep bailed out of storage on the other side, driven back to them in Matamoros, and hitched to the trailer. Then he and the children, with the animals and the rest of the luggage, would drive jeep and fully loaded trailer across the border and out of Mexico without incident because, he reasoned, when the Mexican customs officials inspected the trailer and came across the layer of *falsos,* they would look no further and let the whole load go through—satisfied, I guess, that Trumbo was just one more gullible American who didn't know a *falso* when he saw one.

The whole scenario, of course, was a recipe for disaster.

Trumbo's letter, all twelve pages of it, described in one catastrophic detail after another what had gone wrong, starting with Trumbo's discovery in the Matamoros warehouse that the trailer had been badly damaged during shipping and some of the pre-Columbian pieces broken.

Then the arrival of the jeep from Brownsville raised the suspicions of the *aduana* (customs) officials, who suspected, quite wrongly, that Trumbo had actually been driving it all year without the proper documents. So during final departure, when they began to examine the contents of the trailer hitched to the jeep, they were loaded for bear.

Straightway, they decided that all the *falsos* were the real thing.

And as if that weren't enough, they found on Trumbo's manifest a reference to Cleo's silver fox furs (another relic of better days), and no amount of argument on Trumbo's part could persuade them that "silver" meant anything except the ore. Convinced, then, that there must be some precious metal in there someplace even if they couldn't find it, they placed a temporary hold on the entire load.

That wasn't all.

Trumbo now faced the necessity of repacking, by hand, at midnight, in the yawning warehouse, all the pre-Columbian items for shipment back to Mexico City to avoid their surrender to the Mexican Department of Education (to be brought out at some future date, I suppose, in some future piece of derring-do by one of his friends, though of course he made no mention of this in his letter).

And finally, when he and his much diminished load, and his children, and his animals tried once more to set out—a dead battery in the jeep. (It was now well *past* midnight.) And when that problem was solved and they managed finally to get across the border into Texas— a near arrest by a Texas highway patrolman for expired license plates before they could get on the road, at long, long last, for California.

In fact, however, Hugo and I hadn't been able to give our undivided attention to any of these matters—the good-bye party, or the Colliers' wedding, or even Trumbo's *faena* at the border. We had something else on our minds.

Just before the new year, a phone call from Hugo's father had shifted our attention northward.

Chapter Twelve

AS I REMEMBER, it was a night between Christmas and New Year's. Closer to New Year's, I suspect, because while our Christmas tree still stood in the corner by the fireplace, its ornaments were beginning to get a bit dusty and its needles crisp. At the other end of the room, in the little dining L, we were just sitting down to supper when the phone rang. Isabel had gone to answer the ring and had come back in to tell us it was *"larga distancia"* for the señor; so supper had gone back into the oven as Hugo had disappeared to take the call. He'd been gone almost half an hour, so I knew it was something important.

When he rejoined us, somewhat abstracted, he gave us a report. Warner Brothers, it seemed, had asked his father to adapt Max Reinhardt's extravaganza *The Miracle* for the screen. They wanted something epic and handsome—but the original material, about a nun who breaks her vows, was on the Catholic Index. If Frank accepted the assignment, he'd have to find a way to get it off. . . .

Normally he would have been unfazed. He'd been writing hit movies since the late 1920s. He'd won an Oscar for the screenplay of *Going My Way* and been nominated for another for *Wake Island*. He'd even been chief executive at Paramount for a while, and he'd made what looked like a full recovery from the heart attack that had cut that job short. But this, as we knew, was a badly troubled time for him.

The first years of our exile, Hugo had exchanged frequent letters and an occasional phone call with him, both men trying to get past their political disagreements with wry, amusing reports on life as it was being lived north and south of the border. But lately Frank, ever the most private of men, had been letting drop a few unhappy remarks about the state of affairs at home. And at some point—I've forgotten whether in a letter written surreptitiously or a phone call placed in his wife's absence—he seemed to indicate that if matters weren't resolved, his marriage might be in jeopardy. A close family member of Ethel's, it seemed, had recently married an amiable, good-looking ne'er-do-well who seemed to have no intention of taking a job, and the couple's continuing need for support (from Frank, of course) not only outraged Frank, but had even made his old ulcer flare up.

That situation, however, had not been mentioned in this evening's phone call. Frank had merely indicated that he didn't feel well enough, or strong enough, to tackle a difficult writing assignment by himself. He'd phoned to sound Hugo out: By any chance could Hugo come north and work on the picture with him—under the table, of course?

And Hugo, aware of the subtext and sensing Frank's need for an ally in his domestic troubles, had told his father he'd need a couple of weeks to wind up his current work, and then he'd be on his way north. Reassured, Frank had decided to accept the assignment. The rest of the conversation had dealt with logistics.

Not until dinner was over, and I'd gotten the children to bed and we were upstairs getting ready for bed ourselves, did Hugo make any reference to his own feelings about the whole matter. But as he was pulling on his pajamas, he said thoughtfully, "You know? I think this is the first time Dad's ever turned to me. For anything."

Of course things didn't work out as we thought they would.

Just after the Colliers' wedding (and the arrival of Trumbo's letter) and just days before Hugo was due to leave for the north, there was another phone call from his father, which, since Hugo was out at the moment, I took.

Frank was audibly upset. He had indeed accepted the job offer. But apparently he and his wife had not thought it necessary to keep news of Hugo's impending visit from the whole family, and it had reached another, more distant in-law (this one on Frank's side, not the ne'er-do-well who had so upset him). The distant in-law had announced that if Hugo set foot across the border, he (the in-law) would notify the U.S. Marshals' office so Hugo could be served with that long-standing subpoena—or, more accurately, a new one.

I could tell from his voice on the phone that Frank was almost weeping. "I can't do that to him," he said. "We can't take the chance. I don't know what to do. . . ."

Hugo's response, on his return when I reported this, was a grim look and a shake of his head. Relatives!

But something had to be done. And as had often happened before when Hugo was offered a job he couldn't take, he proposed the obvious alternative—me. And in this case, since the American School was still in the midst of its long winter vacation, Mike could go up with me and get acquainted with his grandfather. What did I think?

It seemed a good plan.

Actually, there was another reason for my going north right now: my mother's health.

For the last few months, she hadn't been well. She had gone to Palm Springs for the winter, hoping the crisp, dry air would make her feel better, but both Hugo and I suspected that she needed more than a change of climate. She'd had a mastectomy six or seven years before, and the possibility of a recurrence of cancer, though unmentioned by either of us, could not be ruled out. Hugo merely pointed out that if I went north, I could make a side trip to the desert. . . .

And so, some ten days or so into the new year, Mike and I found ourselves on a plane bound for Tijuana, where Frank and his wife would meet us.

Of course that didn't work out as planned either. There was an unusual cold snap over the West Coast that year; the plane's wings iced over just below Tijuana, and the pilot couldn't land. We circled the airport for a while, then turned south to Hermosillo, on the coast, to spend the night in a hotel (courtesy Aeronaves de Mexico, SA).

So it was a day later than anticipated when Frank and his wife, Ethel, met our plane, and whisked us across the border and up the coast to the lovely little cluster of Norman-French houses (named, appropriately, St. Malo) where they lived, and shepherded us inside, bag and baggage. If neighbors spotted us in the next few weeks, they would be told we'd just come up for "a little visit."

Circumstances seemed beguiling. The house, though not large, was filled with beautifully kept antiques. Beyond the windows, beds of blossoming ice plant sloped down to a pristine and lovely beach. And before the day was out, our Mike, then not quite fourteen, had fallen altogether under the spell of his witty, charming grandfather and his way of life. The fact that the colony, a private corporation, observed the strictest of restrictive covenants did not reduce its charm for Mike, nor was he aware that the apparent harmony between Frank and his wife covered a wrenching ongoing disagreement about that ulcer-causing family member. He settled in to keep Ethel company while Frank and I began our conferences on *The Miracle*.

These went smoothly from the outset. The plot line the church had objected to was solved with almost embarrassing simplicity. Instead of a nun who broke her vows, we made our heroine a novice, and instead of her vows, she would break a personal promise to a statue of the Virgin Mary. The story would be set during the Napoleonic Wars, and since the studio wanted a broad, sweeping canvas, we gave our runaway heroine a series of lovers: a gypsy, a matador—guess whose idea that was—and an aging roué, all of whom would be killed off one way or another, convincing our heroine that her broken word to the Virgin was the cause of all these catastrophes. Of course, there'd also be an unconsummated romance with a handsome British soldier, to be played by a young English actor named Roger Moore. It didn't trouble us that the story we worked out was old-fashioned, unwieldy, and embarrassingly romantic; we just let our characters swashbuckle to their hearts' content, and Frank was delighted with the whole collaboration.

Inevitably, our story discussions sometimes digressed to include Frank's domestic woes, and at times when I found myself alone with Ethel, I heard her side of the problem. I'd known of her background, of course. She'd been a poor girl, daughter of an oil puddler in Oklahoma, and her mother and brothers all counted on her good looks to get them out of the oil fields. She had married up twice, and now, I realized, she had an almost tribal loyalty to her flesh-and-blood family members. She identified with them, wanted them to be happy. . . .

I listened to each partner separately and felt for them both. Whatever the merits of the case, it was troubling to see this marriage of almost a quarter century on the brink of collapse. And there was one sad, revelatory little moment when we were all at lunch one day, at a table looking out toward the quiet, shining January ocean, when Ethel, asserting her right to a contrary opinion about something or other (I've forgotten what), said defensively, "After all, I'm a—an *entity* too, aren't I?"

Which told me much about her occasional private thoughts, in her husband's world of the busy, the competent, and the successful.

Within a couple of weeks, Frank and I had evolved a workable story synopsis and step outline and were feeling triumphant. And then while he, an old hand at this, sat down to polish a final draft for Warner Brothers, Mike and I took the train to visit our belongings in the storage warehouse where they had spent the last four years. Since Frank was paying me twenty-five hundred dollars (ten percent of his story money), we could now afford to ship home to Mexico those items we had missed most: our books, our children's favorite toys, a few kitchen utensils, our sofa, and our favorite armchairs. Once that was taken care of, we took another train (there was one, in those days) out to Palm Springs to see my mother.

She had rented a little house under the long, early-falling shadow of Mount Tahquitz. She didn't say much about her symptoms, but the one most apparent was a marked swelling of one arm, where the lymph glands had been removed at the time of her mastectomy. Still, no mention was made of any grim possibilities. She was spending most of her time reading—George Eliot, mostly, and trying to write, in much the same style, a biographical novel of her childhood in Mormon Utah. For the most part, that was what we talked about. I found that even now, a married woman with five children of my own, I couldn't allow her to get too close or too personal. I still felt the same desperate need for distance that I'd felt when I left her household to marry Hugo: I had to get away or that strong, admirable personality would swallow me whole. . . .

Otherwise, though, the visit went well. Then it was back to St. Malo for final conferences with Frank, and Mike and I took off for Mexico again. If Warner Brothers approved our story line and gave Frank a go-ahead on the script, Frank and I had agreed that I would write the first-draft screenplay at home in Mexico, mail it up to him scene by scene, and he would revise and polish.

Fortunately, Warners was no more critical of our florid story line than we were; they were, it seemed, delighted. Frank relayed to me the few changes they had suggested, and I settled down happily to work—again, to be paid ten percent of Frank's salary. It seemed like riches to us.

I was feeling inordinately pleased with myself. I loved knowing that

I had been useful, that I was doing (I thought) a competent job on a difficult assignment, and that the money I was earning helped support the family. It was also wonderful to be home again with Hugo and the children, to be eating Ramona's wonderful cooking, and to be waking up again to those lovely clear Mexican mornings. Little Debbie was a delightfully happy child; the bigger girls, who seemed to have thrived in my absence, were back in school now, as was Mike, and Mike, afternoons when he got home from school, had begun a voluminous correspondence with his grandfather.

—Something that Hugo found almost impossible to accept.

Yes, he had wanted his father and his son to get to know each other. But now it seemed to him that Mike in his obvious enchantment with Frank, St. Malo, and Gracious Living was thereby rejecting Hugo and all that Hugo believed in. More than that. Hugo found it wrenchingly ironic that he was losing his son (or so it seemed to him at the time) to the very man who had abandoned his mother and himself all those years ago.

Like most crises, this one ended not with a bang but a silence, with words unsaid, feelings unexpressed. Hugo became impatient with Mike about other, less important matters but held his tongue about the major one, hoping, I suppose, that Mike would outgrow it.

Years later, in the 1970s, Lynn Redgrave would have a line in *Georgie Girl* that could almost be the leitmotif of our lives: "No matter how good things seem to be going, Fate always has a custard pie up her sleeve." Our particular custard pie, the next few years, was that while Mike did outgrow his fascination with his grandfather and would spend much of his youth and young manhood seeking Hugo's unqualified approval, there seemed to be something in Hugo that demanded an impossible perfection from his only son.

Whatever the cause, there was beginning to be something fiercely competitive in Hugo's verbal jostling with Mike at the dinner table. There were times he seemed more a judge than a loving parent, and in the end, Mike was left searching for *his* father as Hugo had searched for his.

In a few weeks our shipment from the north arrived, to the children's delight. A couch to jump on! The waffle iron: we could have waffles for Sunday breakfast now! Books they'd forgotten they had. Toys given them that last Christmas in Hollywood, with only a month's wear on them. . . . Of course, that was four years ago, so each child was too old now for those particular toys, but ownership passed down to the next child in line, so it all worked out. And best of all, the packing crates! The children climbed in and out of them ceaselessly, turning them into oversized dollhouses. Mike finally assembled them all in the driveway and made them into a submarine with a conning tower, which stayed there for weeks.

And Hugo, in his own burst of creativity, decided it was time to enlarge our rented house.

It had always been these between-job intervals, or times when he was having story trouble, when he had gone plunging out house hunting in California; in the fourteen years between our marriage and our departure for Mexico, we had rented four successive houses and bought and lived in seven more. And since I was usually the one who did the packing, I took a dim view of these peripatetics. But this time I agreed with him. Debbie's crib was still in Mike's room because there was no room for it anyplace else, and Mike was tired of having her wake him in the morning by slinging her early-morning bottle halfway across the floor to get his attention. And we all needed more storage, work, and breathing space.

We sounded out the O'Gormans, who had no objection to our building on so long as we paid for it. A general plan was agreed upon, and in due time Hugo was roughing out specifics with Don José, the master *albañil* (mason) Juan O'Gorman had sent us. Our overhung front veranda would become a dining room, thank goodness: French windows would comprise two of the new walls enclosing it, with a waist-high fireplace at one end where we could barbecue. We would extend the southern wall of the house itself to make a study downstairs for Hugo and a bedroom and bath upstairs for ourselves. And of course, since local carpenters in those days were perfectly willing to use secondhand lumber, all this would be astonishingly cheap. *¡Viva México!*

In the ensuing weeks, while Don José was beginning to line up workmen and materials, Hugo (still between jobs and feeling restless) was finding it hard to get my undivided attention. He suggested a cure: that I take a few days' holiday from my screenplay and go with him to Veracruz, which we had never seen and which was reputed to be picturesque and interesting. He got the name of a hotel on the beach, made reservations, and we had started packing—when my mother telephoned from California.

Weary of feeling no better and tired of being away from home, she had returned to her house in Palo Alto, checked in with her doctor, and been given the expected diagnosis. He had given her from two to six months.

I stood there at the wall phone on the landing halfway up the stairs and couldn't think what to say. The stairs, with their red-painted treads and their dark-blue-painted iron-tubing balustrades, looked singularly functional and cold. I remember looking at it and thinking absently that it was the only unattractive part of the whole house. . . .

I told Mother not to worry about her book; I would try to finish it if she wanted me to (a promise I didn't keep, but perhaps someday one of her grandchildren will). And I said we'd be up to visit her. She said she didn't think there was any such immediacy.

But the idea of going off on a holiday with Hugo had lost its appeal. I hoped that Hugo, when I told him about the call, would change his plans, but to my surprise he didn't. I finished packing abstractedly and was brushing my hair at the bathroom mirror preparatory to leaving when Emily—now five and a half and home from kindergarten—drifted in. She studied me a moment, her great brown eyes (as always) looking at me from a long way off. After a moment, she said, "Do you have to go to Veracruz?"

I said yes.

She watched my reflection in the mirror and I saw hers, a few feet behind me. She looked like a very young, very beautiful gypsy seeress. After another long moment she said, in an even dreamier voice, "You'll be driving along, and the car will go off the edge, and you'll go down, down, down . . . And you'll never come back anymore."

Now I really didn't want to go. But we went.

Of the four or five hours' drive to the coast, I remember nothing. The hotel where we checked in, I remember only dimly: a rambling stucco place on the beach, egregiously pseudocolonial. We unpacked and changed into our bathing suits and went out onto an unattractive, scrubby-looking beach for a late-afternoon swim in water that was surprisingly warm and sticky and filled with shreds of seaweed. When we had showered and dressed, we drove into town for a look around and to have dinner. Hugo, fascinated by all things Mexican, seemed to find the flavor of the place interesting. I can't even remember it. I found myself inexplicably worried about the children. I wanted to go back to the hotel so I could phone them.

Hugo was beginning to find my preoccupation annoying. We chose a restaurant—I think it was just off the *zócalo,* but except that it seemed to me singularly unappealing, I remember nothing about it—and ordered drinks and something to eat. Midway through, he said abruptly, "Oh, for Christ's sake, if you're so worried about them, find a phone and call them!"

I went straightway to a public phone near the entrance and put in a call for Mexico City.

Our line was out of order.

Hugo was remarkably unsympathetic about my worries. Ramona and Isabel were there, he pointed out. And the phone was out of order almost as often as it was working. What in the world was there to worry about?

I couldn't put words to it. But he wasn't the one who'd received that call from California that morning, and he hadn't heard Emmie make her eerie, Cassandra-like prophecy. The world seemed to me, that night, fraught with some vague, indefinable threat. I couldn't understand how Hugo, with what had always seemed to me his remarkable, almost feminine intuition, couldn't understand why I was upset. But he only grew increasingly annoyed with me. Before we'd even finished eating, he pushed his plate back and called for the check, and we went back to the hotel.

From a pay phone in the lobby, I tried Mexico City again while Hugo went on to our room.

Our number was still out of order. With growing desperation I phoned our nearest neighbors, the Druckers (home again long since with their rapidly improving daughter), and asked if they'd mind going over to our house to see if everything was all right. Then I waited the ten minutes the errand would require and phoned them again. Yes, they'd gone around to our place and spoken to Ramona; the children were in bed, and everything was fine. An electrical storm had knocked out our phone line, that was all.

My curious anxiety somewhat but not altogether allayed, I went to our room. Hugo was already in bed, his back to me.

We went home the next day.

But Hugo never altogether forgot or forgave me.

However, as summer neared, it was Hugo who suggested that we go to Ensenada for July and August if we could get the children's school assignments for the classes they'd miss. I would be closer to St. Malo in case Frank needed me for conferences and within closer striking distance of Palo Alto if needed there. In fact, maybe I should take the children there for a visit with Mother on the *way* to Ensenada while he went on ahead to find us a place. What did I think?

I thought it was a good idea.

Chapter Thirteen

AND SO, four years after our last arrival in Ensenada, an afternoon in late June of 1955 found us rounding the low, dry hills of inland Baja and then reaching and following the still mostly undeveloped (thank heaven) coastline above Ensenada Bay. The weather was bright, the air was clear, and as we neared the outskirts of town, the ocean stretched out beyond us blue and vast and it all seemed wonderfully familiar.

The children and I had come from a visit to my mother in Palo Alto. We had found her in what seemed surprisingly good health, still mobile and not in pain, though quite thin. She had enjoyed our stay there, had made sure her housekeeper-caretaker fed us well, and feeling, I suppose, that bloodlines needed to be reestablished while she was still there to do it, had taken our unwieldy group to visit an assortment of relatives living in the area whom I had known barely or not at all. Mostly, however, she had spent hours at a card table in her living room playing a card game she called Memory Test (Concentration?) with her grandchildren, as she had once played it long ago with my brother and me.

And when our visit was drawing to a close, I found a subterfuge to get out alone to a pay phone and call her best friend to ask her—coward that I am—to be on hand for our departure in order to avert any emotional leave-takings. I also promised, next day, as I herded children and baggage out the door to the waiting taxi, to come up again later in the summer—although the unstated "if" was large in all our minds.

From there we'd trained south to Oceanside, where Frank lent us one of the family cars not currently in use, and I'd driven on down to meet Hugo at the Ensenada motel he'd been using as a base while he house hunted. With Ramona in tow, he had flown straight from Mexico City, and while she'd been bustling about town, renewing old friend-ships, he'd been scouting for a two months' rental—one that would house not only us but also his mother, Margaret, who'd be arriving any moment to spend the summer with us too.

Initially, the hunt hadn't been promising. As the children scuttled about, exploring the motel grounds, he told me about his first seemingly futile searches. Every available rental in Ensenada, he discovered, was so small, we'd have burst at the seams. All over town, even at the bank, he'd asked, "But aren't there any *bigger* houses?" And all over town, even at the bank, the answer had been the same: No. Except maybe (and this was always said somewhat dubiously) Minnie's place . . .

It was this note of doubt in everyone's voices when they mentioned Minnie's place that kept Hugo from checking it out straightaway. Fi-nally, however, when it seemed there were no other choices, he had arranged a meeting with Minnie at the bank, where she was appar-ently an old and valued customer, and she had taken him to look at her minimally furnished but commodious two-story house south of town, a few hundred yards down the road from the secondary school. To his infinite relief, the place was indeed big enough; there were even enough bedrooms for guests. In fact, Minnie's own bedroom on the ground floor just off the front porch would do nicely for his mother, who'd had a heart attack and shouldn't climb stairs.

He had liked the place on sight. And Minnie had explained why it was so well known all over town: "When the bars close, the fellows like to come here for a drink, you know?" By "the fellows," she meant the American sports fishermen who came down to Ensenada for a weekend of fishing and drinking. "Cristina (her friend) and me, we cook some lobsters, give them some beer; they like that, you know?"

Hugo, busy counting bedrooms, had said yes, he knew.

But as it turned out, he didn't.

He had made a deal on the spot, giving Minnie a check for five hundred dollars for two months' rent, and she, quite pleased with the arrangement, had immediately hired workmen to build her a one-room cottage in the front yard.

Before the day was out, Freddie had pulled up in front of our motel, delivered Margaret to us, hugged his stepgrandchildren, and left, and soon after, complete with luggage, we were heading by car and taxi south through town toward our summer's rental. Ensenada was virtually unchanged, we found: yes, it still smelled of dust, and the fish canneries, and the nearby ocean. Except for a mole built out from the shore to protect the burgeoning little harbor, everything seemed just as we'd left it, though Minnie's semirural "colonia" was new to us. We were on a dirt road now, out in what seemed almost country; we passed what must be the secondary school (which looked newly built), drove on a bit farther; and, when we reached a big white box of a place with a red door and red-trimmed windows, pulled to a stop.

A few small dwellings were scattered about the fields on either side of it, and the dunes across the way, which hid the ocean from the view here, were wild and overgrown with scrub and a few dwarf pines, but it was, I thought, a rather pleasant outlook. The house itself was set on a graveled lot, with a trailer parked in back (where Minnie's friend Cristina lived, Hugo said), and at the front corner of the yard a couple of locals were already working on the foundation for Minnie's new quarters. (In Ensenada you don't expect zoning ordinances, for heaven's sake. Anarchy reigns, and you expect it to.) Across the front of the house, above the red door, we noticed a wide oblong where the paint looked less weathered, as though a sign had been removed. (And sure enough, the children found it later when they were exploring the yard. It said, of course, Minnie's Place. And when Minnie herself dropped by later to see if we needed anything, she explained that she had taken it down because "it didn't look right for the boys at the school, you know?"

And once again we said yes, we knew.

But we didn't.

The children tumbled out of the car and in a moment were swarming delightedly all over the house. It was bright and clean, if a bit long on Ensenada's own special linoleum-floor-and-wallboard decor—though Minnie's room, just off the living room and immediately beside the front door, where we settled Margaret and her suitcase, had a sort of bargain-basement elegance about it. The kitchen, though sparely furnished, was twice the size of our kitchen in San Angel, which pleased Ramona. And the children were delighted to find a pinball machine in the living room.

We were a bit puzzled, though, to discover numbers over the

bedroom doors upstairs; the place must once have been used as a hotel, we decided—or maybe a boardinghouse. Half a dozen small bedrooms had clearly been carved out of larger rooms by wallboard partitions, one of which even had a hole in it, just at eye level. The former residents couldn't have cared much about privacy, I thought, and reminded myself to hang a picture over it. For ourselves, Hugo and I chose a big bedroom at the front of the house, with a pleasant view of the dunes. And as the children were choosing rooms for themselves, Ramona disappeared with her market basket to provision the house for supper.

Margaret, meanwhile, was busy making herself at home in Minnie's former bedroom: putting her *lares et penates*, her silver comb-and-brush set and her little silver-framed pictures of the family, and her various bottles of medication in place on Minnie's dressing table. Once the most proper of Englishwomen, life with Freddie had taught Margaret to make the best of things, and she was so happy now at the prospect of spending the summer with her grandchildren that she accepted Minnie's interior decoration, and indeed all of Ensenada, with equanimity. From her *Mrs. Beeton's Cookery Book* at home she had brought down a recipe for soused mackerel and was promising to make it for us at the first opportunity; a seaside town like Ensenada should certainly have plenty of fresh mackerel. . . .

After dinner I read to the children and put them to bed, and by ten o'clock we grown-ups, tired from traveling and moving in, fell gratefully into bed too.

But not for long.

From midnight on the visitors came ("After the bars close, you know?") singly or in twos or threes, making it all too clear why Minnie's place was such a landmark in town—and why no one had been very wholehearted about recommending it as a family rental. Mainly Americans (since the locals had already learned about Minnie's change of address), they pulled in off the dark road in front, parked in the graveled yard, and came bounding up onto the front porch to bang exuberantly on the door, a few pausing en route to announce themselves by knocking on Minnie's (now Margaret's) curtained window, one of them bleating loudly, "Minnie! Mi-i-i-nnie!" like a desperate ram calling for its ewe. Hugo's mother, after turning away the first caller indignantly, ignored the racket and kept to her bed, but no one got much sleep. It was a lively night.

In the morning, tireder but wiser, we considered our options and found we didn't have any. The five hundred dollars had already been paid, with the excavation in the front yard to show for it. Anyway, there was no place else to go—no place that was big enough for all of us. In the end, we simply covered the front door and Minnie's/Margaret's window with handwritten signs saying MINNIE DOESN'T LIVE HERE ANYMORE! and ¡MINNIE NO VIVE AQUI! After Minnie's cottage was finished we added, to the latter sign, a postscript: ¡MINNIE VIVE ALLÁ! with arrows pointing toward it.

Actually, as the summer wore on, Minnie proved a model of neighborly discretion. Where her former employees had gone, we had no idea—except for Cristina, who having reached middle age had trimmed her lamps and taken over the job of janitor-caretaker instead, glumly raking the gravel in the yard and tending to the halfhearted flowers around the place. But Minnie herself, nearing her sixties, had merely opted for a less active life. She had, apparently, reduced her clientele to one per weekend, usually one or another of the sports fishermen who swarmed into town every Friday evening. Since we rarely saw anyone coming or going, we assumed that Minnie kept her chosen customer cozily in her cottage from Friday to Sunday, cooking for him, serving him drinks, and generally making him happy.

She was a trim, businesslike woman with a quantity of jet-dyed hair, a good deal of black mascara, and bright red lipstick against a startlingly white skin. She wore stiletto heels, sheer black hose, a tight girdle, and black lace blouses that gave peeps of a mountainous bosom. And as landladies go, she was remarkably good-natured. It was she who told us about the fishermen's enclave in the gully near the beach just to our north, where you could buy live baby lobsters for three pesos each (about a quarter); she even explained to Ramona (who listened inscrutably) how to cook them. As for her exuberant misdirected visitors, they tapered off in time as word got around; by midsummer we were only bothered once, by some John-come-lately who came prowling around the side of the house one afternoon to knock on the kitchen door and ask Ramona hopefully, "*¿Hay muchachas?*" ("Are there girls?")

To which Ramona snapped angrily in Spanish, "Yes, there are girls. And they're all under ten years old!"

The children, who had changed lifestyles so often by now that nothing seemed strange or unusual, had simply christened our earlier visitors "Minnie men" and never given them another thought. They had also, prowling through the end-table drawers in the living room soon after our arrival, come upon a red lightbulb, which rather interested them ("Why would anyone want a red lightbulb?"). But by that time we grown-ups didn't need any further confirmation of what we already knew, and since the children couldn't figure out any possible use for the lightbulb, they left it where it was.

In any event, we quickly settled into a routine of half work, half play. I was still busy with the first-draft screenplay of *The Miracle,* mailing each scene as I completed it up to Frank for revision. Hugo was working on a screen adaptation of a Spanish-language novel, *La Escondida (The Hidden One)*, for a Mexican producer friend, and in his spare time was beginning to haunt Ensenada's modest little marine stores. A sailor since boyhood, he was getting the itch to own a small boat, one we could use here all summer for fishing expeditions and, when we left, have shipped to Acapulco. . . .

But mornings, before our day's work began, we took turns driving Margaret and the children (as soon as they had completed that day's share of homework) to the beach or to the still accessible and wonderful lagoon. And families from Los Angeles came down in ever increasing numbers to visit. We learned from Cleo Trumbo, who arrived early on with her children, that she had taken a secretarial course so she could speed-type Trumbo's many under-the-table assignments (of which he currently had three at once). My girlhood friend Marie Rinaldo and her children came down too, though her husband, Fred, who had gone from writing highly successful Abbott and Costello comedies (preblacklist) to selling job lots of paper (postblacklist), was too busy on his rounds to come with them. And actor Jeff Corey and *his* family came down; he told us that studios that still blacklisted him as an actor were now inviting him onto their sound stages to coach their lead players. Other visitors included a diminutive character actor named Shiman Ruskin (who had played charming bits in several of Hugo's pictures earlier but was now driving a bakery truck) and his wife and son, and other friends and friends of friends, many of whose wives were helping ensure their families' survival these days by going door-to-door, doing market research. There were weekends that summer when even Minnie's place could hardly handle the influx.

As for meals . . .

I had learned, our previous summer here, that I could go down to the icehouse early in the morning and buy freshly harvested abalone, wait for it to be filleted, sliced thin, and pounded, then detour on the way home to buy still-hot, freshly baked French loaves at La Guadalupana, which together with wonderful Mexican coffee and the lightly sautéed abalone steaks made a glorious breakfast. I also followed Minnie's directions to the gloomy little hollow where the town's lobster fishermen lived, to buy quantities of baby lobsters and bring them home still wriggling in a tin laundry tub in the back of the car.

We ate well that summer.

Through all of this I had, of course, kept in touch with my mother, who by late June had had to have her lung tapped. Like the determined woman she was, she had driven herself to the health center, refused any painkiller (convinced she was allergic to it), endured the procedure stoically, and driven home again. My engineer brother, who lived with his family an hour's distance from her, was driving over on weekends and kept me apprised of her progress.

As for the boat: Hugo had decided it would be too expensive to buy one, and anyway, those he had seen were all too big. Combing the boating magazines, he had found a diagram of a little sailing dinghy that looked about right and had been directed by local sailors to the town's one little boatyard or what passed for it. By early July, he was deep in conference with a boatbuilder and the little craft was under construction.

He was so busy with the boat, in fact, that he had made no mention of my birthday, which was coming on apace. In fact, nobody had mentioned my birthday. In our family, birthdays had always been made much of, and it occurred to me that for the first time, mine had actually been forgotten. To be sure, Hugo and I were both spending every spare moment at our typewriters, and Hugo's mother had finally assembled all the necessary ingredients and made the soused mackerel (a major event), and the children were swimming and reading and playing and (except for the homework) as happy and busy as children could be. And our streams of visitors had made for a good deal of confusion as well. So maybe it had just slipped everyone's minds . . .

I didn't want to bring it up; it was a matter of pride with me. *But how could they forget?!*

July 7—the day before my birthday—came and, like its fellows, went. Hugo drove the children to the beach and left his mother there to keep an eye on them while he came back to the house to work—but he kept abandoning his typewriter to rush off to the boatyard and check on the progress of the boatbuilding, which was now well under way. I sat resolutely at my own typewriter, feeling more and more aggrieved, forming in my mind a scenario of what I would do tomorrow morning. I would get up as usual, go downstairs for breakfast as usual, and in the middle of breakfast, when everyone was assembled around the table, I would say, ever so mildly, "Happy birthday, Mother." And they would feel *terrible*.

Dinner came and went, and still nobody mentioned the Big Day. Afterward I read to the children, still keeping my offended feelings to myself, and finally, with no word spoken, Hugo and I turned in too, and I tried not to care.

But I cared.

I was still asleep when the first strains sounded:

"Estas son las mañanitas, que cantaba el rey David . . ."

In one bound I hit the floor five feet from the bed and raced barefoot to the front windows. It was still dark, but a hint of day was just showing at the edge of the sky; the dunes and scrub were faintly visible across the street—and below the window, looking up at me and grinning as I looked down, were five tatterdemalion musicians in caps and sweaters, playing guitar, base, xylophone, and trumpet and singing:

"—A las muchachas bonitas, se las cantaban así . . ."

It was, I think, the loveliest moment of my life.

The size of the conspiracy emerged when the song ended and Hugo and I went downstairs in our bathrobes to invite the musicians in; they would expect, he said, to have breakfast with us. And lo and behold, Ramona was already at work in the lighted kitchen, making a mountain of refried beans with *chorizo* and beating up a sea of scrambled eggs. Hugo had given her instructions days before, and she had been smuggling in supplies without my even knowing.

The musicians, a cheerful, raffish-looking lot whom Hugo had hired at Hussong's Bar during one of those supposed trips to the boatyard, settled themselves at one end of the living room and asked us what songs we wanted to hear and, when we gave them carte blanche, took us on a musical tour of Mexico's history, with waltzes from the days of Porfirio Díaz (which is how we learned that "Over the Waves" was originally *"Sobre las Olas,"* written by a Mexican composer), through the songs of the revolution (*"Jesusita en Chihuahua,"* and the Villistas' army song *"La Cucaracha,"* and the Carranzistas' *"La Malagueña"*) as Hugo kept them supplied with tequila and beer. The children, who had been drifting downstairs in their bathrobes too, loved every minute of it, pleased especially that no one had let the plan slip and spoiled the surprise, and Hugo, of course, was the cat that ate the cream. Ramona brought in heaping platters of food, and the musicians joined us around the table—there were a dozen of us, as I remember—and shoveled away Ramona's *frijoles con chorizo* as though they hadn't eaten in weeks.

There were more Mexican folksongs after breakfast; at the musicians' insistence and to the children's embarrassed hilarity Hugo and I even danced to a few of them in our bathrobes and slippers, and then at last, our guests packed up their instruments and drifted off down the road, the sun now higher on the horizon and the town beginning to pull itself together for another workday.

The last afternoon of July, my brother phoned me that Mother had slipped into a coma and that I'd better come up. Hugo drove me to the San Diego airport, but there were no planes until early morning. By the time I had reached San Francisco and taken a bus down the peninsula to Palo Alto, she had already died, and the mortuary van had come and gone.

My brother and I plunged into arrangements. Mother, the most organized of women, had left no instructions about where she wanted to be buried (here? Utah?), but this was the only difficult decision she had left us to face. Otherwise her will was specific, sensible, and scrupulously fair. Her funeral, at a local chapel, was well attended; some of her neighbors, contemporaries mostly, came, and a few lifelong friends from Stanford or Utah, and a number of cousins and half cousins and cousins once removed, who drove in from all over the state. The minister, at our request, read a sonnet from a sonnet sequence she had written late in her life, and the local papers treated her accomplishments with respect. Mother would have approved of every moment of it, we thought.

That night after the funeral, I set out by train for San Diego, where Hugo met me and drove me back to Ensenada. The children, he said, had responded in various ways to this first loss of a family member, but it had been nine-year-old Mary who, when he told them the news, had gone upstairs and cried until dinnertime.

And Emily, almost six, had said little until several months afterward, when we were back in San Angel Inn again. Then, one day when we were en route on foot to some errand in the neighborhood, she had detoured just outside our gates to climb the little crooked-limbed tree that stood sentry out there, and while I waited, not impatiently, for her to come down, she paused on one of the middle branches and looked down at me oddly.

"You," she said, "don't have any mother."

Chapter Fourteen

THE YEAR BEFORE our return to Ensenada, the U.S. Supreme Court had issued a historic opinion banning segregation in public schools.

Absorbed as we were in our own survival and in the exploration of and adapting to Mexico and its ways, we were hardly aware of the fact. We'd read about it in the newspapers, of course. But perhaps we felt so much cynicism about our homeland by now that we viewed such a decision as no more than a gesture. Nothing substantive would be done about it, we thought. Certainly in this political climate, ways would be found to maintain the status quo, the court dictum notwithstanding.

So, in the months that followed, that landmark decision was nowhere in our consciousness. We'd come home from Ensenada and our brief visits in the States still with no notion whatever that *Brown v. Board of Education* in Topeka might actually presage a watershed change in stateside life.

In fact, the only news story north of the border that had really caught our—especially my—attention was about the development of the Salk vaccine for polio (which had claimed large numbers of victims in Mexico back in the early months of the decade). On my most recent trip north, I'd been careful to bring back enough little vials of the vaccine, kept cold in one of the children's lunch box thermoses, for our Mexican pediatrician to inoculate all our children.

In any event, when we returned at summer's end to our newly built-on house with its plenitude (at last) of bedrooms, bathrooms, and closets, life in Mexico was, increasingly, our reality. We had even given up our American meal schedule and now, like Mexican families, had a light supper (*cena*) at night and *comida,* the big meal of the day, in midafternoon when the children got home from school: all of us about the big dining table that Hugo had commissioned from George Oppen, with Hugo presiding like Zeus at the head, in our new French-doored veranda-turned-dining-room, a fire blazing away in the waist-high fireplace and, often, rain or even hail pummeling the windows around us.

Or on warm clear days, we ate outdoors in the *jacal,* a sort of rustic, thatch-roofed gazebo that Hugo on our return had had built in the far corner of the backyard, against a thick stand of bamboo that completely obscured our neighbor's back wall. Partially screened by trees from even our own backyard, we found meals out there gave us a wonderful, primitive Swiss Family Robinson feeling, and the children loved it.

Hugo and I were less anxious about survival these days. My two recent screenplay jobs and Hugo's work with George Pepper's little company, plus an occasional offer from Mexican producers, reassured us that one way or another we'd both be able to make a living in the foreseeable future. We wouldn't even have to touch the money my mother's will had left me but could save it for Mike's and Susie's college. It would even put Mary halfway through. After that—well, that was too far off to worry about.

There were holiday trips to Acapulco too, with predawn fishing trips arranged with one or another of the local motorboat owners. With our children safely buckled into Mae West life jackets (*salvavidas*), we trolled the dark, rolling waters outside the bay for bonito and yellowtail and watched the darkness pale and the world being born all over again as the western horizon, water and sky, began to reflect the first faint glow of daylight from the east. And after Hugo's little sailing dinghy (christened *El Traguito,* "The Little Drink") had arrived from Ensenada, Hugo and Mike acquired impressive sunburns from their daylong explorations of the bay and its inlets.

Then there was the vacation trip, also to Acapulco, when within an hour of our arrival Mike and a friend plunged into the ocean to try out Mike's homemade fish spear (inspired by his reading of Cousteau's *The Silent World*) and, cutting loose the first fish he'd impaled, Mike gave himself such a gash on the thumb that I rushed him to the local doctor for a tetanus shot, which in turn gave him hepatitis—proving again (if we needed proof) that nothing in Mexico ever happens singly; it always sets off a chain of events and you never know where it will end.

Actually, in the normal course of our lives back home in San Angel, more changes were taking place. We had a new car, or rather a new used car, bought in desperation when our tall, sixteen-year-old Cadillac gave up the ghost once too often on a hot, busy Sunday afternoon on the main street of Cuernavaca. We had traded it for a hundred dollars' credit with our neighborhood upholsterer, who didn't yet know how to drive but was thinking of learning.

And, acquired from a family who were returning to the States, we now had a dog named Pablo, half collie, half St. Bernard, a bumptious, cheerful creature who'd been trained to roll over and bark wildly when anyone played or sang "Roll Out the Barrel." During the children's absence at school he spent his time stalking rats or other small game in the lot next door to us, and he was curiously class-conscious, friendly and tail wagging to any scoundrel in a business suit but savage to any-one in working clothes. Despite his snobbery we loved him dearly, and he and our aging cat, Baby Roo, had the good sense to ignore each other.

As for our friends, there were changes here too.

We'd made friends with a family named Zykofsky, left-wingers from the Bronx who'd arrived in Mexico with their daughters a year before we had. Lacking working papers, they'd had no recourse but to bor-row family money and open a small TV-components business—and soon found themselves so successful, they'd been able to build a house in the Pedregal. The wages of misfortune.

And our exuberant friend Bart van der Schelling had had a heart attack from trying, at age sixty-three, to maneuver a piano he had tuned up a flight of stairs. But idleness, even during his convalescence, was impossible for him. Instead he used the time to teach himself to paint, thus beginning (again, the wages of misfortune) a whole new career as a primitive. Hugo bought one of his early works, a childhood memory of a Dutch fishing village, with little boats at anchor along the waterfront and a bevy of stiff little houses looking down at them from the shore. We hung it over our fireplace, where, in the early morning, sunlight streamed in to set its wonderful bold dark blues and greens and reds and yellows ablaze and filled the whole room with Bart's own love of color and light.

There were new arrivals, too, to our exile community.

Since Cold War hysteria continued unabated up in the States, newly minted refugees from various parts of the country, or in some cases past or present left-wingers who merely thought it wiser to be out of the hurricane, continued to make their way to Mexico. Frederick Vanderbilt Field, a China specialist who had been much badgered by the FBI and who had served time for contempt at Trumbo's alma mater the federal penitentiary at Ashland, Kentucky, had arrived with his then wife and her children. And *three* families had come down from Florida to avoid further persecution under that state's "Little Smith Act." Happily, the paterfamilias of one of these families was a skilled dentist, and as soon as he acquired credentials to practice in Mexico, the whole left-wing colony made appointments with him to get their teeth fixed.

But the Floridians who would become closest to us were the Smalls (née Smolikoff).

They were quickly taken under the wing of the Fields and the Maltzes, and we would learn, bit by bit over the next few months, as they moved into our neighborhood and Mrs. Small (the family athlete) joined our Saturday morning ball games, that their political adventures prior to their flight made our own pale by comparison.

Charles, roughly Hugo's age, had been raised in Hell's Kitchen, and only a yearlong attack of rheumatic fever in his late teens had saved him from the kind of finish that was claiming most of his boyhood friends: jail or death by drugs or gunfire. During his enforced bed rest, he had begun to read, and his discovery of Karl Marx had given him, finally, a goal—of a world better than the one he'd been raised in. When he was on his feet again, he became a union organizer, joined the Communist Party, and was soon a party "functionary." His heart, permanently damaged by his illness, left him physically fragile, but the education he'd given himself made him literate enough so that he'd even written and sold a few short stories to the pulps. Fair-haired, with a thin, angular face, he was also tough-minded, wise, and a staunch friend, and Hugo admired him extravagantly.

Berthe ("Bert" to us) had met and fallen in love with Charles at age fifteen and had never looked back. She too was fair-haired, and such flesh as she had on her bones was pure muscle; for a time during her marriage she had taught physical education in Florida, and she was still lean, athletic, physically disciplined. Her years with Charles had made her as tough-minded as he was, and like Charles, she was a sponge for all things Mexican, the country's history, its folkways, its arts.

And about life at home, she had few illusions. A few years before their arrival here, during one of Charles's periods of subpoena ducking, she and their firstborn boy (then quite small) were home alone one night when the Klan paid a visit, burning a cross on their lawn and racing their cars up and down in front of the house, yelling invectives and shooting off rifles. Bert, pregnant at the time with another baby, miscarried.

They'd had another child since then, and during Charles's incarceration Bert too had been subpoenaed and jailed for a time. Now the family were here in Mexico, waiting out Charles's appeal of a sentence for contempt of court (specifically, Florida's grand jury). Charles knew that his heart condition could probably not withstand the conditions of a Florida prison, but neither he nor Bert wanted a life underground for themselves or their children, so Charles had determined that if his appeal failed, he would go home and serve his term.

Meanwhile he and Bert were opening a little souvenir shop down in the city's fashionable tourist district, the Zona Rosa. Like the Zykofskys, they would find themselves surprisingly successful as entrepreneurs, but they would also become, in the following years, the family most of the refugees would come to rely on for advice, for friendship and support.

However, when a real crisis arose in our community later that year, they were still too newly arrived to be involved in it.

It began with the breakdown of our photographer friend Timmy.

We hadn't known her very well. She was the wife (or significant other; we were never quite sure) of Charles Humboldt, a former editor of *Masses and Mainstream,* whom we both liked. But he was in the States at the moment, seeking treatment for a complicated neurological problem at a VA hospital, and for the last month or two, as far as we had known, Timmy had been off in the jungles of Chiapas, working as still photographer on a picture adapted from a B. Traven novel, *Rebellion of the Hanged.* So we were doubly puzzled when, early one morning, Mike, in his pajamas and bathrobe, roused us to tell us that Timmy was outside our gates. "And she's crying," he said. "Pretty hard, too . . ."

Fearing she'd had bad news about her Charles, we threw on our own bathrobes and rushed down. Timmy was indeed at our gates, with a coat thrown over her nightgown and wearing a flowered straw hat over flowing, disheveled hair. She was sobbing hysterically, but not about Charles. About herself. She seemed to think she was dying.

As we brought her inside, sat her down, and gave her coffee, all we could make out was that she'd spent the night at the Maltzes' (how did she get there from Chiapas? we wondered). And for whatever reason—perhaps because she couldn't sleep—she'd taken some pills she'd found in the guest bathroom. But she wasn't sure what they were or how many she'd taken, and now she was afraid they might prove fatal. She was adamant, though, that we not call the Maltzes (*why,* for heaven's sake?) and even more adamant that we not call her (and our) family doctor, Jake Levine, toward whom she seemed suddenly to have taken a violent dislike.

But she was also clearly in no shape to be wandering the streets of Mexico City alone. I gave her more coffee, hoping that caffeine might somehow restore her to sanity, and went off to call another doctor used by some of the American community. Afraid of being overheard, I gave him a cautious report, but the doctor sensed the problem straightaway. "Does the lady seem emotionally disturbed?" he asked. "Irrational?" I gave a cautious yes. "I'm sorry," he said. "That's not my field. I suggest you try someone else."

So I repaired to the living room again, and both Hugo and I urged her to let us call Jake. At that, she transferred her anger to *us,* demanded we call her another cab, and left in a fury—to land, we suspected, on someone else's doorstep.

The children, who had never seen anyone in this condition, had been hovering within earshot in the hall, altogether fascinated. Now, with some urging, they began to get themselves dressed for school while Hugo and I, hopelessly confused by the morning's events and without the faintest idea what should be done, phoned Jake and then various of our friends to try to figure out the best course of action.

From there, matters escalated. Word spread. Other friends, hearing of the situation, began to call us. First the Oppens, to whose apartment Timmy had fled when she'd left us. Apparently when they too proposed getting her medical help, she'd stormed out to seek out yet another friend's house and from there still another, leaving each household reeling from the visit.

Phones never stopped ringing. Self-appointed rescue parties began to turn up, starting at our place and then tracking her from one house to another, missing her at each one. One refugee wife, on the phone, pointed out a problem that had never occurred to us: if Timmy was truly as paranoid as she seemed, she was clearly capable of thinking, and alleging, almost anything about anyone in the exile community. . . .

But now a fresh problem was opening up.

Jake Levine, who as a veterinarian had served with the Aftosa (hoof-and-mouth disease) commission in the States but who had since come down to earn a medical degree in Mexico—and who by virtue of an almost paternal interest in our community had become the doctor of choice for most of us—arrived in the midst of the turmoil to get a fuller report on Timmy's condition. And soon after his arrival, Hans Hoffman (a psychologist, after all) arrived too. Hugo by now had repaired to his study to work, and I, busy tending to the children's breakfast and departure for school, left the two men in the living room with coffee while they discussed what should be done.

I came back into the living room to find them at sword's point.

Jake was addressing Hans witheringly as "*Doctor* Hoffman," knowing full well that Hans had not yet got his Ph.D., though he'd been functioning with some success as a therapist for several years. And Hans, livid, was warning that if Jake put Timmy into one of Mexico's *manicomios* (mental hospitals), which he considered draconian at best, she'd almost certainly be given electroshock, to which he was bitterly opposed. Jake, for his part, simply dismissed such objections, as though Hans lacked the medical qualifications to claim any expertise in the field whatsoever.

I was afraid they'd come to blows. It was a vast relief when they both, one after the other, stormed out—each, I suppose, bent on solving Timmy's problems his own way, depending on which one caught up with her first.

After that, there was a brief lull. Then in early afternoon, Anne

Hoffman phoned me, clearly upset. Did I know which sanitarium Hans had taken Timmy to?

I was relieved to hear that Timmy was in custody somewhere, though I had no idea where. Why? I asked. What was the problem?

It seemed that our mutual friend Waldeen, a dancer of some renown as a teacher of Mexican folkloric dancing and whose classes the refugee wives had been taking since their (our) arrival, as had our daughters, was being held in the San Angel *delegación* (station house) for being, apparently, an accessory to a kidnapping.

A *what?*

Specifically, for kidnapping Timmy. Moreover, the policemen at the *delegación* wanted to know where to find Hans, whom they also wanted to arrest or at least question about where he had hidden the missing lady.

By now we were wholly bewildered. How had the police come into the picture?

Not until evening, when we'd finally heard that Hans, after spending several hours getting Timmy settled in a reputable sanitarium, had gotten home to learn from Anne of Waldeen's predicament and sped over to the San Angel police station to straighten it all out, did we find out how the police had gotten involved in the first place.

It seemed that after ricocheting from one San Angel household to another, bringing chaos with her arrival and leaving confusion and bewilderment in her wake, Timmy had reached the Liebers' apartment, a mile or two away from us. Hans, arriving there soon after, had urged her to let him take her to a sanitarium. Instantly hysterical again, she had refused, and so, with her husband away and she herself clearly in desperate need of care, Hans had seen no recourse but to sedate and commit her himself.

Alas, the Liebers' building at this moment in history was being painted. And two painters, out on a second-floor deck with their paintbrushes, had had a clear view through the windows of the Liebers' apartment: of Hans's arrival, of his putting some sort of proposal to Timmy, and of her hysterical refusal. They saw Hans inject her and looked on as Hans (and, I guess, Max Lieber) supported the now heavily sedated woman downstairs and out to Hans's car on the street below.

Convinced that they'd just seen a white-slave ring in action, the two painters had put down their buckets and rushed off to the San Angel *delegación* to report it.

The police went forthwith to the apartment, where by now they found only Minna Lieber and her small son, Butchy—and Waldeen, who just minutes ago had arrived to see if she, as Timmy's oldest friend, could help in any way. Convinced that foul play had been done and someone had to be arrested, and since Minna clearly had a small child to take care of, the police could find no one to arrest except Waldeen, whom they packed off to jail, where the poor woman (by now totally baffled about why any of this was happening) languished until Hans arrived and cleared things up.

Over the next several weeks we were able to piece together (from gossip) a version of events in Chiapas that might have precipitated Timmy's breakdown: a film company marooned in or near the jungle, with shooting halted by unseasonable rains; much drinking in the enforced idleness; and (according to hearsay) a brief, abortive romance between Timmy and a company's assistant who called himself "Hal Croves" but who was probably the mysterious B. Traven himself. And when Timmy's breakdown began, "Croves" putting her aboard his small private plane and flying her up to the Maltzes' in Mexico City—where, without being too specific about her condition, he left her.

The Maltzes, having no idea of the possible trouble they had on their hands, gave her dinner and put her to bed in their guest room. But at dawn, apparently, she'd wakened, in great agitation, and seeking sedatives or sleeping pills had taken whatever pills she could find in the guest bathroom—then, regretting the action, she'd set out on her mad odyssey about San Angel.

Apart from the curious fact that she refused to speak or even to understand Spanish while she was recuperating, she seemed to recover uneventfully at the sanitarium. A few weeks into treatment, she telephoned me with a rueful apology for her behavior, sounding perfectly sane and truly, deeply embarrassed and ashamed.

But in the meantime, something subtle and unsettling had happened to our community.

As of the morning of her breakdown, a rift had opened up between those who took Jake's side in the matter of Timmy's care (hospitalization) and whatever treatments the neurologists recommended) and those who agreed with Hans (psychotherapy, in a protective environment), and it refused to heal. Suddenly there were subjects we couldn't discuss with each other, islands in our conversations that had to be avoided. Arguments threatened to bubble up when we least wanted them to. Timmy's improvement notwithstanding, those of us (like Hugo and me) who took the old-line Marxist position that psychiatry was self-indulgent and ineffective found it better not to discuss the matter at all.

And by the time her Charles was well enough to come home, Timmy was altogether recovered, and they were making arrangements to move back to the States. But by then it was mid-1956, and history was *really* giving us something to disagree about.

Chapter Fifteen

AND NOW, a difficult chapter to deal with.

The year was 1956. We felt good about ourselves, good about the life we had made for ourselves here, and our new surroundings seemed steadily more beguiling. Well, there might have been a few faint warnings that the world (even our own immediate part of it here in Mexico) was changing, but we managed to keep such notions at bay.

The air over the valley of Mexico, for instance.

One of the wondrous things we'd found about our new dwelling place when we'd first arrived had been the astonishing clarity of the night sky. We'd never seen so many stars. Year by year since then, though, the stars seemed to dim. In fact, as the population, and correspondingly the lights of the city, increased, the stars were beginning to be ever so faintly outshone.

But it was happening so gradually that we gave it little thought.

Actually, a few other, subtler differences were beginning to manifest themselves. One afternoon on our return from a brief jaunt with the children to Cuernavaca, as we reached the summit of the mountain range that divided the valley of Morelos from the valley of Mexico and had started down the homeward side, we realized that our view of the valley spread out below us was just faintly obscured, as if there were a very thin, brownish haze hovering over a portion of it, though up here it was a fine, clear day.

On subsequent trips during the next several years, this odd opacity seemed to increase, ever so slightly.

At some point, I suppose, we arrived at the obvious. Ever since our arrival, we'd been reading newspaper statements by government officials urging the industrialization of the valley of Mexico; jobs were needed, if only to support its ever-increasing population. No one seemed to take into account that the mountains ringing the valley would cut off all escape for the smoke, the exhaust, the pollution that development would inevitably bring. At mid-decade, however, the haze was still so faint that it must hardly have seemed worth mentioning. . . .

But apart from those small hints of problems to come, our lives seemed to be progressing smoothly enough. Mike had apparently outgrown his early anxiety about our politics. The children were all enjoying life, or seemed to, and school was going well. Our ball games, though less frequent, still filled an occasional Saturday. Since Timmy and Charles Humboldt's recent return to the States, the edginess her breakdown had caused in our midst was diminishing bit by bit, though Jake Levine and the Hoffmans still avoided each other, and there were a few other coolnesses.

This summer would also mark the start of my fortieth year, but I managed not to think about that too often. And though Hugo and I had both been working hard on recent jobs, there came a point early in the year when neither of us had a project. We had a little money in the bank by now, so we felt no particular pressure; in fact, the respite gave Hugo the chance to discover a new literary idol.

One night quite late, I'd wakened to find that he hadn't yet come upstairs to join me, so I'd climbed out of bed and gone downstairs to find him. He was in the living room, pacing in the lamplight, with a paperback book in his hand. "Damn!" he said to me as I came in. "That's the best story I *ever* read!"

It was Chekhov's novella *The Duel*, about an impecunious young urban couple living aimless, self-indulgent lives in a vacation resort in the Caucasus and a conflict with one of the locals that leads to their regeneration. For the screen, Hugo thought, it could be updated and laid in Acapulco. He was enormously excited by the notion, and by next morning, after a few hours' sleep, he was busy at his typewriter on a narrative adaptation. We would also, the next few months, fall altogether in love with all of Chekhov's prose and for a time read little else.

For my part, I seized the chance to appropriate, for a novella, a project Hugo had put aside: an incident in his mother's childhood in the Oxford countryside when she and her siblings, with the help of their old blind nanny, had spent a frightening night hiding from their charming, alcoholic—and momentarily homicidal—father. I was translating this story too to Mexico and changing Margaret's family to a consular family assigned here during the early days of the revolution, and I would use, I thought, our own four girls as models for the protagonists. (This story would sell eventually, but Hugo's Chekhov adaptation, which we both thought the best work he'd ever done, did not.)

In any event, it was during this period, with none of our friends or family facing any major crises and when we had a little breathing space and were working on projects simply because we loved them, that history began dealing the left-wingers of the world some painful surprises.

True, there'd been rumors recently about anti-Semitism in the USSR that we'd refused to believe. But on a visit to the Oppens' apartment sometime during the recent past, I'd found George and Mary reading an English-language transcript of some sort of political trial in the Soviet Union in which the prosecution's anti-Semitism was open and incontrovertible.

Badly upset, they gave it to me to read, but I have no memory now of its substance or even of its date. Looking back, I think it must have dealt with the 1953 trial of the nine Jewish doctors who'd been charged with being "Zionist conspirators" and who, it was alleged, had by means of "harmful treatment and bad diagnosis" caused the deaths of certain Soviet dignitaries over the preceding years.

But this is only a supposition. All I actually remember is my unease as I read it. If such a trial actually took place, I remember thinking, it had to be a fluke—some hideous vendetta conducted, perhaps, by one rogue anti-Semitic official; it certainly couldn't represent official government policy. More likely, I thought, was that like a lot of Cold War news stories, it was a complete fraud, a piece of out-and-out anti-Soviet propaganda so well wrought that it could fool even George and Mary.

I'm sure, though, that when I handed the material back to them, my comments on it were safely ambiguous so they wouldn't take offense at my disbelief. And for whatever reason, the Oppens didn't mention the subject again; nor did I. Perhaps they too began to wonder if it were true or not. . . .

Then a short time later—again, I can't be sure quite when—we were confronted with another disturbing piece of reportage, this time first-hand.

George Pepper had met a Czech filmmaker visiting from France, had taken a liking to him, and had invited him for dinner, along with the Maltzes and Hugo and me.

It promised to be a pleasant evening, and like most evenings at the Peppers', interesting. George was an agreeable host and Jeanette a fine cook; as we arrived, we could smell tantalizing smells drifting out from the kitchen. In the living room, some of the Peppers' handsome pre-Columbian figures looked down at us from niches in the walls. The Maltzes were feeling affable, Albert perhaps because he'd just finished another book, *A Long Day in a Short Life,* which was now up in New York, either looking for a publisher or already sold (it would, in fact, be published before the end of the decade), and his wife, Margaret, still busy researching Mexico's legal system for her book on the plane bombing, regaled us with tales of the ongoing trial of the bombers as George gave us drinks.

So by the time we reached the table, conversation flourished. The guest of honor (whose name I've also forgotten, except that he being Czech, it had no vowels in it) was a vigorous, not unattractive man, dark haired, wide cheekboned, and broad shouldered, and his English was fluent. Over dinner we learned that he'd been a Communist since his youth, that he'd fought with the Republican Army in Spain, and that with the fall of the Loyalists he had escaped to France, working there in the film industry until the German occupation of World War II, when he'd been interned. Released after the liberation of Paris, he'd gone back to work in French films again. But when Czechoslovakia had joined the Warsaw Pact of 1955, he'd begun to think at long last about going home. And had telephoned a Czech government official to offer his services to Prague's budding film industry.

The official, who seemed familiar with his name and his film career, had listened to his proposal in polite silence. And then, "Well, let's see," he had said. *"You're a Jew, aren't you?"*

Albert Maltz—who had spent ten months in a federal prison for his left-wing faith—stared at him, almost unbelieving. The Czech gave him a wry, philosophic shrug. And Albert put his head down on his arms on the table. I couldn't see his face, but he may have been weeping.

By mid-March of 1956, news stories were appearing that could not be ignored or rationalized.

Reports in the American press, admittedly hearsay, said that in the final days of Russia's Twentieth (Communist) Party Congress a month before, in a closed session, the party's new leader, Nikita Khrushchev, had given an emotional, four-hour speech about the hideous excesses of the Stalin years.

Secret though the meeting had been, word of it by now seemed to be spreading around the globe. The first (and apparently semiofficial) "leak" had been at a reception in France; copies (the news stories said) had been circulated to local Communist parties worldwide. There'd even been a report on it issued by the U.S. State Department, which the Russians never denied, and the details were—or should have been, to those of us on the Left—appalling.

Stalin's purges, begun in the 1930s, had included many of Russia's top army officers, leaving the country tragically vulnerable during the early days of the German invasion. His secret police had conducted other purges, extracting confessions from their victims by torture. Of the 139 members of the Party Central Committee elected by the Seventeenth Party Congress in 1934, for instance, roughly three-fourths had since been arrested or shot. There had been deportations of "whole national minorities," evils that had continued, apparently, until Stalin's death in 1953.

Curiously, I have not only forgotten the experience of reading about this for the first time; I don't even remember discussing it with Hugo, though for days we must have talked of little else. But looking back, I think—I *think*—that initially we both regarded the whole story as one more Cold War invention, as did many (but not all!) of our friends. However, I do know that sometime during the subsequent weeks, we and our fellow exiles, for whatever reason, began slowly to change our minds.

But I have no memory of how we came, finally, to accept what we had been so vigorously denying to ourselves. Was the story covered at some point in one of the Communist papers? (We hadn't subscribed to the *People's World* for a long time, but I'm sure some of our friends still did.) Or was there just too much corroborating evidence coming out of Eastern Europe? *What finally convinced us?*

Nor can I learn from our friends, those who still survive, how they reacted initially or how they came to change their minds. Almost no one remembers. The fact that most of us have forgotten the relevant details seems to me in itself significant. The only exceptions, the only people who do remember, I've found, are those few who believed the reports from the outset.

For my own part: once convinced, I suspect that as was my wont, I grasped at straws. All right, perhaps it was true that Stalin had indeed been paranoid for years and the system had supported him. But if Khrushchev had made such a confession, that meant the situation was being corrected, didn't it? Or did it? Round and round I (we?) went, struggling to maintain a battered faith. Trying to separate culture from economics, Stalin from Marxism. Socialism could exist under any political structure, couldn't it? One tyrant's thirst for power needn't discredit a whole philosophy, need it . . . ?

Still later that year, the coup de grâce. We found ourselves reading news stories about Soviet tanks rolling into Hungary to quell dissent.

Altogether, it was a bad time in history.

But what country was pure?

Right here on Mexico's southern border, for instance, there was Guatemala, still reeling from a U.S.-engineered rebellion against its democratically elected president, Jacobo Arbenz Guzmán. Stateside papers insisted that the uprising had been indigenous, but word-of-mouth reports insisted otherwise. Just as Mexico had provided asylum for Spanish Loyalists, Jews fleeing Hitler, and U.S. leftists, it had been sheltering recent Guatemalan refugees, and from these new arrivals (including one talented Guatemalan musician who'd married a friend of ours), Mexicans had been getting firsthand reports of what had *really* happened (as Americans would too, eventually). Apparently the CIA, considering Arbenz's land-reform measures too radical by far and urged on by the agri-monopoly United Fruit, had orchestrated, trained soldiers for, and largely fought the whole "rebellion," setting up a minor military figure, Castillo Armas, as dictator and returning the country to its feudal status quo ante.

Nor were things much better on the domestic front, back in the States.

HUAC hearings had resumed in 1955, and doctors, lawyers, and teachers, as well as members of the entertainment industry, were still being hounded out of their livelihoods. Pete Seeger, whose folk songs our children were playing endlessly on our little portable record player, was appealing his 1955 contempt citation, and the fight to stay out of jail would cost him his livelihood and eight years of working life. And we'd heard last year that Phil Loeb of the popular TV show *The Goldbergs,* after struggling to survive his blacklisting for a time, had committed suicide. During the decade as a whole, there were other actors, like J. Edward Bromberg, Mady Christian, and John Garfield, who died of heart attacks or cerebral hemorrhage as a direct result of HUAC or FBI harassment.

So going home didn't seem a very likely alternative either.

But oddly, as we struggled to weigh these events against the changing political landscape in Eastern Europe and absorbed as we were in our own right of dissent, we had paid almost no attention to news stories coming out of Montgomery, Alabama, since the end of last year, about a weary, black forty-three-year-old seamstress who had refused to give up her seat in the "whites only" section of the bus, precipitating a black boycott of the bus line led by a black minister we had never heard of (but of whom we would hear a great deal in the years to come). Nor would we be as impressed as we should have been when, later in this year, the Supreme Court declared Montgomery's bus-segregation law unconstitutional.

Nor did it occur to us to be surprised at the contradiction between these two series of events—the early salvos of the black civil rights drive, as against HUAC's continued hearings—or to wonder which more truly represented the States at that moment in history.

It did, however, seem to us that no matter where we looked, there seemed to be inconsistency, illogic—madness, almost. Israel, with the support of England and France, had just invaded the Sinai; Anthony Eden stoutly defended the act and in the same breath denounced Soviet aggression in Hungary. No country, it seemed, was above reproach. For ourselves and our refugee friends, politics were rapidly changing from black and white to different shades of gray.

As for the Khrushchev revelations, we still wrestled with them. Even in our most fervent days, Hugo and I had thought of the USSR not as utopia but simply as a place where socialism was at least being *tried*, so we could comfort ourselves a little now with the thought that Russia, a tyranny for millennia, was in a state of cultural lag, that was all. It would take more than a few decades of any new political system, we reasoned, to eradicate a thousand years of authoritarianism and prejudice. . . .

But others of our friends, with more years and a profounder passion invested, were less exculpatory, we sensed, and more deeply hurt.

Whatever accommodation each of our various families struggled to arrive at, however, most of us seemed, subconsciously, to reach the same conclusion: *friendships, here in exile, were more important than doctrine.* Perhaps the rifts that had appeared among us during Timmy's breakdown had made us cautious, but politics were now almost disappearing from our conversations. We didn't want to test the boundaries beyond which disagreement became acrimony. If we differed from each other now in any important way, we didn't want to know. We drew back. We changed the subject.

And when, a couple of years later, our friendship with the Oppens (of whom we were deeply fond) came crashing down, it wasn't over politics at all, but over our daughters' social lives.

In any event, spring was moving on into summer that year of 1956; Hugo and I were still struggling with our balancing act and choosing not to ask ourselves too many philosophical questions, any more than we let ourselves worry about that thin, brownish haze that had begun to form over the valley of Mexico or the stars that were disappearing from the night sky—

—When suddenly we woke to another fact, less world-shaking, perhaps, but close at hand and inescapable. Our son, Mike, had turned fifteen, and we were the parents of a full-blown teenager.

Jean Rouverol in a Paramount Studios publicity photograph in April 1937.
(Courtesy of the author)

With W. C. Fields, Kathleen Howard, and Julian Madison in *It's a Gift* (1934). (Courtesy the Academy of Motion Picture Arts and Sciences)

(top left) Jean Rouverol (and false eyelashes) with Norman Foster in Republic Pictures' 1936 mystery *The Leavenworth Case*. (Courtesy of the author)

(bottom left) Jean Rouverol (and the eyelashes, again) with John King in the Universal Studios release *The Road Back* (1937), a sequel to *All Quiet on the Western Front*. (Courtesy of the author)

Hugo Butler in the mid-1940s in a photograph taken by his father, Frank Butler. Hugo and Jean married in 1937. (Courtesy of the author)

(top right) Hugo Butler as presenter of the writing Oscars for 1945, with master-of-ceremonies Bob Hope. The award would go to his father Frank Butler for the screenplay of *Going My Way*. (Courtesy of the author)

(bottom right) *One Man's Family* radio cast is televised (c. 1948), with Jean Rouverol as Betty Carter Barbour, and Page Gilman as her husband, Jack. Jean's daughters Susie and Mary *(left and center)* are loaned for the occasion. (Courtesy of the author)

Dalton Trumbo and daughter Melissa ("Mitzi") with their sheepdog next to the trailer they towed to Mexico City. (Courtesy of Cleo Trumbo)

(top left) Jean Rouverol in the summer of 1951 packing up to leave Ensenada, Mexico. She, Hugo, and the children would meet up with the Dalton Trumbo family in San Diego and together the two 'blacklist families' began their car trip to Mexico City. (Courtesy of the author)

(top right) Ten-year-olds Chris Trumbo (*left*) and Mike Butler check out the water in the Trumbos' jeep before the families start into the Mexican desert. (Courtesy of Cleo Trumbo)

(bottom left) A lunch stop in Chihuahua. Hugo Butler helps some of the children. Jean is to far right. Cleo Trumbo took the photograph. (Courtesy of Cleo Trumbo)

On the way to Mexico City, a stop near the volcano at Paracutín. Seated (*left to right*) Mary Butler, Susie Butler, and Mitzi Trumbo; standing (*left to right*) Mike Butler, Nikola Trumbo, and Chris Trumbo. (Courtesy of Cleo Trumbo)

Luis Buñuel (*left*) and Hugo Butler work on the script during the shooting of *The Young One* (1959). (Courtesy of Robert Gardner)

On location in a swamp near Acapulco during the filming of *The Young One*.
Seated (*left to right*) Zachary Scott, Luis Buñuel, and Hugo Butler. Standing
(*second from left*) is actor Crahan Denton and (*second from right*) is assistant
Harry Kapoian. (Courtesy of Robert Gardner)

Chapter Sixteen

THE FIRST STRAW in the wind had been early in the year, during Easter vacation. In honor of leap year, three different girls in our neighborhood had invited Mike to go steady. He, too polite to say no, had said yes to all three and then hidden in the house for the balance of the vacation for fear of bumping into any one of them.

Now, however, with the sudden alchemy of adolescence, everything was changed. Where had Mike learned to dance? I didn't teach him. All I knew was that out of the blue, it seemed, there were dances at school for Mike's classmates, and other parents and I were taking turns driving carloads of our young to the high school gym in all kinds of weather, the boys unwontedly scrubbed and shining and the girls in bouffant skirts over layers of crinolines, looking like so many suddenly blossomed flowers. Or Mike and his peers were holding sock hops in our dining room to recordings of "Unchained Melody" and "Cherry Pink and Apple Blossom White"; to Bill Haley's "Rock Around the Clock" and, of course, Elvis and his "Blue Suede Shoes."

On those evenings I imported quantities of pizza or barbecued chicken and hovered nervously around the punch bowl to make sure nobody spiked it. Nobody ever tried, as far as I knew, but Mike had told me hair-raising tales of parties given by the more "official" American families (consular or industrial) among his classmates, where unsupervised youngsters had gotten into their parents' liquor cabinets. And of some who, according to rumor, had "made out" in the bushes.

So I encouraged the sock hops, figuring that if they took place at our house, I didn't need to worry about what was going on. And as for chauffeur duty when there was a dance at school or someone else's house, I found the carloads of teenagers delightful, and, in fact, I was eternally grateful that the legal driving age in Mexico was eighteen; it limited the amount of privacy these eager, curious, hormone-driven fourteen- and fifteen-year-olds had with each other.

Mind you, I didn't have anything *against* sex. I just thought the sophomore year in high school was a bit early for it.

Age fifteen was bringing other changes. Mike had begun (*a*) to study, something he had rather neglected from the third grade to the tenth, and (*b*) to go steady—in all seriousness this time. Her name was Nancy Gast; she was a lovely, fresh-faced teenager a year younger than he, and she played a good game of softball. Busy by now not only with my own writing but with early researches into Getting Your Child into the College of His Choice, I didn't realize at first how serious the new attachment was, but abruptly, Mike stopped dating other girls and Nancy was eating *comida* at our house after school as often as she ate at home.

So far, well and good. Nancy's parents, however, may have taken a dimmer view of the budding romance, because that summer, when friends of theirs arrived from the States with their teenage son, they urged Nancy to be nice to him, and the young man, taking a big shine to her, became understandably resentful of the competition—namely, Mike.

Initially there didn't seem to be a problem; Nancy's heart belonged to Mike. But the young visitor found reinforcement at the trailer park where his family was spending the summer. He met a much tougher young man who had the use of his father's pickup truck.

Dating-wise, this gave the interlopers a slight advantage over Mike: more mobility. Actually, Hugo had taught Mike to drive on a stretch of abandoned road down in Ensenada the previous summer, but up here in the Federal District, where traffic laws were strictly enforced, it seemed wiser for youngsters under eighteen to be driven or to use taxis on social occasions. Even this seemed to present no great problem: Nancy lived in the Pedregal, only twelve to fifteen minutes away from us, and taxis in Mexico were nothing if not affordable.

And so, routinely, the afternoon of Mike's next date with Nancy, he called a cab, and when he heard its honk outside the gates went out— to find not only the cab but the pickup truck too, parked on the edge of our road with the two young visitors leaning against it, the older one, an archetypically tough-guy type with a ducktail haircut, ostentatiously cleaning his nails with a switchblade.

Taken aback, but aware that discretion was the better part of valor, Mike moved to get in the taxi and go. But he was halted by the two interlopers, who warned him flatly to stay away from Nancy.

Mike's athletic skills included tennis, swimming, and baseball but not fisticuffs (and anyway there were two of them and only one of him). He dismissed the taxi and, with as much dignity as he could muster, retreated through our gates and, white-faced, searched us out and told us what had happened.

Hugo, who from viewing movies like *Rebel Without a Cause* and *Blackboard Jungle* was already convinced that all American teenagers these days were juvenile delinquents, was livid. He climbed into our car and, trusting in the fabled corruptibility of the local police, drove straight to the San Angel *delegación,* where, with the encouragement of a discreet twenty-five-peso bribe, he persuaded one of the policemen to investigate this bit of teenage gangsterism.

In the meantime Mike, reassured by the prospect of reinforcements, had called another cab and set out once more for Nancy's. At the gates to the Pedregal, as he expected, he found the pickup truck, which had preceded him there and been waiting in ambush. As he made the turn, it pulled onto the road to follow.

By now, however, Hugo, fresh from the *delegación* and with the policeman in the front seat beside him, was driving toward the Pedregal at a good clip.

By the time Mike's cab had reached Nancy's gate and Mike had gone inside to get his date, the pickup truck, a bird of prey, was pulling "casually" into position on the street outside, and when Mike and Nancy came out to climb in the waiting cab and set off, the pickup truck swung into place a few yards behind them and stayed there.

But now Hugo's car had caught up with them, had swung around, and was following, third in line.

For a few moments the procession continued, and then, abruptly, Hugo's car accelerated, swerved in front of the pickup, and forced it to the side of the road. As Mike's cab (with Mike watching, fascinated, from the rear window and Nancy beside him, aware that something was going on but not quite sure what) drove off, leaving the Pedregal behind them, the policeman was just climbing out of Hugo's car to confront the two young malefactors and to take them, with Hugo as a silent driver at the wheel, back to the police station in San Angel.

There the two terrified young gringos underwent a simulated booking, all the while protesting, "Hey, you can't do this to us—we're Americans!" and then, in tears, "Hey, DOESN'T ANYONE HERE SPEAK ENGLISH?"

To which Hugo, hovering nearby, still unidentified and still furious, snapped out, "Yes. *I* speak English!"

At last, when the boys were sufficiently scared and repentant, the police released them and sent them home. They never showed up at the Pedregal again, and Mike's romance resumed without further interruption.

There is something to be said for a wee bit of corruption.

In spite of Hugo's and my political preoccupations (which we were still trying uneasily to deal with) and in addition to the time we spent at our typewriters, the teenage doings around our house managed to capture a good deal of our attention that summer.

For one thing, the Trumbos sent their Chris, half a year older than Mike, and Melissa (Mitzi), half a year older than Mary and still quick, bright, and imaginative, down to visit us. Chris, though he'd gone from preadolescent to teenager, hadn't changed much since the family's departure. Angel faced, with his blue eyes and curly blond hair, he was still engagingly maladroit; at an early age, he was the only child I ever knew who'd had to be brought to the emergency room twice the same day for different accidents. Like Mike, he also played the trumpet, and like Mike, he was fond of books.

But he wasn't the only addition to the local adolescent set. Mike's other friends the Kilian boys, whose family (in the process of divorce) had also moved back to the States in 1954, came down with their mother for the summer too: gangling, bespectacled Crawford, who was already trying to write science fiction, and his shy, silent brother, Lincoln, who was still a Civil War buff and who'd taken to wearing at all times a battered gray wool Confederate army cap (for its historic value, not as a sign of any special partisanship). With the frequent addition of Nancy, the Oppens' Linda, the Zykofskys' Diana, and sometimes another girl or two to even out the numbers, there were now parent-chauffeured trips to the pyramids or to a hotel pool in Cuernavaca, or journeys even farther south to Las Estacas to swim and picnic. Days spent at home, there were rarely fewer than twelve or thirteen around our table at every meal as the boys (as competitive as their fathers) tried to top Hugo's or each other's jokes. It was a busy season for all of us.

And if I had feared that Mike and his friends, for want of a sense of identity and with no way to sublimate their new energies and emotions, might fancy themselves rebels without a cause, I needn't have worried. They had decided who they were. They were writers. Intellectuals, even. They were, I realized, wonderful kids.

By the winter holidays, though, a new problem had arisen. What kind of Christmas present do you get for a boy Mike's age? Toys and mechanical gadgets were out of the question. There were always books, of course, but he'd already read all of Cousteau and Thor Heyerdahl, his two favorite authors. And clothes were a necessity, not a treat. What would he *like?*

Hugo did a little subtle questioning and came back with the answer: Of all things, a bullfighter's *capote.* (That's the large red-and-yellow cape with which a torero capes the bull on its entrance to the bullring to learn its idiosyncrasies and to train it to his command.)

Hugo had discovered during the shooting of his bullfight movie, however, that *capotes,* being handmade and usually of heavy silk, were very expensive. He got in touch with Luis Procuna's brother-in-law and asked if the *torero* had a cape he wasn't using any more that he would consider selling. The brother-in-law said he'd find out.

Which is how it happened that by December 20, we still hadn't bought Mike any other presents. We learned that the brother-in-law might be able to deliver Procuna's second-best *capote* for five hundred pesos (about forty dollars), a sum that substantially exceeded our usual Christmas budget for each child, but we figured it was worth it. It would be, we told ourselves, a present our aficionado son would never forget.

There was only one problem. The deal had not actually been closed. As the next few days came and went, and our tree was trimmed and the pile of presents under it (all for the girls and none for Mike) grew, we began to get nervous. Our days now were studded by phone calls from the brother-in-law—some from his home, some from the bull-fighters' café where he seemed to spend a good deal of time—to say he was "working on it." But he didn't really have it yet.

At last, it was the afternoon of Christmas Eve. The girls were in the kitchen with Ramona, decorating sand tarts, the record player was keeping up steady renditions of "Jingle Bells" and "Oh, Holy Night" and "The Little Drummer-Boy," and Hugo and I had taken time out from work and present wrapping to confer anxiously in the living room when Mike drifted downstairs to join us. He had, I supposed, sensed that something had gone awry with our Christmas plans; whether he knew they involved a *capote*, we weren't sure, but he seemed to know a present for *him* was somehow in jeopardy, and he tried, "casually," to reassure us. Christmas presents, he commented, were really for little kids, didn't we think? They weren't too important for someone his age. As a matter of fact, he felt as though he'd outgrown Christmas. . . .

His gallantry only made us feel worse.

Ostensibly, our Christmas Eve observances were just as they always were. I read the children the end of *A Christmas Carol*, which we'd begun several days before. The four girls Scotch-taped their stockings to the molding of the fireplace as on other Christmas Eves, and we all sat with the lamps off, looking at the lighted tree for a few quiet moments, and then the girls went off to bed. Mike, getting more depressed by the moment but still trying to cheer us up, went upstairs with a show of nonchalance. I stuffed the girls' stockings with candies and small gewgaws, which would keep them quiet in their bedrooms for a little while when they woke up the next morning, and Hugo and I stayed up till eleven, hoping against hope that we'd hear word of the *capote*, but it didn't come.

At last, discouraged, we went upstairs, put the girls' now bulging stockings at the foot of their beds and went to our own.

At midnight, the gate bell rang.

Hugo was yanking on his bathrobe as he raced downstairs to answer it. I tiptoed into Susie's room (which overlooked the driveway) and peered out to see Hugo open the gate to a small group of cheerful, raffish-looking, and slightly drunken men, one of whom held out a bulky package wrapped in brown paper. "*Hola*, Hugo!" he said cheerfully. "*¡Aquí tengo la cosa!*"

And so, by late the next morning, when the trash bins outside were filled to the top with crumpled Christmas wrapping and the girls in happy satiety had taken their goodies upstairs to put them away, Hugo and I had fled to the dining room for coffee and a moment's respite. From here, through the French windows looking out on the little front garden, we could see Mike with his *capote*, making graceful passes at an imaginary bull.

It had been, we decided, one of our better Christmases.

But adolescence, we also discovered, was not necessarily all sock hops and puppy love and tauromachian dreams of glory.

One day early in the following term the school nurse phoned me to say that Mike had had an episode of double vision in one of his classes. "It's probably just a growth spurt," she said. "But you'd better check it out."

By now our GP and friend Jake Levine had left for the States, planning to work toward getting his medical degree up there, and we hadn't found a replacement yet. We took Mike to the Oppens' physician, who was not inclined to be as casual as the school nurse about the episode. He ordered cranial x rays and an EEG.

And while Mike was out of the room getting dressed after the examination, the doctor told us what the possibilities were. "It could have been a petit mal seizure," he said, though he knew Mike had never had a history of epilepsy. "Or," he added after a slight pause, "it could be a brain tumor."

The next few days, while the necessary appointments were made and kept, and the days following, while we waited for the results to come in, were the worst days of our lives. All we had told Mike was that "it might be an episode of petit mal," but my first act when we'd gotten home had been to bury our copy of John Gunther's *Death, Be Not Proud*, the story of his own son's brain tumor, behind my desk drawer where Mike couldn't find it. Even without such reinforcement, I knew his natural hypochondria would make him suspect the worst.

After school a few days later, the three of us went back to the doctor's office for the diagnosis.

The doctor checked over the sheaves of laboratory test results, saying, "Well, these look normal," and then, looking at the EEG, "But this . . . isn't."

We waited, sick. Mike looked very pale.

Then the doctor looked at one of the cranial x rays and again at the electroencephalogram. Had Mike ever had a concussion?

No, we said—and then I remembered a day in 1951, our last day in Los Angeles, when I'd been getting ready to drive the children down to Ensenada to meet Hugo; Mike had gone to the Y pool with a friend, dived into the shallow end, and hit his head on the bottom. He had come home with a bad headache, nausea, and a temporary loss of peripheral vision. But after a day's rest on doctor's orders, he was his old self again, and we'd driven south as planned.

Now, however, the x ray the doctor showed us revealed a thickening of the skull in the area of that early concussion. It was probably pressing, he said, on the cerebral cortex, and if, as sometimes happened with adolescent boys, the cortex became slightly inflamed, the resultant pressure could cause neurological symptoms. He put Mike on a medication to calm the cortex, told him to avoid athletic or other vigorous activity for six months, and dismissed him.

We were still worried, afraid the doctor's diagnosis might not prove to be the whole story. It was the Hoffmans who gave us the ultimate reassurance. Hans had observed, at the Hospital Infantil, where he did a little consulting, that an inflamed cortex was not uncommon among teenagers. It was usually of brief duration and occurred more often in boys than girls, which may say something about the relative intensity of the emotions of the two sexes at that age.

In any event, Mike had no further manifestations of the problem, nor did we ever find out what variety of stress—scholastic, amatory, or what—had caused it in the first place. Nor did it occur to us, as it would to sophisticated parents nowadays, that a few sessions with a psychotherapist might give him relief from whatever was troubling him. We were still Marxist enough to disapprove of Freud and all his works.

And by the following summer, when the Kilian boys arrived again, this time to stay with us (and importing, by easy stages, their fast-moving, fast-talking friend Danny, another literary type from their high school who had come down to Mexico to visit a former stepfather but who had ended up eating all his meals at our house), and the son and daughter of two other stateside families *also* arrived for visits of various lengths, our lives at Palmas 81 once more became a blur of teenage activity and the whole incident faded, like most nightmares, into oblivion.

Anyway, by that time we had other things on our minds. Hugo had begun to prepare a new docudrama, and by late summer I found I was pregnant again.

First, though, there was the earthquake.

Chapter Seventeen

IT WAS A NIGHT in late July. We had a houseful, as usual. The Kilian boys were sleeping on camp cots in Mike's room, our girls were asleep in their own various rooms, and Ramona and Isabel had turned in hours ago to the monastic little structure next to the garage out in back that served as a maids' room—when abruptly, out of total stillness, windows and doors began to swing, beds to shake, and in a bound the whole household was on its feet and milling about excitedly in the hall. As Hugo and I yanked on our bathrobes and raced to join them we could hear, above the barking of every dog in the neighborhood, Diego Rivera and *his* household out on their rooftop next door, crying out, *"¡Mira! Mira!"* ("Look! Look!") as all over the city transformers were shorting out in bursts of blue light.

It was only moments till sirens began to sound. Now it seemed as though their wails, rising and falling, were coming from every direction, telling us that all over the city fires were being fought, power lines restored, injured taken to hospitals. Mike and the Kilians, excitement quickly replacing fear, were estimating the force of the quake.

Hugo and I made a quick appraisal of the masonry, but O'Gorman's wisdom in building a beehive of small rooms had paid off: no cracks anywhere nor, astonishingly, had there been much breakage. When we decided that the shaking was over, and the dogs' barking quieted and the voices on Rivera's rooftop faded away—and our own hearts stopped pounding—we all went back to bed. But we slept uneasily.

Even before breakfast next morning, Mike and his guests taxied downtown to view the damage. They came back to report that in addition to a couple of collapsed buildings (where there had been, it seems, several fatalities), there was one other catastrophe: the winged statue of the Angel of Independence, who for almost half a century had stood atop a pillar on one of the *glorietas* along the Paseo de la Reforma, had come crashing down and now was nothing but a mass of wire and plaster and a few fragments coated in gold leaf.

The Angel was not just any public statue. Gold burnished (albeit a bit tarnished), she had had an airy if somewhat dusty beauty, and Mexicans who over the years had come to take her for granted now mourned her as we did. In the months to come she would be rebuilt and anchored more securely to her perch. But our feelings about her would be changed. Ten years later, when our Mary was struggling through a depression in college, she would publish a poem in the Harvard *Advocate* about the earlier, dustier, more fragile Angel poised so dangerously on her pillar—identifying, in effect, with her very precariousness. As for the rest of us, we would always be aware that the shiny new Angel up there was an impostor. A good imitation, but not the same.

What was important, though, was that we all *cared* so much. Mexico and her symbols had become important to us, part of our lives.

Some three weeks after the quake, I made my customary early-morning pilgrimage to the gates to get the paper and discovered that Mexico's Little League baseball team, which under a new rule had for the first time been allowed to compete in the World Series, had somehow or other managed to reach the final play-offs in the United States. And had won the world championship.

Not only that. Their pitcher, a shy, handsome, ambidextrous twelve-year-old named Angel Macías, had pitched a perfect game, the first such win in the series' history.

Reading the reporter's account of it, it seemed to me incredible. How in the world had it happened? The players, boy for boy, were the smallest and family for family the poorest of any group of Little Leaguers ever to reach the finals. Mexicans—indeed, baseball fans everywhere—were beside themselves, already hailing the boys as *"Los Pequeños Gigantes"* ("The Little Giants"). They were being flown to Washington to meet President Eisenhower and the Mexican ambassador; after that they would be flown to Mexico City for a triumphal reception and to meet their own president, Adolfo Ruiz Cortines.

Even more than our feelings at the loss of the Angel, the news brought home to all of us—to me, and to the children, when I told them, and to Hugo when I went upstairs to wake him and put the newspaper in his lap—how profoundly we had all come to identify with our adopted country. In the whole history of Little League, we wondered, could there ever have been such a David-and-Goliath triumph? And wouldn't it make a lovely docudrama?

Minutes later, Hugo was on the phone to George Pepper, and plans for another movie were under way.

By the time he was ready to leave for Monterrey, Nuevo León, where he and George would be getting acquainted with the city and the boys and scouting locations and setting up a shooting schedule, Hugo and I were both a bit uneasy with each other. The problem was my pregnancy.

Although our small Debbie had indeed arrived "with her own bread" (in the form of fairly steady work offers for her parents) and had proved to be a delightful, happy little girl whom everybody adored, Hugo had met the news of one more baby with dismay. *Six* children to support, and the blacklist still governing our lives? He would be almost forty-five when this one was born. How many more years of work would it take to raise them all and put them all through college? The road ahead of him, I knew, must seem endless. Not to mention the fact that I was already so occupied with the other five, he pointed out, that we rarely had any time alone. . . .

All this, then, was hovering in the air between us when I drove him to the airport for his Monterrey flight. I found myself feeling irrationally guilty, as though I had played the old army game and gotten pregnant deliberately. (And since, in those unenlightened times, husbands took no responsibility for such matters as contraception, in effect I *was* responsible for the four of our eight pregnancies that were accidental). Fortunately, the word *abortion* was never mentioned between us, neither then nor at the time of our previous surprises; perhaps he thought any such suggestion should come from me. Or perhaps, in spite of his dismay, he was too philoprogenative even to suggest such a choice. In any event, when we kissed good-bye in the airport lobby and he disappeared into the passengers' waiting room, I couldn't help remembering the pause that had greeted me when I'd broken the news to him. Or what he'd finally said, lightly but in earnest: "Well . . . you're on your own with this one, kid."

He was gone for most of the rest of the summer. Our young guests began to leave for home singly and in twos, and the children's lives returned more or less to normal. I hadn't told them yet about their new sibling-to-be, and I was doing some private worrying of my own about having another baby at almost forty-three, as well as about Hugo's reaction to the prospect. So of course when Mike announced that he and his friend Rafael Buñuel (Luis's younger son) were going down to Acapulco on their own for the September holidays and would find themselves an inexpensive hotel to stay at, I had an extra load of anxiety to devote to the problem.

I tried to argue it out with myself. Why shouldn't they go? Both boys were sixteen. And reasonably sensible. In another year, after all, Mike would be going away to college. . . .

Nevertheless, I decided it might be wise if the girls and I had our own separate Acapulco holiday, to be on hand there in case of emergencies. And when I checked with Rafael's mother, Jeanne, I discovered that she—just coincidentally—would be spending that week in Acapulco too.

Two nervous mothers.

In fact, the boys got along famously. Mike got ptomaine from eating *ceviche* bought from a vendor on the beach, but Rafael told him to drink milk as a cure, and it seemed to work. Rafael fell off his rented motorbike and took much of his skin off, but no bones were broken. The boys deigned to visit their families once or twice that week, out of courtesy, but it was clear they needed us a good deal less than we needed them. And they were both, I knew, making an important statement about independence.

For me, the week in the tropics with Hugo absent was a curious experience, removed from time, removed from reality. I had loaded Ramona and the girls into the car and driven down to a house I'd rented sight unseen; it proved to be perched above one of Acapulco's smaller inlets where a recent hurricane had torn away part of the supporting cliff, making access and egress, we discovered, a perilous adventure. I solved the problem of getting in or out of the driveway by making the girls get out and walk while I maneuvered the car to a safer stretch of road.

The days, clear and hot, we spent at the beaches, but by evening the storms that had already damaged the cliff side came sweeping back over the Pacific to drench the coast again while we hovered under cover. Our living-dining area was really a covered, three-sided porch, open on the west to the view and the weather. Translucent little geckos, which on earlier Acapulco visits the children had christened *"qüiquas"* because of their tiny squeaks, darted up the walls and across the beamed ceiling, snapping at insects, but we knew they were benign and ignored them. Evenings, when Ramona put our mosquito-bitten little Debbie to sleep in one of the bedrooms, the other girls and I clustered under a living-room lamp, fending off more mosquitoes and reading aloud. (That week I read *A Tale of Two Cities* and Rostand's *Cyrano de Bergerac,* ostensibly to Susie and Mary, but Emily, who had just turned eight, listened too, enthralled, until she fell asleep upright in her chair.) The rain was heralded by gusts of moist wind, and by the time night had altogether blotted out the view of the bay, its blackness was broken by lightning and then, always with startling abruptness, a downpour.

I was still worried about my pregnancy, but huddled together with the girls in that yellow pool of lamplight, as the geckos darted and squeaked above our heads, I felt a curious kind of nervous excitement and a cautious triumph that we were safe and dry while the storm flashed and thundered and poured down in sheets at the roof's edge just a few feet away.

Up in Monterrey, in the meantime, Hugo was having an altogether different kind of experience.

In that bustling little industrial city, he and George Pepper had checked into a local hotel and, preliminary to drawing up a shooting schedule, had set about exploring the barrios where the boys lived and the back streets and empty lots that had nurtured them. Certain key decisions had already been made, of course: The title of the Mexican version of the picture would be *Los Pequeños Gigantes* (changed to *How Tall Is a Giant?* later for its stateside release on TV). But checking with newsreel companies, the two men were finding that most of the picture's events would have to be restaged, because unlike *Torero!*, there was very little news footage available. How could there have been? What news photographer in his right mind could have predicted that this undersized, mostly underfed bunch of contestants would achieve the impossible?

So, as in *Crusoe*, it was decided that most scenes would be shot with guide track only, then dubbed later in both Spanish and English, with a narration in both languages added later too. This, however, raised a crucial question: *whose* narration? From whose point of view should the picture be told?

During the planning (and later, the shooting), Hugo would become friends with the boys and their families and come to like and respect the two Monterrey residents who had helped create the team: middle-aged, blond, blue-eyed "Lucky" Haskins, half blinded at Omaha Beach on D day and now in business in Monterrey and the father of a Mexican family, and head coach César Faz, with his long, olive-skinned, seriocomic face. César had once been a batboy with the St. Louis Browns and as a "Tex Mex" had learned the nature of prejudice from the receiving end. He was also photogenic. Hugo decided the team's story should be told from César's viewpoint.

In the first place, though, he needed to know how in the world it had all come about to begin with. How had this extraordinary team even come to be?

Under the aegis of the local chapter of the American Legion, it seemed, Lucky and César had gotten together with a few other city fathers, announced the formation of a Little League team, and been overwhelmed by the response. As it happened, only two of the boys who qualified came from middle-class families; most of the others had not even owned *shoes* till they'd been issued their Little League spikes. Hugo dramatized this by restaging the application scene, lining the boys up on the street to sign up for the team as they'd done earlier and having the camera pan slowly along all those bare feet, which were then joined by two pairs of feet that were neatly shod.

The Mexican censors, alas, ordered this shot cut from the finished picture; they didn't want the rest of the world to get the impression there were children in Mexico too poor to own shoes. (In fact, a few times on their original trip north, some of the boys had to break Little

League rules by practicing in their uniforms because Lucky was at the laundromat washing the only other decent clothes they owned.)

Hugo also learned that even getting the team to its first stateside stop in McAllen had presented Lucky and César with major problems in both logistics and economics. The team had gotten as far as Reynosa, at the border, by second-class bus and then, a necessary economy, had crossed the International Bridge on foot (a journey Hugo restaged for the camera). Once on the other side, Lucky had combed McAllen to find cheap motel accommodations and a friendly restaurant that would cut its prices for this small, voracious army. It was in McAllen, by the way, that the boys had discovered a new taste sensation—southern-fried chicken—and also in McAllen that the whole team, hearing the local band at the playing field strike up "The Eyes of Texas Are Upon You," had leapt to their feet, caps off, on the assumption that this was the *norteamericanos'* national anthem.

Of their first three original stateside games, in the heat of a Texas summer, the boys had scored three wins, and from there on, with fans at home (increasingly excited by each new win) scrounging to send them funds and an occasional Texan Little League family coming to the rescue with a dinner invitation for the whole bunch, Lucky had bootstrapped them from victory to victory. Throughout he and César had maintained a remarkable discipline: even in the hottest weather, they'd insisted, no colas and no swimming, on the theory that such indulgences softened the muscles and slowed up the boys' game. The boys had protested these injunctions, but they'd obeyed them finally because nothing in the world mattered more to them than winning.

And then, at last, they'd reached Williamsport, Pennsylvania. It was the final scenes of the picture, a restaging of those last days of the contest, that made the picture (at least to this viewer, at its first screening some months later) almost unbearably moving.

Under Little League rules, the same pitcher cannot be used two games in succession. With the final two games looming, Lucky and César faced a choice. They knew that in young Angel Macías, who among his other talents could pitch either right- or left-handed, they had a sure winner. But if they used him in the semifinal against the Bridge-port, Connecticut, team and won, they couldn't pitch him in the finals. What to do?

Williamsport was teeming that week with excited visitors from home:

Monterrey's city fathers, officials from the Mexican Embassy in Washington, Mexican businessmen from New York City, and anyone else who could afford the time and the plane fare. Many of these influential figures urged Lucky and César not to gamble. Forget the championship, they said. Be prudent. Use Angel for the semifinal game, they said, and make sure of a second-place win, even if it meant losing the championship game.

The boys were outraged. "*No, César!*" they said. "For us it's *always* second place!" Unlike their cautious elders, they wanted to go for broke. They begged Lucky and César to take the big chance, pitching their second-best pitcher in the Bridgeport (semifinal) game and saving Angel for—they hoped and believed—the final play-off. They had not come all this way, and fought so hard, to settle for second place.

Legend doesn't relate how much persuasion it took to convince the two coaches. But the rest is Little League history. In the semifinal game against Bridgeport, the team's second-best pitcher, tough-minded little Fidel Ruíz (a fine player in anybody's league) gave Monterrey a narrow 2–1 win.

And in the championship game next day, the boys took on a team from California—the biggest, tallest, heaviest boys in the play-offs—and with Angel at the helm achieved their perfect game. For a country that had lived so long in the shadow of the colossus of the north, it was a glorious moment.

That was the moment Hugo set out to capture in *How Tall Is a Giant?*

Chapter Eighteen

HUGO WAS STILL in Monterrey when I came down with some worrisome symptoms in November and a hematologist diagnosed hepatitis.

There is no good time to get hepatitis, but when you're forty-two and pregnant, it's especially not a good time. The doctor ordered me to bed for a month and told me to drink quantities of *jugo de carne* (beef tea) and eat as much fruit sugar and sugar candy as I could tolerate. Also, on the chance that my illness was the infectious type, he lined up Ramona, Isabel, and the children and injected them with gamma globulin. He also gave me a prescription for chloral hydrate to be taken nightly because, he said, plenty of rest was urgent to recovery and chloral hydrate was the only sleeping medicine that was nontoxic to the liver.

I had followed instructions to the letter, discovering in the process that a month's doctor-mandated bed rest is a wonderful time to reread Thomas Hardy, any Chekhov one may have missed to date, and all the Dickens one has never gotten around to. I was jaundiced for only a few days, and the only crisis that presented itself had nothing to do with medical problems but arrived in my bedroom one morning via the bank of windows that looked out on the greenery of our backyard and were brushed by the upper branches of a loquat tree.

The children had just gone off to catch the school bus, and I had gotten myself comfortable for a morning's reading when Ramona came in to pick up my breakfast tray. Abruptly she told me not to move and snatched up my quilt by its four corners—

—But not before I caught sight of a very large, very pregnant black scorpion that (in its excitement, I guess) was birthing a quantity of scrabbling babies on the quilt. How Ramona, who was portly and no longer young, could move so fast I will never know, but without a wasted motion she was at the window, shaking the quilt and its occupants out into the garden below. (And just for the record, we never saw any of them again.)

But thus far, that had been the only momentous occurrence during my illness. Hugo had come home for Thanksgiving, fortified by his own injection of gamma globulin, but during his few days with us he was abstracted, his mind almost entirely on the film project, and he'd gone off again without ever having quite tuned in to the family doings.

Now it was nine o'clock of an evening soon after, the children were off in various parts of the house doing homework or asleep, and I had tired of reading and had just stirred my sleeping draught into its glass of water when there was the sound of our gate bell outside, and in a moment Isabel came upstairs to say that one of the señoras from next door wanted to speak to me.

I had met Teresa Pruenza once before. Middle-aged, Cuban, she was one of Diego Rivera's two secretaries—both, I suspected, working for him as volunteers because they idolized him. Isabel brought her in and sat her on a chair near my bed and disappeared again. We exchanged courtesies, and then my visitor said in Spanish, "Señora, you know the maestro is very ill. . . ."

Yes, I said, I knew. I think everyone in Mexico knew. Gossip had it that it was cancer of the prostate, and local doctors had told him that they could save his life by surgery. But this, of course, would mean an end to the maestro's fabled sex life, and (gossip had it) he had refused, saying in effect that life without that important activity wasn't worth living. Later we heard he had applied for a visa to the States to get radiation, but the State Department had refused him entry, citing his long career as a radical. So, when the Soviet Union had offered him the services of their doctors, many of whom had worked with patients badly burned by German bombs and artillery fire during World War II, he had accepted their invitation.

On his return, he had announced that cobalt treatments in Moscow had cured him, and what's more, he told newsmen, *"Muchachos, todavía estoy completito"* ("Fellows, I am still whole"). But was he really cured? Soon after his arrival, he'd gone down to the Hotel del

Prado, where his 1948 mural—a medley of dream and memory and Mexican history—had been covered over by a movable screen since its completion, because one of its characters, Reform leader Ignacio Ramirez, was painted holding a scroll with the words *"¡Dios no existe!"* ("God does not exist!"), and the Mexican archbishop had refused to bless the newly built hotel till the mural was concealed. On this nine-year-later visit, Rivera, never one to miss a grandstand play, had alerted the press, mounted the scaffold with bucket and brush, and calmly painted out the offending slogan. When he'd climbed down and the astonished onlookers had asked him why he'd done it, he had simply shrugged and said, "I am a Catholic."

Not long after that, we'd heard that his painting arm had become badly swollen, and remembering that this was one of my mother's later symptoms, I suspected that his cancer was no longer in remission, that it had, in fact, metastasized. These last few weeks there'd been rumors that he was very sick indeed, confined now to his bed in that upstairs studio room where, through the floor-to-ceiling glass windows that faced our Mike's glass wall across a few feet of garden and tall stand of organo cactus, we could see lights burning at all hours, highlighting the maestro's easels, the life-sized "Judas" figures dangling from his ceiling, and the people (family? attendants?) moving back and forth. Too, Ramona had been getting fairly frequent reports on the maestro's condition from Mariquita, the maestro's short, vast, devoted house-keeper.

I didn't tell Teresa Pruenza that I hoped he would recover soon, be-cause it seemed clear he wouldn't. I said we were all very sorry he was ill, and hoped he wasn't too uncomfortable, and was there anything we could do?

Yes, she said. Our porch light, which we left burning at night to discourage intruders, shone through the maestro's windows and kept him awake. Would we mind very much turning it off?

Of course not, I said. And then, "How about our son's trumpet? Does it bother the maestro when he practices?"

"Well . . . perhaps if he played on the other side of the house . . . ?"

I said I would see to it. We exchanged good-byes, and she left.

We had never officially met Rivera—well, not exactly. Early in our life here, friends had taken me to Bellas Artes to watch him work on the drawing (a stage in the work called, for reasons I still don't understand, the "cartoon") for his new "Peace" mural, commissioned for Mexico's upcoming exhibition in Paris. Our little group had stood at a respectful distance watching him work for a while and had seen his stunning, dark-browed wife, Frida Kahlo, herself a painter, wheeled in in her wheelchair to bring him his lunch, which was packed in one of those multitiered galvanized lunch tins with a container for hot water at the bottom. (Day laborers in Mexico bring them to work so they can have a nice hot *comida* on the job.) She and Rivera had kissed and greeted each other as "amor"; they had been extraordinarily tender with each other. Frida Kahlo was dead now, and he was remarried; our glimpses of him in recent years were usually as he stood at his windows looking down over our yard when one or another of our children was having a birthday party; he would stand up there smiling down at them like a Buddha as they played musical chairs.

We'd actually spoken to him only once. On the eve of his last pilgrimage to Europe, Hugo had wondered aloud to me if, stricken as he was, Rivera would live to come home. What a shame, Hugo said, to live so close to someone and never to have let him know how much we admired him. . . .

And so, that last day before his departure, Emily and Debbie and I had joined a constant stream of admirers (all women!) climbing the cantilevered staircase that led up to his studio. We had introduced ourselves (yes, he said, he knew us) and wished him well. And this extraordinarily ugly man with his squat figure and his bulging eyes, whom Frida Kahlo had called her "frog prince," had kissed the hands of our eight-year-old Emmie and our four-year-old Debbie in the most courtly manner possible, as though they were charming grown-up young ladies. They had come away altogether entranced.

And now he was dying. I called Mike in and explained what was happening and suggested that he do his trumpet playing on the far side of the house; in Susie's room, perhaps, since she was in Valle de Bravo with the Hoffmans that night. Mike was sobered. Of course, he said.

He went off about his own business, and I drank the glass of water with its bitter taste of chloral hydrate and turned out my lamp and waited to get sleepy. (When you have a liver ailment, you are never sleepy when it's time to sleep or hungry when it's time to eat.) There were still a few cars passing along Avenida Alta Vista, up at the corner, but for the most part it was a quiet night, clear and cool. As the chemical began to take effect and I was beginning to drift off, I could hear Mike, off in Susie's room, playing not his trumpet but his harmonica, very quietly. He was playing "Jamaica Farewell."

In the morning, when Ramona went outside to sweep the dirt in front of our gates (a morning routine), she saw, up at the neighboring gates, Rivera's Mariquita sweeping the dirt too, and crying. Mariquita told Ramona that the maestro had died in the night.

I've never known what time he died. But I choose to think he was ushered out of this life to the quiet, distant strains of a harmonica playing "Jamaica Farewell."

Chapter Nineteen

THE NEW BABY heralded its arrival a couple of weeks early.

I had wakened one March morning long before daylight to a substantial twinge and at four-thirty had gone downstairs to wake Hugo's mother, who had flown down to be with me this last month while Hugo continued his shooting in Monterrey. Maybe she should have a cup of coffee, I suggested, while I called a cab.

For someone who had never delivered a baby in less than twelve hours (it usually took twenty-four), I don't know why I was always in such a rush to get to the hospital. Perhaps the excited departure into a cool, dark predawn lent an extra feeling of adventure to what was now becoming something of a habit. In any event our taxi driver, having been assured that he wouldn't be faced with an emergency delivery in the backseat of his cab, drove at a leisurely pace along streets that at this hour seemed almost uninhabited. It was a delicious time of day, Mexico City at its quietest and most lovely, and as always at these moments I felt an unreasonable joy. At the hospital (the American-British hospital this time, where my present OB practiced), the admitting nurse wisely refrained from calling the doctor until a more sensible hour; Margaret had a proper breakfast at the hospital coffee shop and then put in a call to Hugo's hotel in Monterrey while I settled down to time contractions.

Apart from the jaundice, and perhaps Hugo's concern at our having another baby in our middle age, it had been an agreeable pregnancy. There had, of course, been the visit by that pregnant scorpion to my bed that morning a few months ago, but no one, except perhaps the scorpion, was any the worse for the encounter. There'd also been a troubled day or two in late November when Mary's graduation from Spanish *primaria* was coming on apace and neither I (still in bed) nor Hugo (on location with the picture) could be there to attend it. But we'd recruited the Oppens, who had taken Mary shopping for a graduation dress and gone with her to the ceremony, and Mary, shining and rosy cheeked, made no complaint. The ceremony had gone off without a hitch, the Oppens said, except when the school band had struck up "The Marine Hymn" and one of the school's American trustees, mistaking its opening bar ("From the halls of Montezuma . . .") for the Mexican national anthem, leapt to his feet respectfully and then, realizing his mistake, sat down in confusion.

Even Christmas had not presented any insurmountable obstacles. The children had done my Christmas shopping for me, and the arrival from Hollywood of our friends the Coreys added a pleasant confusion to the holidays. Jeff, whose career as a character actor was still on hold since the blacklist, arrived feeling exuberant. His new reputation as an acting coach, it seemed, was thriving. Even Gary Cooper, one of the leaders of Hollywood's anti-Communist crusade, had sat in on several of Jeff's classes during the preparation for *High Noon* and later had recommended them to his daughter.

And soon after the new year there had been, of all things, *snow*, mantling the mountains between the valleys of Mexico and Cuernavaca and giving the children of the Federal District a once-in-a-lifetime chance to plunge knee-deep in snow alongside the Cuernavaca highway and throw snowballs.

And then, in February, when I was very pregnant indeed, the Little Giants had come to lunch.

A chartered bus had brought them to our gates and disgorged them; they were in town for pickup shots at a local sound stage, and Hugo had invited them over for Sunday *comida*. Ramona had learned to cook southern-fried chicken for their special benefit; Hugo's blacklisted writer friend Eddie Huebsch, feisty, brilliant, and not much taller than the team's players, was in Mexico working with Hugo on the film's narration and was with us then too, and our own children helped me serve up. It had been a lovely day, sun flooding the front garden and pouring in the dining-room windows; the *campeoncitos,* crowded around the table, were resplendent in freshly washed uniforms, their olive faces shining, brown-black hair slicked down, and caps, for the most part, still placed securely on heads. They were eager, ravenous, polite, and adorable, and our children fell in love with them and would have liked us to adopt the whole bunch. After lunch (and, for a wonder, surfeited), they drifted out to the front yard for a few practice throws or to chat with Hugo or Eddie but at a signal from César had gathered into a half circle, crouched down, and on cue had delivered three rousing cheers for Ramona, who had been so pleased that she'd been smiling quietly to herself ever since.

That, then, had been the high point of my pregnancy. And as for those ceramic storks that had stood by our bedside . . .

We lent them—as a joke, of course—to the Hoffmans, who'd been anxious to have one more baby before Annie's childbearing years were over but somehow or other hadn't been able to manage it. Within weeks Annie was pregnant, her housekeeper was pregnant, their dog was pregnant, and their lovebirds (sterile since their purchase months before in the San Juan market) laid eggs.

Our new baby was another girl.

"And dear," said Margaret, whom I found just waking from a nap on a trundle bed next to mine when I came out of the anesthetic, "she's the *cutest* thing!"

She was indeed. I made my way down the hall to look at her through the nursery window and saw a tiny creature, pink cheeked, with a few soft wisps of hair that might someday be reddish like her father's. She looked, those first few hours, oddly vulnerable and altogether irresistible. Having learned from Debbie's birth, when we'd gone to the hospital trusting in the law of averages and thus prepared with only boys' names, that the law of averages doesn't mean a thing where babies are concerned, I had a name already picked out for this one, so when the congratulatory telegrams began to arrive from the film company in Monterrey, they addressed the new arrival by name. The wire that came from the picture's cameraman (a refugee from Hitler and a veteran of Spain's Republican Army) read, *"Todo el equipo grita, '¡Viva Rebecca!'"* ("The whole team shouts, 'Hurray for Rebecca!'")

And the following week, when Hugo came home to meet her, already ensconced snug and tiny in her wicker bassinet at Palmas 81, he didn't seem at all displeased.

She was three months old when my stepmother phoned from St. Louis that my father was in the hospital and in and out of a coma.

I had known it was coming. He had phoned the last day of the old year to tell me his doctor had diagnosed cirrhosis. Although I'd only come to know him the last decade or so, and then not well, it had seemed to me he was not an alcoholic, but just an enthusiastic "social drinker," and I thought it singularly unjust that he should fall victim to, and be stigmatized by, such a disease. I conferred by phone with my brother in California, and we both agreed we'd rather visit him now while there was still a chance, however slight, that he might recognize us, than wait for the funeral.

I was still nursing Becky, however. I bought a manual breast pump at the drugstore, figuring I could use it on my trip so I'd still have milk when I got back, and it was in my carry-on when Hugo took me to the airport to catch my plane. It seems almost repetitive to mention that over Texas we flew straight into the eye of a storm and dropped thirty-five hundred feet in thirty seconds. I remember thinking, as I flew out of my seat (the seat belt having been pushed partway open by my purse and only caught by the buckle at its farthest end), that it was singularly fitting that I should be killed on my way to St. Louis.

St. Louis. To my mother, who had literally kidnapped my brother and me when we were a year-and-a-half and three years old respectively, it had stood for heat and cold, domestic drudgery, and all that was petit bourgeois and ugly. Our father's family, she had drummed into us when we were growing up, were not only anti-intellectual, they were *ungrammatical,* to her mind the most egregious sin of all. She'd had twilight sleep when she'd delivered me, she said, but when my brother was born, she'd refused any painkiller at all because she was afraid she would die under anesthetic and we'd be brought up by our paternal grandparents.

How had that unlikely couple ever gotten together?

It was a freak of time and geography, really. The youngest child in the large family of a soon-to-apostate Mormon, Mother had gone from

Utah to Stanford (where she won $25 for writing the lyrics to their "fight" march, "Come Join the Band"). From there she'd gone to study playwriting under George Pierce Baker (then at Harvard) and from there to New York to look for acting jobs. She'd landed the job of understudying, and later replacing, Alice Brady as Meg in the Broadway production of *Little Women* and had then joined the road company. It had been a long tour, at a time when "no nice girl goes on the stage," and by the time the company reached St. Louis, my mother was turning thirty, desperately lonely, and beginning to be afraid she'd never have any children. She wasn't afraid of being an old maid; she was too much of a feminist for *that*. But she did want children.

Road companies, in those days, traveled only with their principal actors; smaller parts were played by local talent wherever they stopped. Joe—my father—worked as a bank clerk in St. Louis, but his parents had been itinerant actors in French and German productions there; he was stagestruck and at night moonlighted as a walk-on in any theatrical company that came to town, including *Little Women*. He'd had only a sixth-grade education, his family having put him to work as a runner for a bank when he was twelve. But he played a good game of bridge, he was an entertaining conversationalist, and his wavy, copper-colored hair might just prove a dominant gene. So when the road company moved on, my mother stayed behind, and her brief married life began.

For three years and nine months she suffered amid the alien corn; then, under the guise of taking my brother and me to visit her family in Utah, made her escape, and only after my father had waved our train good-bye did he go home to learn we were gone forever. It would be thirty years before he saw my brother and me again.

All through our childhood, while Mother worked her way from schoolteacher to drama coach to playwright, she used to say to her friends with pride, "I've been both mother and father to these children," and we believed her. But we'd both grown into adolescence with a sense that something important was missing from our lives and we didn't quite know what.

On my graduation from junior high school, I had decided—almost idly, I thought—to send Joe one of my graduation announcements. He sent me back a lovely little silver compact on a finger chain, with a nice card, and though I was touched by the gift and sent a thank you note, there'd been no further word between us until my Susie was born, when it occurred to me that it was a shame for a man to have two grandchildren and not know anything about them. So I'd written him and learned in return that he'd kept up with me during my acting days through studio publicity releases and had been listening to *One Man's Family* ever since I'd joined the cast.

We'd kept in touch thereafter, and in the late 1940s he and his second wife had come to California for a bankers' convention. My brother had come down to Hollywood for their arrival and we had all, finally, gotten acquainted.

Well—more or less. Joe by then was vice president of a trust company (and in a few years would become commissioner of finance for Missouri; so much for the disadvantages of a sixth-grade education!). Slight of build, he was attractive and told funny stories (*dialect* stories, to our dismay) . . . and oh, the gulf between his way of life and thought and ours!

But he *was* our father, the father we'd been missing all these years, and meeting him at last went far toward filling the vacuum we'd felt in our lives. He was still more or less a stranger, but at least the stranger had a face. From the time of that visit, we'd corresponded and had sometimes spoken by phone, but neither my brother nor I felt we really knew him, nor he us.

So the trip to his bedside, as he lay dying, was our last chance to fill in the gaps.

It was a vain hope.

At the St. Louis hospital where he was a patient, our stepmother took us up to his room. He was dozing. The three of us sat chatting quietly till he showed signs of waking. Then my stepmother went over to his bedside.

"Joe!" she said loudly, as though he were deaf. "It's Bill and Jean. They've come to see you."

He looked at us, confused. After a moment, a fleeting smile crossed his face. *"Hassenpfeffer,"* he said.

"What?" his wife shouted.

"Hassenpfeffer," said Joe. "Isn't that a funny word? *Hassenpfeffer . . ."*

That was all he said. The next time we came, he said nothing at all; he was either asleep or in a coma. There seemed no point in staying longer. Our stepmother insisted on driving us around St. Louis and showing us the sights, and then we left.

When I reached Mexico City and a taxi brought me home to San Angel Inn (with the breast pump still in my carry-on), I came straight through the house out into the yard, where the nice Mexican nurse I'd hired to take care of Becky in my absence had put her, bathed and baby oiled and swaddled, in her kiddie coop in the afternoon shade of the house. Tiny, still vulnerable, she looked up at me a moment and then gave me a little wiggly smile of recognition.

This small newcomer, who had arrived unbidden in our middle age, would prove an unexpected delight to the whole family. She would lose her own father, however, before she was nine. A decade after that, in college, she would win a regional prize from the Motion Picture Academy for best student film from the New England area: a film about a young woman whose father had died with a cognitive dysfunction when she was young, as Becky's had. The little fifteen-minute movie told of the young woman's trying to reach backward in time, to remember what he'd been like before the dementia that had turned him into someone almost unrecognizable.

In the film, she finally remembered. In life, she never could.

Chapter Twenty

MEANWHILE, through small Becky's earliest weeks, life at Palmas 81 had become more intense than usual.

Mike was seventeen and in his last term of high school. He had taken the college boards, submitted applications to several colleges, and was keeping in close touch with his stateside friends Chris Trumbo and Crawford Kilian to see where they might end up going in September. Coincident with this, the American School was about to hold its annual literary contest, and Mike, Susie, and Mary had been busy in various corners of the house, writing their entries for it.

By now almost a college man (we hoped), Mike had begun to cultivate the undergraduate look. His new glasses were horn-rimmed, like his father's, giving him a sober, intellectual air; he had taken to smoking a pipe and wearing a bohemian-looking Guatemalan vest; and afternoons, when he wasn't down in our dining room with his buddies, involved in the oldest-established floating seven-and-a-half game in San Angel, he was reading. Mostly poetry, these days; having abandoned his early diet of Cousteau, Heyerdahl, and Rachel Carson and worked his way through our whole play collection (an interest that had resulted from our having taken him and Susie up to New York two years before to expose them to a week of good Broadway theater), he had discovered Keats—"When I have fears that I may cease to be," naturally—and then moved on to Dylan Thomas, who had inspired him to start writing poetry of his own.

A major dividend of our exile was that our children hadn't been exposed to television; they'd been forced to *read* for entertainment.

Well, they might have become readers anyway; from their earliest days I had read aloud to them at bedtime almost every night of their lives: for the littlest, family favorites like *Wind in the Willows, Mary Poppins,* and the Little House series (which the whole family identified with, not surprisingly), and books I knew the older ones would love but were unlikely to tackle, like *Puck of Pook's Hill,* and *Westward Ho,* and Dickens—and I always flatly refused to read them anything I didn't like myself. Still more important, however, had been Hugo's storytelling. Every Saturday night at bedtime, the whole bunch of them piled onto his lap and the arms of his chair in the living room while he told them one pie-in-the-face funny story and, with the lights out, one scary story. (That's how the distant moan of the little produce train that plied between the valley of Morelos and Mexico City's wholesale market became, in our family mythology, the howl of a carnivorous monster named The Swamp Worm.)

And without our realizing it, what all this had done for the children was to give them, from the time they were barely out of their infancy, a sense of structure.

For instance:

Long ago, before we had ever dreamed of coming to Mexico, when Mike was an energetic four and a half and Susie a small, cautious, pigtailed three, they had curled up in Hugo's lap one Saturday night and waited for their story as I sat nearby, darning socks (my one domestic skill). Hugo began:

"Once upon a time there were three little rabbits . . ."

"Who's after them?" Mike demanded.

"What do you mean, who's after them?" Hugo asked.

"That's the way it's got to be," said Mike reasonably.

Hugo shot me a look and resumed. "Once upon a time, there were three little rabbits. And they were happy little rabbits . . ."

Susie gave a deep, throaty chuckle. "Soon they won't be," she gloated.

That's what I mean. A sense of structure.

As they grew older and their numbers increased, reading came to serve a different purpose for each child. Thus Susie a few years ago at age eleven, when she had just finished reading *Little Women* to herself and to whom I had just finished reading *David Copperfield,* was overheard to say as she prowled the bookshelf in her room, "I want a book to get lost in."

Or Mary, who used books as a security blanket and could usually be found on her stomach on bed or floor with an apple, a glass of milk, and a cookie while she read, for the hundredth time, *The Secret Garden*.

Or Emily, who must have heard me reading *Hamlet* to the older children, because at age seven, pestered beyond endurance by her little sister Debbie, she had whirled on her and cried out impatiently, "Thou wretched rash, intruding fool, farewell! I took thee for thy better!"

In any event, by midspring of 1958, Hugo and I were feeling good about our family. The first five were doing well in school; each one seemed his or her own person, unique in his or her own way, and they were all fun to be with. I found myself wondering if this would have been possible if we'd spent those years in the States and our young had been molded by television, pop culture, and their peer groups. What would have been the gains, what the losses?

For the moment, there seemed only gains.

By mid-April, Mike had heard about his applications: he'd been accepted by three colleges and wait-listed at a fourth. He conferred long distance with his two stateside friends and learned that though they had both been accepted by their first-choice colleges, they had both, like Mike, also been accepted by Columbia. Being together superseded all other considerations. The three boys decided to go to Columbia.

And one morning a few days after this decision, Mike phoned me from school. "Ma?" he said. "Get this. In the literary contest, Mary won first prize for best character sketch. Susie won first prize for best short story. And in poetry, I won first, second, and third prize and honorable mention."

Truly, there is balm in Gilead.

And then, graduation day.

It was a midafternoon in June, and the school's "multipurpose building," gym or auditorium as needed, was teeming with parents in their festive best. Nancy, still a year away from her own graduation, sat with us, and just a few seats away sat the Oppens, whose daughter Linda—today's salutatorian—would be going to Sarah Lawrence in September. Up onstage, the dignitaries/speakers were taking their places; behind them rows of empty chairs waited to be filled by the about-to-be graduates, while piled on a table near the footlights was a mountain of diplomas in readiness. There on the stage and down on the floor the excitement, the anticipation, were almost palpable.

And finally the school band, which had to make do without Mike and his trumpet today, struck up "Pomp and Circumstance."

On cue, and exactly like every mother in every high school north or south of the border on that occasion, I started to cry, even before the students appeared at the doors behind us. And then there they came, in their rented, plum-colored caps and gowns. At measured pace, in time to the music, they filed past us, looking scrubbed and proud and awesomely adult, while the faces of their parents turned toward them like flowers to the sun, reflecting their progress down the aisles. Suddenly we caught sight of Mike, looking astonishingly handsome in his horn-rimmed glasses and his mortarboard. *How had he grown up so fast?* He scanned the audience, caught sight of us, and gave us a quick smile as he strode by. . . .

So, by the time summer and the rainy season were well upon us, Hugo and I were feeling rather like the coaches of a football team whose quarterback has just carried the ball into the end zone for the winning score. Mike's college acceptances and graduation were the targets we'd been aiming for, planning toward, for the last two years: this summer we could all relax.

Or could we?

With no further need to concentrate so hard on our eldest, parental focus shifted to the next in line, Susie.

Born eighteen months after Mike, a slender little brown-eyed blonde, she had grown up very much in his shadow. In his ebullient early years he had so teased and tormented her, I was afraid she'd be forced forever into the classic role of martyred second child. But one day when they'd been swimming, he had teased her once too often, and she had turned on him suddenly and raked him from shoulder to swimming trunks with five sharp little fingernails. From that day on he carried the scars and treated her with cautious respect.

Through the next decade, as he continued to occupy the family spotlight, she had been developing very much on her own: reserved, with a kind of instinctive dignity and a wry wisdom that occasionally produced a comment about Mike's vagaries or our own so impious and perceptive, we began to suspect she was really more grown-up than we were. Now a willowy fifteen and a half, the straight fair hair darkened to ash brown and, in place of pigtails, a single long braid down her back, she had somehow managed to skip the awkward age altogether and had developed instead a grace and symmetry that were lovely to behold. Her sisters adored her, as did her teachers, and Hugo and I regarded her with awe—and bafflement. For all her directness, she had such a sense of privacy that we never knew what she was feeling. We were sure of one thing, though. She obviously hadn't the faintest idea how beautiful she had become and might only have been terribly embarrassed if anyone had pointed it out.

But to my old-fashioned romantic mind, there was one problem. She hadn't yet shown the slightest interest in boys.

I told myself she was just a "late bloomer." But I kept remembering my own fifteenth year, the year I discovered dating and school dances and falling in love for the first time, and perhaps I wanted to go through it all over again with Susie. Or perhaps I simply felt she was *missing* something.

In any event, wanting to push things along a little, I invited the Kilians' exuberant friend Danny, our volunteer visitor of the summer before, to spend a few weeks with us before he too went off to college. He arrived with a friend (teenagers never come singly) named Pete whom the Oppens, as involved with their daughter's social life as I was in Susie's, were happy to take on as a houseguest, and the summer whirl began once more.

But again, not as planned. Danny tried to date Susie, but to no avail; she enjoyed the group excursions to Las Estacas or the pyramids—but spent her spare time at home locked in her room or, when really desperate for privacy, up on the roof in the shadow of the water tank, reading.

Matters at the Oppens' were also going awry. After a brief romance between their Linda and Danny's friend Pete, Pete was distracted by a new arrival from the States in the form of the Oppens' attractive, slightly older niece, and Linda was left in the lurch.

At this point, either Linda met the rebuff by switching her attention to Danny—or her parents did, on her behalf, and to Danny's delight he now found himself being assiduously cultivated by two sets of parents.

I was, in fact, furious. Even though Susie hadn't shown the slightest response to Danny's attentions, still, he was the nearest thing to a boy-friend she'd had yet—and anyway, we were the ones who'd invited him down. So I regarded the Oppens' usurpation of Danny as an incursion onto Susie's turf and their open wooing of him as the ultimate violation of our friendship.

Yes, I know this is all comic opera, and before long I could view the summer's events, and my vigorous interventions on Susie's behalf, with laughter. But the deeper significance of it all was that our friendship with the Oppens was drawing to an end, and for Hugo and me it was a wrenching loss.

As we had learned during the political upheavals of 1956, friend-ships in an exile community are fervent and indispensable. Life in Mexico until now had been a happy time because we had, almost unconsciously, been avoiding political disagreements with those closest to us. We may have been trying not even to think too much about politics. It was enough now that we all had more or less shared experiences; our friends' children were our children's friends; we were all one large extended family.

And friendship with George and Mary Oppen, those years, had been something even more. It had seemed to us a little like being admitted into an enchanted kingdom.

There had, of course, been that curious discovery the previous year. Reading William Carlos Williams's autobiography, I had come upon his mention of "an earnest young poet named George Oppen," who had been part of Williams's coterie of poet friends of the 1930s. Not quite able to believe that this was *our* George, I had mentioned it to his wife, Mary, and she, almost reluctantly, admitted that George had indeed been part of that group.

In other words, George had been an honest-to-goodness, published, recognized-by-his-peers poet. "But why didn't you tell us?" I asked.

Mary simply shrugged. "Why?" she asked. "What difference would it have made?"

That was a hard one to answer. We were already close friends with a man we had assumed was a cabinetmaker, albeit a highly literate one. Would our friendship have been any closer if we'd known he'd had a whole other life?

I couldn't see how. From the time we'd first known them, we had fallen in love with the simplicity and contentment of their lifestyle.

They had long since discarded any attempt at middle-class appearance or housekeeping; George still did a little wood sculpture in addition to his cabinetwork, and Mary was still painting, but they didn't seem to be trying to achieve anything with this work; they merely pursued it because they enjoyed it. It was *living* they were skilled at. They explored the whole countryside in their well-worn old panel truck, so they knew all the best picnic places and excursion spots. It was they who had taken us picnicking in a wild area of the Pedregal just when the fragrant little white *estrellas*—star flowers—were blooming in every hollow, and it was they who, on a joint holiday in Acapulco, took us on our first evening fishing trip around the bay, with George baiting our children's hooks and Mary detaching them after a catch if any of the girls were too horrified by the gaping, gasping fish to do it themselves. Afterward we'd had a wonderful two-family picnic on the dark sands of Roqueta beach, and someone had seen a water snake appear for a moment at the water's edge and then disappear into the next wavelet. . . .

It was also George who, early in our stay, had taught Mike carpentry, a skill our son practiced with pleasure forever afterward.

We knew, of course, of all the boy babies they'd lost—perhaps from sudden infant death syndrome or perhaps from a defective gene affecting only boys, and we could only conjecture that this must make them passionately protective of Linda, the sole survivor. And we'd been aware, during the years we'd known this little family, that their warmth and approval, cautiously granted, could also be rescinded. Sometimes it was one of Linda's classmates who was "adopted" for a period and then, found wanting perhaps, abruptly dropped—something that had happened to Nikola Trumbo during her family's last year in Mexico. Sometimes it was a whole family who, for whatever reason, were found to be unworthy and abandoned. George and Mary had even fallen out with the Hoffmans, close friends since their arrival here, over the philosophic point of whether art was or was not therapy, with George, passionately, taking the negative.

Safe in the glow of their favor, we had in all such instances sided with Mary and George; anyone who earned their disapproval must almost by definition be a philistine. But bit by bit this past year, it had begun to happen to us.

Over such small matters, it seemed! Hugo and I had gone to see our first Fellini film, *La Strada,* and been captivated by it. The Oppens, on the other hand, had hated it. Or had their curiously indignant judgment of the film been symbolic, a statement that they had decided to disagree with us, and *La Strada* was simply the arena they had chosen? We were puzzled, unsure. There were one or two other such instances. Their preemption of Danny this summer, I felt, was the final statement that Hugo and I were expendable as friends.

History would solve one of the mysteries for me. I would learn, from an encounter with Linda four decades later, why George Oppen the poet had been replaced by George Oppen the woodworker. Back in his days as a radical, when he had become a party functionary, the Communist Party had taken a position that "art is a weapon"; artists who were Communists had a duty to bend their skills to serve the cause. But this apparently was something George could not bring himself to do. He could not, or would not, make his poetry merely the tool of his political beliefs. He had chosen instead to stop writing altogether.

But why he concealed from us (even from Linda, she told me later) his former life as a poet, I never learned. And I couldn't help feeling aggrieved at the deception.

Also, in the same four-decades-later encounter with Linda, I would learn, or be forced to remember, something else about our relationship with the Oppen family during the fifties that fills me with shame.

"Do you remember," she asked me, this attractive fifty-six-year-old with whom I was renewing old ties on a visit to the San Francisco Bay area, "telling me I would no longer be welcome at your house?"

What? I had said *that*—to a teenager? A perfectly nice teenager who'd been my children's friend and who certainly could not have earned such treatment? I couldn't believe it.

"It was really kind of okay," she said quickly. "The way you explained it . . . You said that Hugo had insisted on it. And you said you didn't agree with him, but that his word was law in your house, and you were afraid that was the way it had to be. So I sort of understood."

However angry we had been with her parents, it still seemed almost impossible—and absolutely unforgivable.

But over the next few days I dug into the realms of the long-forgotten (or perhaps the deliberately forgotten) and remembered fragments of my discussion with Hugo when he had issued this ukase. Whether our growing schism with her parents had any part in it or not, I'll never know. But what he had *said* was, *"She's too much competition for Susie!"*

I'm sure I protested—I must have, but he was impatient and angry as he seemed to be more often those days, and since our domestic harmony had always been based on my agreeing with him about everything, I must finally have acquiesced. I do remember, though, that I insisted I be the one to tell Linda, figuring, I guess, that at least I could find some way to break the news gently. And (still trying to piece the whole incident together) I remembered more: that after Hugo's dictum I'd had some bad nights, nerving myself up to deliver this coup de grâce to a teenager who for more than half the decade had been in and out of our house like a member of the family.

No amount of trying, it seems, helps me reconstruct the scene with Linda as it must finally have taken place. As with the Khrushchev revelations, my memory has erased what I found too difficult to face at the time. But afterward, the distance between ourselves and the Oppens became complete. And though during the two and a half years then remaining to us in Mexico we would bump into them occasionally, it would be as mere acquaintances whose lives were no longer joined. The feeling of real bitterness, though, would linger . . .

With one exception.

Summer was ending. Mike's room assignment at Columbia had arrived; he was busy wrapping books, packing clothes, wondering what to take and what to leave. He would fly up a little early, he decided, and spend a few days with the Lardners and the Hunters in New York, and we made sure his bank draft included enough money to buy an overcoat, something he'd never needed until now.

At last the day came, and we all—with Nancy—packed ourselves into the car and drove to the airport. Inside the busy, bustling terminal building (newly built and already overcrowded), we hovered round our about-to-be-fledged chick as he got his seat assignment and checked his luggage through and got his *salida* (departure) paper from the official at the desk. There were hugs, and admonitions, and excitement, and then he went through a door; we could see him through the glass, there in the passengers' waiting room—and then his flight was called, and we watched him disappear.

On the way back to San Angel we swung out to the Pedregal and dropped Nancy off. When we reached home, Ramona had *comida* ready, so we took our places straightaway. The afternoon sun was slanting in the windows; Ramona had done a *filete* of beef on the spit, so the coals still glowed in the fireplace, and the whole room smelled of nicely charred meat. Hugo, at the head of the table, began to carve, and plates were passed, and Ramona came and went with *salsa verde* and *arroz blanco* and *frijoles,* and the girls chattered until Hugo served himself, which was the signal that everyone could start eating.

But no one had thought to take Mike's chair away from the table. There it was, empty, a looming presence. Was *this* what we had worked toward, planned toward, all through Mike's high school years—this empty place at the dinner table?

Hugo looked at the empty chair, and rolled his eyes and shook his head, and I knew he was feeling as aghast as I was. Abruptly, as in an afterthought, "Jesus!" he said. *"The poor Oppens . . . !"*

Chapter Twenty-one

OUR OLD CAT was dying.

She was nineteen—older than any of the children. She had, in fact, been given me, with her twin sister, by Hugo as a surprise the Christmas after we had lost our first baby. Two tiny, wild-eyed Siamese kittens, one blue point, one seal point, he had brought them to me in a basket on that cold, clear California Christmas morning in 1939, having kept them successfully hidden since their purchase in his mother's and stepfather's quarters at our house in San Fernando Valley.

It was a strange, catastrophic time in history as well as in our own lives. I had gone into labor, coincidentally, on the same September morning that we learned by radio of Germany's invasion of the Polish corridor. But labor refused to become "established," and twinges throughout the day were intermittent; we had spent the first night timing them and listening to radio reports of the torpedoing of the British cruise ship *Athenia*.

For the delivery, which didn't happen till a day and a half later, I'd been heavily anesthetized; the baby, much wanted and very beautiful, was too birth damaged to survive more than another two days. It had not occurred to Hugo or me, both of us still young and staunch believers in happy endings, that such a thing could happen. Not to us.

While I was still in hospital it fell to Hugo's mother, Margaret, who had lost her own first baby, to return all our baby clothes and nursery furniture to the stores where we'd bought them. And after the then requisite two weeks in hospital, Hugo had brought me home to the ten-acre walnut farm where we were living—I still trying to cope with the astonishment of the loss and Hugo concealing a private fear (which he didn't confess to me till years later) that he would never have a child.

Then, Christmas morning and the kittens. They had long, strong hindquarters and a powerful leap, and we named them Kanga and Baby Roo. They cut their small, sharp teeth on our knuckles and sharpened their already sharp claws on our furniture; wild and shy, they greeted strangers by clawing their way up the drapes and crouching on the pelmets above the windows, to stare down at interlopers from wild blue eyes.

As the time approached for the birth of our next baby, and in an excess of anxiety that this new child be protected from every possible mishap, we checked with our doctor to make sure there was nothing in the old wives' tale that a cat might get into a baby's crib and smother it; the doctor (with a straight face) assured us he'd never known of such a case. As it happened, the cats would be more in danger from Mike, a lively, curious, exuberant baby who thought cats' tails were for pulling, than he from them.

By the time the two cats were a year old, however, Kanga, the seal point, had wandered across a busy street and been hit by a car, so Baby Roo—Roosie, the blue point—became sole household pet. She grew into a lovely animal, lean and aloof, who ran to answer doorbells and ringing phones and loped out to greet us when we came home and then trotted ahead of us to the door, waving her tail airily and pretending she didn't know us. She had the good sense to stay out of streets, or at least away from cars, and as Hugo continued to meet each story problem with a change of habitat, she accepted each new house with equanimity, as she accepted each new baby.

She saw us through Pearl Harbor and the early days of the States' participation in the war. When gas rationing had driven us out of the western reaches of San Fernando Valley (four houses later than the walnut farm) and into a big old frame house on the edge of the Hollywood hills, she had of necessity become a skilled rat hunter. She accepted, more philosophically than I did, Hugo's absence during his army training; moved with us up to Carmel while he was stationed at Fort Ord, where she sharpened her hunting skills on our neighbors' chickens; and when we moved back to Hollywood again was delighted to resume hunting rats. Two houses after *that*, when the Cold War and the resulting anti-Communist fervor in the States during the late 1940s had precipitated our hurried departure, she had traveled with us in our tall old Cadillac to Ensenada and thence, finally, to Mexico City.

Her life in San Angel was, I think, pleasant. When our great bouncing dog Pablo joined the household, she treated him with a kind of remote tolerance, regarding him apparently as one of life's unavoidable inconveniences. She was still in good health when Debbie was born, but by the time Becky arrived five years later, she was showing her age. She had long since given up hunting. Her coat was dull and scruffy; she moved stiffly and with discomfort. She had a sore on her side that wouldn't heal. The vet said it was cancer.

We all began to watch her with concern—especially Mary, then twelve years old and passionate in her attachments. But there was nothing, said the vet, that could be done.

Jeanette Pepper came by one pleasant morning in late summer; we brought our coffee out to the back garden where the girls were playing and where Becky sat in her kiddie –coop, watching them. Roosie followed us, slowly, dragging her poor, thin, ragged body into a patch of sunlight and then turning wearily round and round, trying to find a posture to lie in that didn't hurt. Jeanette looked at her with horror. "Jean!" she said indignantly. "If that were *my* cat, I'd have her put to sleep!"

Mary was too polite to retort. But she glared at her in silence and never forgave her.

By summer it was clear Roosie had very little time left. One night in late September, after I'd put the younger children to bed and found Mary unaccountably missing at reading time, I came downstairs to look for her. I found her in Hugo's study, sprawled on the daybed, crying, with Roosie—dim eyed and almost motionless—encircled in her arm. "Mommy," she said, sobbing, "she can't even move anymore. She just lies there."

How do you prepare a child for the inevitable? "Honey," I said, as gently as I could, "she probably won't be here when we come downstairs tomorrow."

She nodded. After a moment, her voice muffled, she said, "Do you think she knows?"

"I think so."

"Do you think she *wants* to (die)?"

"I think so. She's very old. She's very tired."

She nodded again. After another minute she kissed the old cat and, tears still spilling out of her eyes and down her cheeks, followed me out of the study and upstairs.

Next morning I came down early, wanting to precede the children. Isabel was dusting in the living room. *"Ya se murió,"* she said quietly. She had found Roosie dead on the daybed, just as we'd left her last night.

I didn't ask where she'd been removed to but only suggested that Isabel ask Don Ramon, the neighborhood gardener who was due to come that day to tend the garden, to bury her.

When Mary came downstairs for breakfast, she asked no questions. Nothing was said; there was no need. Even the younger girls seemed to know without words. After breakfast, in order to leave the coast clear for Don Ramon's sad little task, I took Mary and Emmie and Debbie off to the neighborhood athletic club, ostensibly for a tennis lesson, though I knew from their quiet compliance that they understood very well why it was necessary to be away from the house that morning.

On our return, Mary disappeared into the kitchen to speak privately to Ramona, and Isabel pointed out to me where, in the front garden, Roosie had been buried.

The next time I came outside, I saw that Mary had already visited the spot. Placed there on a little patch of broken ground in the shadow of the bushes stood a small emptied-out tomato can, holding a handful of flowers.

Chapter Twenty-two

BY THE CHILDREN'S *dieciséis de septiembre* holidays we were, once again, refugees.

The children didn't know it. They only knew we had made a sudden decision that we'd all drive to Taxco ("We've never seen it!" we explained) and thrown a couple of suitcases into the car and set out.

At least some of us did. Mike was away at college now. Susie was spending the holidays out of town with the Hoffmans. And we'd left Becky at home being spoiled by Ramona and Isabel. So the only passengers we had now were the three middle girls. Packed happily in the back of the car, they watched the lush Cuernavaca landscape disappear behind us and then, a few miles farther on, when we neared the sugar mill that marked the turnoff to Las Estacas, there'd been a groundswell in favor of a detour. We'd been sorely tempted, but since we hadn't brought our bathing suits, we hewed to the highway.

As the scenery grew browner and more bare, Mary, Emmie, and Debbie vied for a while to see who could count more goats, sheep, cows, or horses (each worth one point if you were the first to sight it), and, when that paled, were sent into happy shudders of fear when Hugo, as he drove, spun them a story about a man who lived in a cave among these dry hills, who captured little children and used their skins to make *equipales* (rawhide chairs). By the time the highway had begun to climb again and reached the higher, cooler countryside that signaled the approach to Taxco, the girls were in an agreeable state of self-induced panic.

We weren't doing too badly ourselves.

On the political scene, there had been worrisome events for more than half a year: a rash of "Article 33" deportations, with frequent government statements headlined in the papers blaming "foreign agitators" for the recent spate of labor unrest that had kept the country in turmoil. The unrest was probably inevitable in a period when (according to the government's own figures) forty-one percent of all children in Mexico were unable to attend school for lack of teachers and classroom space and agrarian reform was admitted to be a total failure.

But as for any part the American Left might have played in the resultant protests: as mentioned before in these pages, every one of us had leaned over backward to avoid involvement in Mexican politics, and few of us even had enough mastery of Spanish to hold a philosophical discussion with our Mexican peers on any subject—let alone do any serious rabble-rousing among them.

Nevertheless, "foreigners" were inevitably targeted in times of domestic protest. Earlier in our stay in Mexico, our biographer friend Ralph Roeder, a gentle, stately—and altogether apolitical—man who had written the definitive biography of Benito Juárez and was now on a subsidy from the Mexican government while he researched and wrote a history of the 1910 revolution, had been peremptorily arrested (by a different branch of the same government) and tossed into the ominous Lecumberri prison during a local strike (of either miners or teachers, I've forgotten which), allegedly for having helped foment the trouble. It had taken his wife a number of frantic visits to their friends among Mexico's dignitaries to get him freed, but four or five days in a cell among Mexico's most hardened criminals had left this aging, fragile scholar badly shaken.

The next wave of scapegoating was equally wide of the mark. Two small-businessmen whom we knew very slightly, who had invested in businesses here, had been picked up just before Christmas last year and unceremoniously shipped to the border. This, however, provoked a contretemps with the American border officials because one of the deportees, a naturalized U.S. citizen, was unable to produce his citizenship papers on demand (not surprisingly, given the involuntary nature of the journey). The Americans had refused to accept him, so he at least had been returned to his family in Mexico City.

There was even some question, in our circles, whether such deportations were really political (there was certainly no evidence that they were) or whether they had been engineered by Mexican business associates. This was a not unreasonable assumption, considering the ease with which a simple *"denuncia"* (even with no proof whatever) could trigger expulsion—which, of course, would leave the deportee's share of ownership in the hands of his Mexican partner. This at least was the current anxiety among those of our friends who had any money to invest.

However, the labor picture this current year, 1958, was even more volatile than the year before. There were nationwide strikes of telegraphers, railway workers, oil and textile workers. Huge red-and-black flags denoting strikes appeared outside union headquarters all over town. Early in September there'd been a parade downtown of striking teachers; police had charged the crowd, and *Cruz Roja* ambulances had picked up fifty injured. Authorities again blamed foreign agitators and ordered the immediate arrest of "all such persons."

The demands weren't just rhetoric. Within a day or two, agents from *migración* had gone to the Hoffmans' house, three blocks away from us, but found those particular birds flown, Annie and Hans having in all innocence taken advantage of the school holidays and driven their children and our Susie to their holiday cottage in Valle de Bravo. Across the street from us and around the corner, at their house in the row of attractive Spanish-colonial houses edging the San Angel Inn grounds, the Druckers had been picked up, questioned, and then sent home again. But deciding not to rely further on the democratic process, David and Esther had climbed over their back fence onto the inn grounds to emerge onto a back street, whence they also headed, with friends, for Valle de Bravo.

Agents had also paid a call at the Maltzes' house, but Albert by chance was in California.

But *migración* agents hadn't always come up empty-handed. A few months before, they had picked up screenwriter John Bright (whom we knew slightly but rarely saw) one midnight while he was babysitting his children and shipped him across the border in his carpet slippers without a cent in his pocket. And they had deported a quite apolitical (as far as we knew) contractor named Bernard Blasenheim, who'd been a partner in the building of two or three rather pleasant houses in a nearby residential neighborhood. ("Red Millionaire Deported!" trumpeted the local papers. "Poor Bernie," sighed one of his friends. "He always *wanted* to be a millionaire!")

But somehow or other, we had convinced ourselves that the agents wouldn't come after *us*. Hugo had, after all, written three pictures for Mexican production, all of which brought dollars into the country in the form of financing and sales and all of which were regarded with pride by the Mexican film industry. Moreover, we had no Mexican business partner; hence no one to benefit from "denouncing" us.

One day soon after Mike's departure for college, however, we had come from home from a lunch downtown at our favorite Yucatecan restaurant to be met by the news that "a señor in a black raincoat" had come to the gates, asking for Hugo or me. Isabel didn't know who he was; he hadn't left a name.

That's when we'd packed and left, our children altogether delighted by this unexpected holiday.

But Taxco, however charming, afflicted the girls with terminal boredom. After an evening and a morning spent admiring the cobbled streets and colonial architecture, and exploring (but not buying anything from) a number of silversmiths' shops, and with the children's complaint "But there's nothing to *do!*" ringing in our ears, we knew we'd have to move on. Afraid to go home yet in case the señor in the black raincoat might still be lurking in San Angel, we decided to vacation elsewhere and by lunchtime were traveling back toward the Acapulco highway and from there, south to the seacoast. It took the children no time at all to figure out, with considerable satisfaction, that because we hadn't brought our bathing suits, we'd all have to buy new ones.

We pulled into Acapulco on that hot afternoon with no hotel reservation and wound up not at our favorite breezy little hotel on the hillside but down in the center of town, across the busy highway from the beach, in a not very appealing motel sheltered from the sun by banana and coconut palms, its outdoor dining area shady but airless, its pool a troubled green. On arrival we had checked in with our friends the Zykofskys, who had spirited Mary away with them to their own holiday rental, so now there were just the four of us, Hugo and I in one bedroom and Emmie and Debbie in another adjoining but not connected, all the bedrooms leading off a tile-roofed porch that extended the length of the building in the rear of the complex.

We heard the shots on our second night there.

It was midnight or perhaps later. We were wakened by a series of staccato blasts coming from the alley behind the hotel, a shout or two, the padding sound of bare feet running—and then silence. We were still trying to diagnose the sounds when Emmie's voice sounded from the porch outside our door: "Mommy? Daddy? Was somebody shooting?"

"Of course not," I said, reassuring myself as much as Emmie. "It was only firecrackers. Go back to bed."

"It sounded like gunshots," Emmie said. But then apparently she'd decided to go back to her room—when only a few minutes later, there was another burst of explosions, now clearly from some sort of automatic weapon, and then many shouts and the nearby sound of a police siren, and then the wail of an ambulance, all muffled by the thick wall at our back. Hugo leapt from his bed and ran out onto the porch in front and along to the girls' room to make sure no wild bullets had gone through their wall. Emmie, who had had the same concern and was now lying on the floor for safety, assured him she and Debbie were all right, and reassured by the sounds of officialdom outside in the alley, Hugo came back to bed. But it was a long time before there was sleep for any of us.

The girls and I were up early. Leaving Hugo to catch up on his lost sleep, I joined them and we made our way through the thicket of palms fronting the veranda, circled the murky pool, and reached the shaded dining area to find ourselves a breakfast table. It was very quiet and the morning still relatively cool. After a few moments a waiter emerged from the kitchen and brought us our menus.

"*¿Que pasó anoche?*" ("What happened last night?") I asked him.

He looked very wise. "*Hay un ciudadano menos,*" he said. ("There is one citizen less.")

The story emerged. Two old enemies, owners of small adjoining coconut plantations, had been feuding for years over their common boundary line. A few months ago, henchmen of the richer and more powerful owner had killed the brother of the other; last night's shooting was in revenge. A sub-machine gun. The richer plantation owner was dead.

"But how about the man who did the shooting?" I asked him in Spanish. "Did they catch him?"

The waiter shrugged. That one got away, he said.

"What will happen to him?"

He shrugged again. In all likelihood, he said, the fugitive would flee into the jungles of the Costa Brava, the wild coast south of Acapulco; people would shelter him; and in a year or so he would drift back to Acapulco and it would all have blown over—though perhaps, for the sake of appearances, he might have to serve a little while in jail. . . .

Not until years later did I learn what else made that night memorable for Emily. Yes, the shooting had frightened her, but it had been, after all, sudden and strange and unreal and hence forgettable. What she remembered most about Las Hamacas was that she and Debbie had discovered, the first day of our stay there, a little hoard of cut-up leaves banked against the wall near their doorsill; the two little girls had puzzled over it and puzzled still more the second morning when they'd found it had grown larger. What was it? How did it get there? What did it mean?

That night—the night of the shooting—when Emmie had been wakened by the shots and had come out onto the porch en route our room to call to us, she had discovered, by the light of the bare bulb overhead, a stream of ants busily carrying little pieces of cut-up leaves along the tile floor of the porch to the cache of leaf fragments near her door. She had watched them a moment in wonder, then come on to our room to ask about the gunfire. On her way back to her room she had studied them again and had gone back to bed still thinking about them—only to be jolted by the second burst of gunfire, which had sent her scrambling with her sister to the floor for safety. She never did discover why the ants were behaving in that curious manner (at least, not until she was older and learned about the habits of leaf-cutting ants), but at least now she knew where the pile of leaf fragments had come from. That much at least of the world's mysteries had been explained.

A postscript. A few weeks after our return home, one of the cardplayers at Mike's former seven-and-a-half games, his friend Peter Neustaedter, dropped by the house and, chatting with us, mentioned that he'd come by early in the September holidays to say hello, but we'd been out for lunch. Actually, he admitted, he'd wanted to talk to Susie but had been too embarrassed to say so, so he'd asked for Hugo or me instead.

Something rang a bell. I looked at the hint of heavy dark beard under his clean-shaven chin and realized he looked far older than he really was. "Peter," I said, "do you by any chance have a black raincoat?"

Yes, it seemed, he did.

(top) Hugo Butler conversing with team captain Fidel Ruíz during the shooting of *How Tall Is a Giant?* (1958). (Courtesy of Walter Reuther)

During the shooting of *How Tall Is a Giant*, with Hugo next to the cameraman Walter Reuther. (Courtesy of the author)

Scene from *The Adventures of Robinson Crusoe* (1954), an early collaboration between Luis Buñuel and Hugo Butler. (Courtesy of the Academy of Motion Picture Arts and Sciences)

Poster for Hugo Butler's film adaptation of *Torero!* (1954) written pseudonymously. (Courtesy of the Academy of Motion Picture Arts and Sciences)

The five Butler children in late 1953 at Palmas 81, their home in Mexico City. Hugo took the picture for a Christmas card. (Courtesy of the author)

A family outing at Xochimilco in 1952 with a boatman and his young assistant in the rear. (*Right, front to back*) Chris Trumbo, Hugo Butler, Emily Butler, and Susie Butler; (*left, front to back*) Nikola Trumbo, Mary Butler, and Katie Lardner. (Courtesy of Cleo Trumbo)

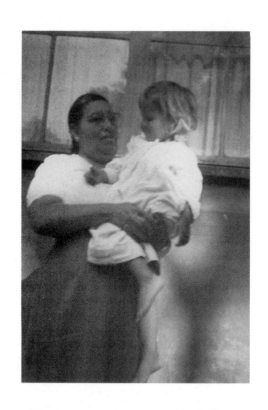

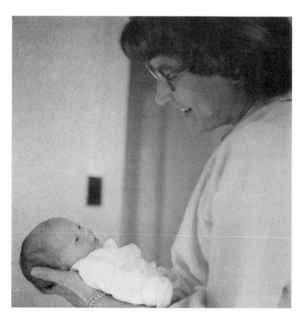

Emily Butler with her dream horse, c. 1959. (Courtesy of the author)

(top left) Debbie (born in 1953) with Ramona, the indispensable family-helper. (Courtesy of the author)

(bottom left) The sixth Butler child, a newborn Becky, with mother, Jean, in 1958. (Courtesy of the author)

Susie Butler in a Saturday ballgame with Cleo Trumbo seated in the background. (Courtesy of the author)

(top right) Debbie in the snow on the Cuernavaca Road in January 1958. (Courtesy of the family)

(bottom right) Emily helps serve some of the team members when the Little Giants come to lunch in 1958. (Courtesy of the author)

Juan O'Gorman, architect, muralist, and the Butlers' landlord, working at Chapultepec Castle on one of his murals. (Courtesy of the author)

(top left) Fidel Ruíz, *beisbolista*, and Mike Butler at Christmastime in 1959. (Courtesy of the author)

(bottom left) Valedictorian Susie Butler and diploma in June 1960. (Courtesy of the family)

Jean Rouverol and Hugo Butler in front of a Roman fountain in December 1960, and the beginning of their three years in Italy. (Courtesy of the author)

Chapter Twenty-three

WITHIN DAYS of that particular crisis, the local spate of scapegoating had calmed down as quickly as it had begun, and we had learned a new lesson. These brief eruptions, it seemed, were simply the price of living as outlanders in Mexico—a minor inconvenience if one could avoid being jailed or deported while the crisis was in progress.

So, as our nervous friends drifted back into town from their impromptu "vacations," life took on its familiar face again. Mexico's occasional unpredictability was still better, we all felt, than the continued blacklisting and Cold War hysteria back in the States. Anyway, we'd grown fond of our adopted country and were inclined to excuse even its occasional vagaries. We felt at *home* here. . . .

But how about our fellow blacklistees at this point in the decade? How about those who had chosen to remake their lives abroad and who, through whatever happenstance, had been able to get to Europe before the State Department had made them turn in their passports? Or those who'd settled for the relative anonymity of living in New York? Or, for that matter, how about those who had dared to stay put in the Los Angeles area, in the very heart of the blacklist? While we were busy adapting to the mores of Mexico, how were *they* getting along?

Their experiences varied wildly.

Since the Hunters had joined the Lardners in New York, Ian and Ring had been doing very well—under noms de plume, of course. Among other jobs, they had written the pilot and become story editors for Great Britain's TV series *The Adventures of Robin Hood*. Happily, its success allowed them to keep a small army of blacklisted friends busy writing episodes, and not just on *Robin Hood* but on their subsequent series (*Sir Lancelot* and *The Buccaneers*) as well. The three series were produced by a sympathetic American producer, Hannah Weinstein, who'd moved to England, where, seemingly, she had cornered the market for TV adventure classics, and in time, when passports became obtainable again, the Hunters lived in London while Ian worked as story editor of another of Hannah's shows, *Four Just Men*.

Ian and Ring had also written a British feature film and the pilot for another series sold in syndication, and by 1958, Ring was also working under the table on a Sophia Loren picture. And, when both families finally settled for good in New York, Frances was picking up an occasional stage job too.

So they at least were thriving. As for Trumbo:

Not only had his producer friends the King brothers funded him for the writing of his modest little bullfight picture, *The Brave One,* but from the first days of his return to the States they, along with other low-budget producers, had kept him supplied with other projects, to be written, of course, under pseudonyms or using unblacklisted friends as fronts. A number of these movies, low budget and well constructed (including *Gun Crazy* and *Lonely Are the Brave*), would later come to be viewed as classic examples of film noir, but at the time they were assigned him, they were simply jobs Trumbo took on to feed his family. He had also written a few scripts for foreign production, and altogether, he was keeping so busy that when Hugo visited him on a brief trip north, he again had three work baskets on his desk for three simultaneous script assignments, which Cleo was busy typing. This seemed to be his average assignment load.

His salary as blacklistee, needless to say, was less than a tenth—perhaps less than a twentieth—of what he had made per script in pre-HUAC days. Nevertheless, he was exhilarated by the challenge of an almost impossible writing pace and at the notion that one way or another he was outwitting his persecutors and making a mockery of the blacklist.

Employment in the States for other blacklistees, though, was still a mixed bag. Most of our actor friends who'd been driven from the screen still worked at any jobs they could get. But a few of our writer friends had, over the last eight or ten years, managed to created new identities for themselves as writers. Early on, our friend Eddie Huebsch had badly miscast himself trying to run a television repair business with the Kilian boys' father, Michael—but now he was also getting an occasional consulting job with Bob Aldrich and sometimes, like so many of our friends, an episode on one or another of Ring and Ian's series. Former agent (and before that, teacher of musicology) David Robison, who had lived quite near us in Hollywood, had only just begun to get writing jobs when the blacklist began, but since then, under a nom de plume, he had created a thriving career writing Ronald Colman television shows. He had even discovered, working pseudonymously, that the disappointments involved in writing TV drama gave him ulcers, but when he switched to comedy shows, his health improved immediately. (His older daughter, Paula, once a classmate of our Mike's in elementary school, would become a world-renowned flautist, but that's another story.)

Our friend Al Levitt, who had struggled as a still photographer when he'd initially been driven from screenwriting, had, with his wife Helen, been reborn as part of a television writing team, "Tom and Helen August," and they were thriving.

And Waldo Salt, who had figured so prominently in the early days of Hugo's and my life together—introducing us and then recruiting us into the Communist Party—was functioning sometimes on the West Coast, sometimes on the East. For a time he had worked on a folk musical with Earl Robinson; he did a few shows for Ring and Ian, and, still pseudonymously, a few TV drama series for an American producer. He was also coping with his own private demons. A few years hence, as the blacklist began to grind down, he would churn out several films for Hecht-Lancaster that he was bitterly ashamed of, his marriage would break up, and by the early 1960s he would be living alone in a New York hotel and drinking heavily.

The moment of salvation for him seemed to come from something his younger daughter said one day when she visited him. "We wouldn't worry so much about you, Daddy," she said, *"if we thought you loved what you were doing."* Somehow, that moment seemed to mark a turning point. With what must have been herculean effort, he halted his downward spiral; his next screenplays (*Midnight Cowboy* and *Coming Home*) dazzled the whole industry with their quality and would go on to win Oscars. He would also, before his death, become a guru for aspiring young screenwriters at Robert Redford's Sundance Institute.

Actually, New York would provide another group of blacklistees with a "bully pulpit" during the dark days of the 1950s. Word had it that a much respected history-based, issue-oriented TV series called *You Are There* was largely being written (under the table) by blacklistee Walter Bernstein, whom we knew only by reputation, and writers Abraham Polonksky (*Body and Soul*, *Force of Evil*) and Arnold Manoff, whom we had known slightly in Hollywood. The show itself was a consistent prizewinner; and in the 1970s, Bernstein would memorialize his blacklist experiences on it for Woody Allen's lovely tragicomedy *The Front*.

Then there was the phenomenon of 444 Central Park West.

Mid-decade, when New York had had a sudden spate of good plays and Hugo and I had taken Mike and Susie up to New York to see some of them, we discovered that three or four families we'd known who'd fled there from Hollywood had all taken apartments in the same building. Later we would learn that at one time or another before the blacklist years were over, at least *eight* such families had sought refuge there. To the initiates, the address became known, wryly, as "The Smolny Institute," after a building in St. Petersburg that housed a military/revolutionary committee during the Russian revolution. Basically, however, I suspect the transplants were seeking, in the proximity of others like themselves, the same kind of reassurance and community that we were finding among our friends in Mexico.

For many others of the Hollywood Left, however, the blacklist had set in motion a diaspora, and early on, those families who were able to had scattered to England, France, Spain, Italy. Much later in the decade, when the Supreme Court decision declared the right to travel a basic civil right, other blacklistees followed. News of some of these expatriates reached us by letter or Christmas card or gossip—and some I have only been able to piece together from personal accounts, in print or told as folklore, long ex post facto.

In England, we gathered, blacklisting seemed a sometimes thing. By 1952 Carl Foreman, formerly a partner of producer Stanley Kramer and author of most of Kramer's socially significant films (and whose work we admired enormously), had been forced out of Hollywood but had found that in Britain he could still, in some instances, work under his own name. Comedy writer Frank Tarloff, whose film career at home had shifted (pseudonymously) to television, found that in England he could get film-writing jobs too, though still under his nom de plume. Bernard Vorhaus (who had cowritten and directed one of my pictures) and Joe Losey (who had directed two of Hugo's) had also moved to England, and in fact, Joe's career would really take wing in British films—without benefit of nom de plume at all. And actor Phil Brown was getting acting jobs there too, and he and his wife were now living, we heard, on a houseboat on the Thames. Actually, Phil had never joined anything but simply happened to have the wrong friends, so the Hollywood blacklist had swept him up along with the others.

Then there were those who went to mainland Europe. By the end of the 1950s and early 1960s, Leonardo Bercovici would be writing and directing movies in Italy and Yugoslavia. Bernard Gordon, who just prior to the blacklist had managed to move from being a "reader" (a screen story analyst) to a modest career as a writer, had had for a time to take a job as a private investigator after being named. Fortunately he was able to write his way (pseudonymously) out of this predicament, and by the end of the decade he and his family would be living in France and then Spain, where he would prove the most prolific of all the blacklisted screenwriters, turning out an astonishing number of films (primarily for Phil Yordan) and enjoying the kind of prosperity he'd never known before. Meanwhile his best friend and sometime collaborator Julian Zimmet, whom we'd known as a screenwriter, had written and published his first book as "Julian Halevy" while he'd been living in Mexico; Hugo and I had both read it in manuscript and found it gentle and charming, and he'd subsequently come close to a fresh Hollywood career under his new name. But then his identity caught up with him, and late in the decade he would move permanently to Italy, where he would do an occasional writing job (including magazine articles) and, in time, marry a magazine editor—a lovely woman, who was also the sister of writer Primo Levi.

France, during the 1950s, would gain a whole clutch of Hollywoodians, including Norma and Ben Barzman (who not only kept very busy writing films in Europe but seemed to be trying to outdo us in the baby department, finally totaling seven to our six); Lee Gold and his wife, Tamara Hovey; director John Berry (who had directed three of Hugo's preblacklist screenplays); and, until he moved on to Greece, director Jules Dassin, whose work in France and then in Greece would become legend.

Additionally, as passports allowed, Paul Jarrico and Michael Wilson (whose wives were sisters) arrived at different times to settle in France with their families. By the end of the blacklist, Paul, after producing *Salt of the Earth* (of which more in a moment), would have written several films pseudonymously for English or American production. And Mike Wilson, who'd done the script for *Salt of the Earth,* would also have written or cowritten, either under the table at home or in England or in France, so many stunning epics (including *Friendly Persuasion; Bridge Over the River Kwai,* written with Carl Foreman; and *Lawrence of Arabia*) that—also taking into account Trumbo's *The Brave One* and Ned Young's cocredit on *The Defiant Ones*—one could only wonder what the Motion Picture Academy would have done for Oscar-winning screenplays all those years if the blacklistees had *really* been driven from the industry!

And apropos, what about *Salt of the Earth*? What had we learned thus far about its makers and its making?

It was a story of such pluck, such determination, against such enormous obstacles that even now, near the end of the decade, Hugo and I still regarded the film's completion as little more than a miracle.

But let's back up a bit. Soon after our arrival here, we'd heard stories about the little group of Hollywoodians who, since no established production company would deal with them anymore, had undertaken the daunting task of fund-raising for and producing their own picture. Spearheaded first by Adrian Scott, who was not well enough to continue and had ceded his post as producer to Paul Jarrico, and by Michael Wilson as writer and Herbert Biberman as director, they'd taken as their springboard the true story of a miners' strike in the Southwest during which, with the jailing of all the husbands, the wives had emerged as the strength behind the ongoing strike (and afterward in their own homes as well).

Most of the shooting had taken place on location in New Mexico. Local law-enforcement agencies and a number of self-appointed vigilante groups had interfered mercilessly with the shooting and, just before the picture's completion, had managed to rig a charge against the film's Mexican star Rosaura Revueltas and have her picked up and deported. Bloody but unbowed, the little company had come down to Mexico sometime in 1952 or 1953 for final pickup shots with Rosaura (although absent the necessary local permits, this too had to be done discreetly).

During the group's brief stay in Mexico City, a reception had been held for them at the Pedregal house of Bolivian artist Roberto Berdecio and his American wife. Our whole refugee community was there, along with a number of Mexican filmmakers and an assortment of artists and other luminaries. We all listened, fascinated, to tales of the company's adventures during shooting. Even the processing of the footage had seemed a near impossibility, with stateside film laboratories flatly refusing to touch it; even this had to be accomplished piecemeal and by subterfuge. . . .

The whole roomful of us were still listening, spellbound, when it came Herbert Biberman's turn to report on his travails as director. But at that point my feelings became, I'm afraid, ambivalent. I kept remembering the last time I'd observed this bespectacled, elegantly tailored gentleman speaking to an audience, up in Hollywood in late 1950, one of the last months before we'd had to go on the run.

It had been an eerie time, the Cold War intensifying by the moment and all of us wondering whether or when we too would become targets of HUAC. Most of the Hollywood Ten were then still in jail, but Herbert, assigned a more lenient judge, had been given a six-month sentence and, with time off for good behavior, had served five. On his release and return to Hollywood, friends and family had held a series of cocktail parties where he could talk about his experiences in jail, and Hugo and I had been invited to one of them. Hugo, I think, was working that particular afternoon, so I'd gone by myself.

There, in someone's house in the Hollywood hills, we guests had listened as Herbert had given us, in these same mellifluous tones, an account of his bitterly unpleasant early days behind bars. But then, he reported, he had discovered the prison library and thereafter had spent all his spare time reading: mostly, he said, the Greek dramatists. "And now," he told us, "when people ask me how I felt as a prisoner, I can only think . . ." (slight pause) " . . . of Prometheus, who for the crime of bringing fire to mankind was chained by the gods to the rocks, with the vultures tearing at his liver!"

That's what was echoing in my mind as I listened to him at the gathering in the Pedregal, some three years later, talking about *Salt of the Earth*. And I'm afraid I had the same feeling I always had in

conversations with Albert Maltz: How do you separate the self-fabricated "hero" from his quite real, and quite admirable, achievements?
Over the months that followed, the various members of this staunch
little group would manage somehow to complete their picture; the story
of their struggles would spread throughout filmmaking circles not only
here on this continent but in Europe too. One *had* to respect them for it.

And yet—oh, dear—*Prometheus?*

But now at last, several years after the company's frantic trip to
Mexico City for pickup shots and even well after its triumphant release at film festivals abroad, we heard that the picture would open in
the capital (despite, we suspected, whatever pressure American officials may have exerted to prevent it). There would be a prestigious
premiere. Hugo and I, dressed in our best, went downtown to join in
the celebration.

It was a gratifying evening. The audience was almost entirely Mexican, boasting many of the city's artists and filmmakers, and at the
picture's conclusion, the whole house rose and gave it a standing ovation. Whether they were saluting the film itself or the courage of its
makers, I wasn't quite sure. But my unease at Herbert's postprison
rhetoric was fast fading. In the face of a triumph like this against such
odds, surely a small touch of hubris here and there can be forgiven?

Meanwhile what about ourselves, as our Mexican decade moved toward the end of its eighth year? How were our own writing careers
coming along?

We were learning, if we had not known before, that in our perilous
professional situation, whether we were working for pay or on spec,
we could count on about one project in three reaching the screen or
selling for publication. In Hugo's case, though his work for George
Pepper's little company and for Aldrich and a couple of Mexican pro-
ducer-directors had kept him fairly busy, the pay was modest, and between jobs he had managed to load up the "unsold" shelf in his study
with a good deal of material—including, of course, his adaptation of
the Chekhov novella. In addition, now there was a dramatization of
Melville's novel *Typee,* which had not sold, and another of Robert
Louis Stevenson's *The Beach at Falesa,* which had been optioned by
John Huston and then, we thought, abandoned before payment of the
final third of the purchase price. Much later we made the painful dis-

covery that the producer representing the material (an American businessman living in Mexico but *not* a blacklistee) had felt he was entitled to a bigger share of the proceeds and had simply kept the final payment, telling Hugo it had never been paid.

In addition, there were a couple of fully worked out screen stories (one of which kept getting optioned but never made), and in 1957 George Pepper had acquired the rights to Evelyn Waugh's *The Loved One,* which Hugo and Luis Buñuel had turned into a deliciously funny screenplay. But that was well before black comedy had come into its own, and when our agent friend Ingo Preminger had tried to market it, the studios had merely dismissed it, saying: "There's nothing funny about death."

(The whole package, however, sold several years later to a producer at MGM, who filmed the material with a different screenplay. But at least Hugo was paid for his labor.)

Our "unsold" shelf also included a couple of short stories I'd written early in the decade, which were (in all honesty) not very good, but now it also boasted my two recent novellas: the earlier mentioned story about the alcoholic father and his four daughters and a second that I had just completed, about an American family living in modern Mexico, with a mother who conducts a guerrilla war on behalf of her teenage daughter's social life—a thinly disguised version of recent events in our household, in which the mother (myself) was treated with the ridicule she so richly deserved.

Both these stories, I felt, were salable—or would have been at a different moment of history; their presence on the "unsold" shelf was a source of much frustration to me. I hadn't even sent them out, primarily because by now I had no literary agent. The agent who'd sold my four novellas to *McCall's* had left the William Morris agency to become a film producer, and I hadn't yet found a replacement. Still more crippling was the fact that I didn't know what name to use as author. Hugo's admonition that day at Prendes over lunch still echoed faintly in my ears: "Nothing with your name on it is going to sell!"

In other words, I still didn't know for sure whether there was or wasn't a blacklist in the magazine market or even if there were literary agents who would handle blacklistees. But I knew I needed *some*one to represent me. Few magazines buy material submitted "over the transom"; they seem to require the imprimatur of an agent to guarantee a work's professionalism. Also, I hadn't sold any fiction in more than ten years, and by now I was desperately in need of reassurance about the quality of my work. It wasn't just a need for someone to get my stories out into the light of day; I needed to know if I could still write readable prose after all this time. . . .

And then, one evening when Hugo was off on his *beisbolista* shoot, the Maltzes invited me over for dinner to meet a visitor from New York: the agent who had just sold Margaret's book (about the bombing of the plane to Oaxaca) to Simon and Schuster, on its first submission.

And while Margaret had used her maiden name (Margaret Larkin) on the manuscript, the agent clearly knew she was Albert's wife and that she undoubtedly shared his politics. But that apparently had made no difference. . . .

Did that mean there was light at the end of the tunnel for me too? I went off to dinner in a state of almost irrational hope.

His name was Barthold Fles: a slight, erudite, and opinionated Dutchman who'd been both an editor and a translator before he'd become an agent. Over drinks, I learned more about him. One of the books he'd translated, it seemed, was *Bambi's Children,* the sequel to one of our children's favorite books.

Then I learned something else. The person who had translated the first *Bambi* was a former client of his named Whittaker Chambers.

At that moment in history, there was no public figure more anti-Communist than self-confessed former radical Whittaker Chambers. It was astonishing enough to find out that such a man had translated that lovely, gentle book. But that the same agent who'd represented him could also represent Albert Maltz's wife in a book sale . . . I waited, hoping to learn what Mr. Fles thought of his former client *now.*

But he made no further mention of him, neither that evening nor as long as I knew him. During dinner, however, he did mention that he was handling other blacklisted writers in addition to Margaret: Phil Stevenson (writing as "Lars Larson") and Guy Endore (*Werewolf of London*) too. So—still puzzled, but desperate to join the ranks of publishable writers again—I set about courting him shamelessly, offering to be his tour guide next day for some of Mexico's tourist attractions (with the private hope that there might be time afterward for him to do a little reading).

Our day of sight-seeing went well. If I had needed a secret weapon, it was provided by my girls, who rode out to Teotihuacan with us and charmed this childless (and, I suspect, often lonely) gentleman altogether. As we trudged along the approaches to the Pyramid of the Sun, he allayed one of my anxieties by stating categorically that there was no, repeat *no*, blacklist in magazines. And after we got home and the girls disappeared about their own business, he settled down in our living room to read my two novellas.

And liked them.

I had an agent. At last.

And within a month or two, when Hugo and I had made an emergency flight to New York because Mike, not having bought that overcoat before the onset of winter, was in hospital with viral pneumonia, and I dropped by Bart's minuscule, book-stacked office near Columbus Square to see how things were going, Bart told me he had just sold the lighter of my two novellas to *Seventeen*. Under my own name.

I was a writer again.

Through all these efforts on both our parts, however, there was an essential difference between Hugo's approach to writing and mine that I had never taken proper measure of and should have because I might then have been more aware of what the blacklist could do, and in fact *was* doing, to Hugo.

I wrote because I loved it, because I couldn't *not* write. As I loved words and reading, I loved the very process of writing, and of course it gave me enormous reassurance when a piece of my work sold, whatever the medium or the genre: film, book, magazine fiction, or even, in later years, TV soap opera. And with household help still so affordable here in Mexico (though not just left-wingers like me but all American housewives tended, guiltily, to bid up the local salaries), my responsibilities to hearth and kitchen were so minimal that for most of every day—at least till the children came home from school—I could write to my heart's content.

Hugo's relationship to his work, though, was another matter altogether.

First of all, while writing was for me a glorious luxury, it was *his* work we counted on to support our ever-growing family. But even so—even though his family responsibilities forced him to view every one of his projects through the prism of its commercial viability—film was still the very center of his life. He visualized every scene, often doing sketches of every shot as he wrote. Yes, he was a writer, but internally he was director, cinematographer, and editor as well. And as he acquired mastery of the technology of filmmaking, he was also testing the boundaries of the medium, trying to give it new dimensions. It was not just that he struggled always to write at the top of his craft; film was, in a way, his language, his *conscience.*

These years of the 1950s, though, faced not only with the never-ending need to support his family, he was also facing the continual frustration of knowing that much of his best work might never reach the screen, let alone bear his name.

And he was burning out.

He was forty-six, he had chronic high blood pressure, and he was tired. Unbeknownst to me, he turned to the worst possible remedy: stimulants. On one of his recent trips to the States, he had dropped in to visit our former family doctor, complaining of fatigue, and the doctor, on the then current theory that they were nonaddictive, prescribed amphetamines.

The side effects of these drugs were not yet common knowledge, but in time they would make more profound changes in our lives than ever the blacklist did.

Chapter Twenty-four

EARLIER IN OUR Mexican decade, when Emily was about four, I drove her downtown with me early one Sunday morning, probably to buy a Sunday *New York Times* or *Herald Tribune* at Sanborn's. The city was still quiet; we were traveling our leisurely way along a tree-lined street divided by an island (Avenida Amsterdam, perhaps?) and found ourselves approaching a corner where early churchgoers were just emerging from services. Emily, small beside me, watched them from the car window as they came out in twos, threes, small family groups, moving down the steps and onto the street and away, and as we drove on by them she said dreamily, "It's a world full of strangers . . ."

Maybe that's why she fell in love with horses.

She was an infinitely gentle child, quite beautiful, with a vulnerable face and huge brown eyes and a (usually uncombed) cloud of curly, honey-colored hair, and she was given to long, thoughtful silences while she tried to make sense of a world that clearly bewildered her. All through her childhood and growing-up years, she looked for larger truths that would somehow explain or make predictable the peculiarities of day-to-day living, the behavior of grown-ups, the social behavior of leaf-cutter ants and other live creatures, and, not least, the utter confusion of school. But why were horses so important to her?

I never really knew. But when she was still little enough to use a tricycle, she used to ride it about our yard, chanting to a tune of her own, "I sing all the galloping songs / but I ne-ver go for a ride."

And by age seven, when she was reading for herself many of the books I'd read aloud to her older siblings, her choice, of course, was horse books. Hugo and I were lingering at the dining table over coffee after *comida* one autumn afternoon when we heard her sudden, anguished cry of "Mommy!" from the living room, where she'd been immersed in *Black Beauty*. She flew in to us, the book open in her hand, her face white and a look of betrayal in her eyes. She tried to talk but couldn't without crying, so she simply held the open page in front of us.

It was the moment when the equine narrator, descended now to a cab horse, catches sight of a cart bearing the body of a horse that looks much like his longtime friend Ginger, whose life had become as miserable as his own. "The head hung out of the cart-tail, the lifeless tongue was slowly dripping with blood, and the sunken eyes!" said the text. " . . . It was a chestnut horse with a long thin neck. . . . I believed it was Ginger; I hoped it was, for then her troubles would be over. Oh! If men were more merciful they would shoot us before we came to such misery."

Emmie had discovered, abruptly, that even in books, characters one loved—horses, too!—could meet cruelty and even death.

And sometime the next year, Hugo and I had come home from an evening out to find her sound asleep on top of our bed with a copy of Katherine Anne Porter's short stories, *Pale Horse, Pale Rider,* open across her chest—something she had apparently found in our bookshelves and figured that with such a title, it *had* to be a horse book. (Undaunted by her disappointment in this regard, though, she'd gone to the American School's librarian the next day and earnestly recommended it as a good book for her eight-year-old schoolmates.)

But she wasn't completely single-minded. She made occasional forays into more cosmic issues, trying always to find a pattern, any pattern, for the curious and inexplicable goings-on around her. The Spanish-language half of her third-grade school program that year, for instance, included biology, which seemed to intrigue her. I remember an Indian summer afternoon when she and her older siblings, just home from school, were eating with us out in the *jacal* in the backyard. The trees, the tall bamboo, and the garden growth that shielded us from the rest of the yard made us feel as though we were all in a small, quiet world of our own, and after a long, contemplative silence in this quiet place Emily, apropos of nothing special, said, "Isn't it funny? Everything in the world has the same things happen to it. Cells, plants, fish, animals, people . . . You're born, and you're young and strong, and you reproduce, and then you get old and weak, and then you die. I think

I'm different, but I'm not; I'm exactly the same as everything else."

Hugo paled, clearly threatened by the concept. "That's not true!" he said. "Everyone in this whole world is different from every other person. You're unique. And don't you forget it!"

Emmie pondered him a moment, as puzzled as ever about grownups and their reactions, and then silently went back to her lunch.

By and large, though, it was clear that if Emmie identified with anything, it was horses. After her repeated pleas for a horse of her own fell on deaf ears, she offered a compromise suggestion: "Well . . . if I can't have a horse . . . can I at least have a *saddle?*"

So at last, the summer she turned nine, it seemed time to do something about her fixation. I'd learned that one General Mariles, of Mexico's prizewinning Olympic equestrian team, had a riding school and stables at the far edge of the city, and when the rainy season had ended, I signed Emmie and Mary up for lessons.

Ah, but that was only the first step. The girls were required, it seemed, to work out in tailored breeches and riding boots and helmets; real live horses would have to wait while I took the girls to the tailor and boot maker recommended by the "Club Equestre." At no small investment, they were equipped, and only then, when they were turned out like proper little English jockeys, did the lessons begin.

To my utter horror, I learned that these would include learning to *jump*. During the hour's wait in my car twice a week outside the stables, while the girls were getting their instruction, I went nearly out of my mind with anxiety. Jumping, for heaven's sake! To keep my mind, for that hour at least, off the hazards facing them, I brought along and read our friend Ralph Roeder's early book, *Man of the Renaissance*. That led to other books about the period and finally to a full-blown interest in Italy in general. It didn't help much with the anxiety, but I learned a lot about Italy.

It was during one such waiting period, when I happened to be between books, that I found myself in a conversation with one of the stable hands and learned that the stable had for sale a little Oaxacan filly, of a breed descended from the small Spanish horses brought over from Spain during the Conquest and since let run wild in the Oaxacan Sierra. I was taken inside the stable and introduced to this small, brown-black, bright-eyed creature and found that her purchase price was remarkably low—about twenty-five dollars American. And when I

discussed it with Hugo at home, we decided that maybe this little animal would make a fine Christmas surprise for Emmie. She (the horse)
was small enough to be kept in the lot next door to our house and also
small enough that if Emmie fell off, the ground wasn't very far down.

That settled, our other preparations for Christmas went on as usual,
and a few days before the big day, the pretty little horse was delivered
by arrangement to the backyard of a friend of Hugo's who lived nearby.
Christmas Eve, with the sand tarts made and the wrapped presents
piled under the tree, I wound up our customary reading of *A Christmas Carol,* which by now the children knew almost as well as Hugo
and I did; we helped the children Scotch-tape their stockings to the
wall above the fireplace, got the younger children into bed and the
older ones at least into the general proximity of bed, and headed out
"for a little walk." We were, of course, bound for our neighbor's to
retrieve the new member of the household and walk her home along
the dark streets of San Angel Inn. She was on a lead and didn't make
too many objections when we brought her in through our gates and
around the house to the back, where we tethered her securely to a post
of the *jacal* in the dark yard and left her with a handful of oats to
munch on.

Congratulating ourselves that we'd managed to smuggle in Emmie's
major present undiscovered, we came indoors and resumed our regular Christmas duties—filling the children's stockings. What we didn't
know but would learn years later was what was going on in the younger
girls' bedroom upstairs in the meantime.

Emmie and Debbie, far too excited by the thought of tomorrow's
festivities to sleep, were still wide awake when they heard a loud and
unmistakable whinny from the darkness outside. "Mommy!" they
shouted. "What's that?"

Susie, in on the plot, hurried into their room to tell them that our
dog, Pablo, had gotten out of the gates and bitten the horse of a passing *leñero* (one of the rascally characters who go from house to house
selling firewood and cheating on the count). The two younger girls
exchanged a look and pretended politely to accept the explanation.
But they were not deceived.

On Christmas morning, however, their parents *were.* Emmie and
Debbie didn't want us to know that our ruse had been seen through;
they didn't want us to be disappointed, so they did a wonderful job of

feigning surprise when the little horse was introduced. That apart, though, there was no feigning Emmie's very real delight at having, finally, her own horse, which she named Dandy.

Dandy seemed initially to be settling in nicely; she followed Emmie and her sisters about the yard like a puppy, pleased by the petting, the oats, and the attention. And all in all, with everybody having tried to fool everyone else but with the centerpiece now firmly established as a family member, it was a lovely Christmas morning.

Alas. Within the next few days, Dandy's true character began to emerge. She was a small, unpredictable, mean-tempered witch of a horse. She couldn't be ridden yet because she hadn't been broken (it never occurred to me to ask about that), and before long she took to biting anyone who went into the lot to bring her feed or water—including Emmie.

Within weeks, we sent her back to the stable to be gentled.

By the time she was delivered to us again, we had bought a small secondhand saddle and watched from the edge of the lot as Emmie saddled her up and mounted for her first ride.

Dandy bucked her off. Emmie picked herself up and started to mount again. Dandy avoided her and cantered to the far end of the field, where she stood watching, tail switching. Emmie tried again to mount, and the whole process was repeated, except that now Dandy began to bite and kick. Boots and breeches and lessons aboard General Mariles's well-behaved stable horses had not prepared Emmie for dealing with a creature as just plain ornery as that dainty little beast.

It was only the first of many disparities Emmie would encounter between the dream and the reality. Six months after our departure from Mexico, at our first breakfast in an English hotel, she would find on the menu kippered herring and, having read about them for years in all our English children's classics, order them in much anticipation. But when they arrived, she would discover with dismay that herring are filled with countless tiny, prickly bones. They're not so much a food as an obstacle course.

But that was still well in the future. At the moment, here in Mexico, though she had not yet found that there could be bones in your kipper, Emmie was learning the hard way a universal lesson: that it was possible to lavish love and tenderness on another creature (man or beast) and not have it love you back.

Chapter Twenty-five

IT WAS EARLY in the new year. Mike, who had arrived home for Christmas vacation bringing a copy of Ginsberg's *Howl,* a bamboo back scratcher for Debbie, and for Nancy a blue-and-white scarf that said Columbia, had gone back to college. And Hugo's father had written suggesting that if we were indeed planning to come to California over the girls' winter holiday, we should visit them in Palm Springs, where they were living now; they could put us up at a nearby motel.

Actually, we had been planning the trip because we did want to see Hugo's family, none of whom, we were aware, were getting any younger. His mother, Margaret, of course, had visited us several times, and she and the children adored each other, but Frank and his wife barely knew our older girls and had never even met the younger ones. And since the death of my own parents, Hugo and I had had an uneasy sense of Time's wingéd footsteps. In another year, Frank would be seventy, and though he and Hugo wrote each other funny, joking letters, Hugo still had a feeling—though he rarely spoke of it—that their relationship was still somehow unresolved, and there wasn't all that much time to put it right.

Also, without quite knowing it, we may have thought of this trip as a testing of the political waters. There'd been a major change up north: we, among others, had been granted passports.

We had applied for them twice before during the decade but had been refused each time by a form letter from the Department of State,

Passport Division, citing our beliefs and associations and saying they didn't think allowing us to travel abroad was "in the best interests of the United States." In June of 1958, however, in the cases of artist Rockwell Kent and a psychiatrist named Walter Briehl, the Supreme Court had voted 5–4 to reverse the right of the State Department to refuse passports on such grounds and stated, in a decision written by William O. Douglas, that "the right of exit is a personal right included within the word 'liberty' as used in the Fifth Amendment."

For us at the time, the matter was more symbolic than practical; we didn't need passports to travel between Mexico and the States, and we had no plans to go elsewhere—but someday we might. Anyway, we agreed with Justice Douglas that there was a principle involved. So once more, we applied.

I have no memory of that particular trip to the American Embassy. I had forced myself to brave U.S. officialdom on earlier occasions to register the births of Debbie and Becky and had each time been so panicked by the experience that I'd come away drenched in perspiration. Why? Were the embassy clerks and officials really as grim as they seemed, or was I simply being paranoid? What danger did I think awaited me within those walls? Or was it just a flashback to that childhood fear of being sent to the principal's office? Whatever the cause, I had been terrified almost to the point of paralysis on each of those earlier visits. This third visit, however, must have been so traumatic that I've blotted it out altogether. But on the evidence of a page in our photo album, with a formal pose of Hugo and me and the girls labeled Passport Photo, Oct. 1958, I know there must have been one awful day when we all went in to file the necessary forms. We had probably restored our spirits afterward by going downstairs to Sanborn's restaurant (which Hugo used to refer to as *Rincón de Gringo* ("Gringo Corner") to have restorative martinis for us grown-ups and ice cream for the children, in the shadow of those lovely Tamayo watermelon murals that on purely social occasions I'd always loved.

In any event, with our "right to travel" now miraculously restored to us and with the money from Hugo's new screenplay for George Pepper (of which more in a later chapter) to cover the plane fare, we were beginning to arrange for our all-family trip north—when we realized that if we took Ramona along to look after Becky, she would need her own passport. So, bowing to necessity, Ramona journeyed down to Mexico's large, gloomy department of *"relaciones exteriores"* and discovered to her dismay that the document would have to bear her legal surname, not the one we'd always known her by. Which in turn precipitated a painful (for her) little scene in our living room soon after.

She came in from the kitchen that afternoon with the little navy blue booklet in her hand and a troubled look on her face. "Señora," she said, "I must confess my shame." She used the word *pena*, which in Mexico means shame or embarrassment or disgrace, or sometimes a mixture of all three. And she showed me the name on her passport: Uribe, her maiden name. "I was not married to the father of my son," she said.

Bless her heart. In a country where so many of the population were born out of wedlock that even the Mexican constitution prohibits any legal distinction between legitimacy and illegitimacy, it certainly seemed to us no great thing, but Ramona treasured her respectability and felt she had to explain. Carlos's father, she said, already *had* a wife and children when she had begun her relationship with him. He had been very good about helping her support the baby, however, and had finally brought him into his own household to be raised with his other children. At about this point Ramona had joined her evangelical church, stopped seeing the gentleman, and begun to feel that there was something shameful about the whole episode.

We had known that Carlos, now grown and himself the father of three children, was a bus driver in Jalisco; he and his family lived on a little piece of property outside Guadalajara that Ramona had been buying on time over the last several years. It had a few fruit trees, and a well, and room for chickens, and, one summer, a baby pig being raised for slaughter. Ramona planned to retire there when she was no longer able to work, and during a recent vacation had even built a room for herself so she wouldn't have to sleep in the kitchen when she went home to visit. But that this little family group, with whom she spent all of her vacations and from whom she returned each year browned, rested, happy, and laden with presents for all of us, represented a period of her life that even to this day she looked back on with *"pena,"* was astonishing to me. She'd been with us almost eight years, and yet how little we really knew about her! I assured her I didn't think it mattered in the least, and much relieved, she went off about her business. Before long I heard her singing "Rock of Ages" in Spanish as she started getting dinner.

On the other hand, Hugo and I had never confessed our own *pena*— our political problems—to her either, and never did. Politics were never mentioned between us, and only in retrospect have I wondered if she knew.

In any event, when we finally embarked on our own family visit north that year, she journeyed up by train and bus to meet us in Tijuana and be with us on all our stops, finding a branch of her church in Los Angeles and falling so in love with the efficiency of the States that her own country paled in her eyes, and when the whole trip was over, though she never managed to learn English, all she dreamed of was the day when we might move back to the States forever and take her with us.

Our own view of our homeland, anno Domini 1959, was more cautious.

On our first stop, in Hollywood, it seemed clear that our friends' professional situations hadn't changed much. Those of our writer friends who had managed to edge back into the industry still worked fairly steadily but for minimum salaries and under other names. But with the exception of Jeff Corey, still not allowed on-screen but whose new career as a drama coach was now thriving, the actors we knew were still banned altogether from the screen and were still driving bakery or delicatessen trucks (or, in the case of one longtime character actor, working as a barber).

Whatever their craft, though, blacklisted families were scattered about the ever-expanding city now, seeing less and less of each other, and a fear of further persecution had driven everyone out of political action. Some, to be sure, had sought fellowship in the Unitarian Church or Jewish community centers, but for the most part, as the Coreys told us, "we make our lives in our own backyards."

And driving past Hollywood High School, on the busiest corner in Hollywood, where our own older children would have been students if we hadn't fled to Mexico, feeling our eyes smart with smog and seeing the high schoolers eating their lunches on the all but treeless patches of lawn adjacent to the teeming streets, made me wonder again about the gains and losses of exile for our own children. I asked Hope Corey, when I saw her on that visit, how public schools in Hollywood had proven for their children. "Oh—it hasn't been too bad," she said. "They survive."

I wasn't sure "surviving" was enough.

After our ritual roast-beef-and-Yorkshire-pudding dinner with Margaret and Freddie in their tiny Hollywood hillside apartment and a flight to Berkeley to see my brother and his family, we made our way down to Palm Springs, where Hugo's father and stepmother spent their winters now on Smoke Tree Ranch, another restricted community like their beachside place.

Truly a "well-run desert," this part of Palm Springs boasted simply designed but expensive ranch houses in sagebrush blue-greens, and landscaping of desert plants, and a guard at the gate to keep out undesirables. There was a clean, clear view of Taquitz mountain, snowcapped, and a faint smell of sagebrush in the cold air, and once again I had the feeling, which I always had in Palm Springs, that it was a kind of exquisite vacuum.

Frank and Ethel, their earlier domestic problems now smoothed over, had bought a small, attractive bungalow but had lately built onto it to make room for Ethel's daughter, who had come home with her little boy to live with them after her divorce. Jamie, now a thin, blond, freckled just-turned-three, was Frank's first experience with a very small child in residence since he'd left Canada when Hugo was a year old. And remembering Frank's anxiety whenever they had invited us to Thanksgiving dinner when our children were little (including sheets of plastic spread under our children's chairs to protect the dining-room carpet) and his less than enthusiastic response to the birth of his grandchildren in the first place (Mary had been three months old before he had even come to *look* at her), we were curious to see how this living arrangement was working out.

To our surprise, it seemed to be working well. Acutely conscious of Frank's need for peace and quiet, Jamie's mother and grandmother made sure that even at this young age, Jamie was a well-behaved little boy—a bit tense, a bit restrained, perhaps, but never a nuisance. During the whole week we spent in and out of the Palm Springs house, I don't remember ever seeing him misbehave, though I do remember hearing once a thin wail from his bedroom that, even at that distance, seemed to cause Frank considerable nervousness.

Nevertheless, Frank seemed profoundly, almost foolishly, devoted to the child. "It's strange," he confided to me, "considering that his father was one of the few people in the world I really hated. . . . But he's such a nice little boy. . . ."

He made a conscious effort with our children, altogether charming our susceptible Emmie in the process; he joked with them and set up all-day chuck-wagon rides for them at the Smoke Tree stables with the neighbors' children while Hugo and I, out from under wraps at last, were introduced to friends and taken to cocktail parties. Frank and Hugo had long talks over Dubonnet cocktails and a good deal of laughter.

Then, one day late in our week's stay there, when Hugo and I were about to leave to rejoin Ramona and the girls at the motel and were en route to the front door with our coats, we passed the guest bathroom, where, through the open door, we saw Frank on his knees beside the toilet, trying to teach Jamie how to urinate standing up, "like a big boy."

It was an unimportant, domestic little moment, but it was also so intimate, so familial, that Frank seemed embarrassed by it. He looked up at Hugo with an apologetic smile. " 'Grandfather . . . ,' " he said.

Hugo said nothing. We took our leave and drove back to the motel, where, with Ramona in charge, Becky and the younger girls were playing with a set of plastic cowboys and Indians we'd gotten for them. Hugo went straight to the bedroom and sank down on the edge of the bed and buried his forehead in his hand. He was silent for a long moment. Then he looked up at me, ashen faced. " *'Grandfather!'* " he said.

A few days later, we were back in Mexico. But Hugo had the certain knowledge now that his stepsister's child was already filling the place in Frank's life that he, Hugo, had wanted so desperately as a little boy to occupy. He was also sure now that he and his children would be effectively disinherited (as, to a less absolute degree, the rest of Frank's own family members would be)—not in anger, but simply because in Frank's thoughts and concern and care, they had all been displaced.

Chapter Twenty-six

IT WAS ALMOST the end of Susie's junior year now, and she had made up her mind about college. Radcliffe.

She had chosen it partly, I suppose, because her grandmother had gone there to graduate school more than half a century before. And partly—why not?—because it was a challenge.

I was delighted at the choice; it seemed the perfect match of girl and college. She was a thoughtful student, serious and conscientious, and though she grew steadily more beautiful, there was also something Victorian, almost bluestocking, about her—a sense of privacy and integrity that seemed to cry out for a New England college. She was putting her hair up now, and still wore no makeup, and was still so shy that most of the boys at the American School were quickly discouraged from pursuing her. But she was also winning the school's annual prize for "outstanding student" with regularity, editing the literary magazine, and winning a short-story award from the States' nationwide *Scholastic* magazine, and her fellow students kept electing her to offices.

So getting Susie into Radcliffe on the early notification plan where the student, putting all her scholastic eggs in one basket, applies to no other college and is notified by Christmastime of her acceptance or rejection, became the family's current project. Once again, as with Mike, I was filling out forms, rounding up recommendations, and driving our own child and those of our friends to school on various Saturday mornings to take the college boards. We had been true to the promise we'd made ourselves earlier and had used my inheritance from my mother only for Mike's college thus far, with the balance still set aside for Susie and then, whatever was left, for Mary. We now felt, more strongly than ever, that blacklist or no blacklist, we would certainly earn enough between us in the future to educate the rest of the children.

Or so we told ourselves.

In any event, it was while our attention was thus occupied and we weren't really worrying, for a wonder, about Susie's social life that the magic moment came.

One of the boys from the American School whom I'll call "Davy" had turned up after *comida* one afternoon to visit, and before the day was out, our small Debbie, then about six, came to us in consternation. "Mommy!" she said. "The most terrible thing! I went in the hall and that boy was *kissing* Susie!"

And after he'd gone home, Susie had come to the supper table wearing a huge, loose-fitting gold signet ring.

Being Susie, she made no reference to it, so we had no idea how she felt about this young man. The wakening of her interest in boys was something I'd been awaiting so impatiently (and often vigorously promoting) that we should have been delighted. Certainly Davy was a very presentable sample of the genre: well scrubbed, even featured, his blond hair in a short, military trim, socially sure and without any doubts whatever that Susie found him as attractive as he found her.

But in subsequent days, as he began to establish a beachhead at our house and to take over our dinner-table conversations, Hugo and I began to have misgivings.

The first glimmering of a possible problem came to us one late afternoon when I arrived home from a trip downtown with Mary, who had outgrown her riding boots and had to be fitted for a bigger pair. Davy asked me whom we'd gone to for the boots, and when I told him said with delighted recognition, "Oh, yes, he's *my* boot maker!"

Hugo and I glanced uneasily at each other. We had never expected to hear that line outside Thackeray—or maybe Noel Coward.

He bore the surname of one of the early heroes of Mexico's 1910 revolution, but there, we suspected, the resemblance ended. Aiming polite questions across the dinner table, we learned more. His father was an executive with one of the big American/multinational firms in Mexico; the family was clearly well-to-do and had, with Davy, done a good deal of traveling in Europe . . .

And then something else came out. Davy couldn't come see Susie on Saturday, he mentioned, because that was the day he played polo.

Polo? Our Susie was going with a boy who played *polo?*

What had we done wrong?

Socially, he was beyond reproach. He brought Susie flowers and to us, small, well-chosen gifts. On Hugo's birthday, having discovered among our gramophone records Hugo's collection of Spanish folk music, he arrived with a lovely, hard-to-find record of *jotas*. And whatever else Susie might see in him, I couldn't fault his appearance; I'm sure the American School never boasted a boy with a more dazzling smile, clearer skin, more disciplined muscles, better manners . . .

Or a more absolute sense of privilege.

Our dismay grew. But we had waited so long for Susie to find someone she liked or could at least tolerate that we knew we had to keep our opinions to ourselves. One night after a particularly trying dinner-table conversation, Hugo and I came upstairs to read (because Davy and Susie had taken over the living room), and Hugo said wistfully as he laid out his pajamas, "You know? We've been wrong about Susie. All this time we thought she was an intellectual, and what she really was, was a princess."

Mike, in the meantime, was nearing the end of his freshman year at Columbia. He had arrived in New York filled with excitement and anticipation, but culture shock at the slums and ugliness of Morningside Heights, the bitter weather, the competitiveness of his fellow students had quickly overwhelmed him. He didn't tell us how unhappy he was, but if illness is a metaphor, his last winter's case of double pneumonia should have been ample proof. Leaving behind the warmth and sun of Palmas 81 and Acapulco and Las Estacas must have seemed, on some deep level, like expulsion from paradise. He had also left behind the affection and admiration of family, friends, teachers—and to ace a course at college was so much harder than in high school! Worst of all, we learned later, was his uneasy knowledge that Hugo and I had limited funds for his and his siblings' education, and it would be unthinkable to let us down. . . .

By the time spring came to New York, however, he was beginning to adjust. He was finding his roommates congenial (one in fact was a budding concert violinist, given to practicing the whole of Tchaikowsky's D Major concerto at his open window on balmy spring evenings). He'd made a few new friends and was occasionally part of a floating poker game that met in his dorm's second-floor broom closet. He had taken a few courses that he liked, and with the used Rolleiflex we'd bought for him last Christmas from Hugo's photographer friend Walter Reuther, he was developing a keen sense of composition, and the campus paper was printing his stills.

So, by the time the term ended and Hugo had come north to re- search a possible documentary about the Wright brothers (another good idea that never reached the screen), Mike's spirits were much improved. En route home, father and son had detoured to North Carolina, where Mike achieved some fine pictures of the sand dunes and work sheds at Kitty Hawk, and when they reached Mexico City by the end of June, Hugo was feeling, momentarily, mellow, and Mike was his old exuber- ant self. And soon, with two of Mike's college friends arriving by invi- tation to stay with us, plus the teenage daughter of two of our stateside friends, we were plunged once more into our regular summer whirl— complicated, this summer, by the almost incessant presence of Susie's young raja.

Our private opinion of this young man hadn't improved. Davy's political pronouncements were becoming, if anything, steadily more reactionary (could he have been testing us?), but for Susie's sake we bit our tongues and said nothing. Debbie reported that she'd been listen- ing recently to a Paul Robeson record in the living room when Davy had come in. "Who's that?" he said of the singer. "Sounds like a nigger." And he strode across the room to turn it off.

It was growing harder and harder to keep our mouths shut—but worse, *how could Susie stand him?*

And then, just as suddenly as he had arrived in our lives, he vanished.

One evening in July, as we were all responding to Ramona's notifica- tion that *cena* was *"servida,"* Susie arrived at the table alone. I asked her where Davy was. She said he'd gone home. Actually, she admitted, she'd *told* him to go.

But no elaboration. I realized she was not wearing his ring. "I gave it back to him," she said. I learned weeks later that she had *thrown* it at him.

Naturally, Susie being Susie, details were hard to come by. But eventually we learned that she hadn't liked him all that much in the first place; he'd simply been so persistent, she hadn't felt she had a choice and, like her brother at an earlier age, was just too polite to say no. On the crucial afternoon, when Davy had unwisely tried to make her jealous by phoning another girl on our phone and talking affectionately to her, Susie had decided the whole situation was ridiculous, torn off his ring, thrown it at him, and ordered him out of the house.

The relief at the dinner table was almost palpable. She herself seemed delivered of a great burden, and so were we.

Thanks to the American School grapevine, it was known almost immediately around town that Susie and Davy had broken up, and within days she was asked out by the boy she really *did* like, a gentle, good-looking young classmate named Miguel, whose father had been an official in the Spanish republican government and who now worked for the United Nations.

By the end of summer Susie and Miguel were going steady, and in her own quiet way, Susie was altogether content.

Word about college came the week before Christmas.

Once again, we were around the dinner table having *comida* when we heard Mr. Flores's *pito* out on the street. The mail had already come that morning, so we knew this must be special delivery. I went out to the gate; Mr. Flores handed me a fat envelope, I signed for it, and he bicycled off.

The envelope was addressed to Susie, and the return address was Radcliffe College.

I brought it back to the table and gave it to her. We all held our breath as she ripped it open. At first she didn't say anything. Then, with the faintest of smiles and only a tiny wrinkle of her nose to show her pleasure, she said, to nobody in particular, "I'm accepted."

So in any event Christmas would have been a major celebration. But this year there was an unexpected addition.

Again it began with the gate bell, which Isabel answered. From the window over the drive I could see she was talking at the open gate to someone slight, dark, and not too well dressed, and I wondered at the length of the discussion. In a few moments, however, she came back to report that a *muchacho* was here to talk to Hugo. One of the *beis-bolistas,* she said.

It turned out to be Fidel Ruíz, the small, direct, earnest former captain of the Little Giants—he who had pitched the semifinals game that had sent the team to the finals for that first wonderful championship contest. But what was he doing here in Mexico City alone, so far from Monterrey and his parents?

He had come down by bus, he said, to see about school.

I figured he must be fourteen by now, maybe almost fifteen, and I knew that after the boys' first triumph two years ago, a private school in Monterrey had offered them all scholarships for *secundaria* (junior high school), and the local Sears Roebuck had donated the respectable clothing they'd need. But that two-year program had just ended, and I suppose Fidel's chances of getting into his overcrowded public *preparatoria* (high school) were slim. So he'd come here, he told us, to visit the military school in one of the city suburbs along the Desierto de los Leones road above us to see if the army, in return for his future enlistment as an army engineer, would put him through *preparatoria* and engineering school. But he'd found the school's offices closed for the holidays.

He was still slight of stature, but how he had matured since the documentary! There was a kind of confidence about him now, a sureness, not a superfluous word or gesture. But of course, this was Mexico, where the children of the poor were lucky to get through primary school and, if they did, were considered almost as adults and expected as a matter of course to get a job to help support their parents. Touched, flattered even, that he had found his way to our house, Hugo and I suggested he stay with us through Christmas—though we'd be leaving a few days after for Acapulco, to meet friends who were arriving from the States. We made up the daybed in the living room and brought him towels and a pair of Mike's pajamas (much too big), and the next morning the girls and I rushed downtown to find Christmas presents to put under the tree for him.

For the first time since we'd arrived in Mexico, our holiday festivities were conducted almost entirely in Spanish.

We also found, as Christmas came and went and he fitted quietly into the household, that our respect for him grew, as did our affection. When it came time to leave for our meeting in Acapulco, we delivered him to the Peppers' to stay till the military school's offices opened and felt a pang of loss as we left him at the curb in front of the Peppers' apartment.

But after that we lost touch with him. In Acapulco, and for several months after, Hugo was busy on a picture, and I was absorbed in the lives of our own children, and he, apparently, was no letter writer. We never found out if the army agreed to his proposal and did indeed put him through school or what became of him in the years that followed. I only hope that if by the wildest chance this book falls into his hands and he has acquired enough English to read it or knows someone who has, he will learn what a special addition his quiet presence made to our Christmas that year. We wondered (I still do) about him often, hoping against hope that his being, however briefly, one of Mexico's local heroes—if not his own integrity, his directness, and common sense—helped him make his way out of the poverty he was born to and finally into his country's still small but struggling middle class.

By now it was late spring again, and Susie's graduation was coming on apace.

The lovely news, not altogether unanticipated by her parents, was that her grade point average determined that she would be valedictorian of her graduating class that year.

The reverse of the coin was that she had been simultaneously felled by a bad case of mononucleosis. She was running a high fever, her throat was too sore for her to speak, and she was confined to bed and altogether too sick even to think about composing the commemorative address.

There was also something she *didn't* know and wouldn't until many years later.

Soon after the school had notified her about being valedictorian, I'd had a phone call from an English teacher she'd had in earlier years—a nice woman, the mother of a boy in Susie's class who had taken rather a shine to Susie but, being even more shy than she, had never asked her out.

The teacher/mother sounded flustered, uncertain, a bit upset. Her son, she said, would be salutatorian at graduation. I offered congratulations. But it seemed there was a rub. Her boy was one of a large family, she worked to help support them all, but they would all need scholarships to get through college. Knowing only that Hugo and I had come from Hollywood (but not why, apparently), she blundered on: "You'll always be able to get your children into college. Mine have to have scholarships to go. . . ." And then, the point of the call: "Being valedictorian would help my boy so much to get a scholarship at one of the good schools," she said, all in a rush. Would Susie be willing to step aside and let him be valedictorian instead?

I was stunned. I knew her son worked hard and was a serious student and a deserving young man. . . . In fact, I was almost dead sure he didn't know anything about this phone call and would never have condoned it for a minute if he had. And my heart bled for this poor mother.

But on the other hand . . . !

I stammered something about having to discuss it with Susie before I could answer, promised to call back—and took the problem straight to Hugo, at work at his typewriter in his study.

He was enraged. Furious. "How *dare* she ask a thing like that! How dare she?"

Lamely, I relayed the poor mother's reasons. "I told her I'd have to speak to Susie first, of course—"

"My God, you're not going to tell Susie about this, are you? You're out of your mind! You know her. She'd feel she'd have to say yes. Even if she said no, how do you think she'd feel? It would ruin graduation for her!" I had never seen him so angry. "How could you even *think* of asking her? Are you crazy?"

Somehow his anger had progressed beyond the issue; the issue had become my disloyalty to my own daughter, or perhaps my thickheadedness, or my cowardice, at contemplating the suggestion even for a minute. Yes, one could be indignant at such a request, but the level of his outrage bewildered me. (In fact, I'd suspected the school wouldn't allow it anyway even if we *had* agreed; I just wanted Hugo to get me off the hook with this poor woman, and here he was, yelling at me. . . .)

And so I made the return call and with deep embarrassment explained that we felt we couldn't ask Susie to make such a sacrifice. The mother, on the other end of the line, sounded close to tears but resigned too, as though she hadn't thought it would work but was willing to try anything to get her son a better chance at a scholarship.

I said nothing to Susie about the matter; and our lives went back to normal, or what passed for normal for us those years—though Hugo's outburst lingered at the back of my mind, with one or two similar ones, reminding me, subconsciously at least, that he was becoming capable of a good deal of anger and I should try not to aggravate him. . . .

At last, the morning of the big day, Susie—still sick, still fevered— went to work on her speech. The source of her theme was Joseph Wood Krutch's book *The Measure of Man,* in which the author challenges modern man's passive surrender of his own sense of free will in the face of the determinist philosophies of Darwin, Marx (!), Freud, and Skinner and urges us instead to take charge of our personal and social destinies while we still can. The book had become a family favorite with us and, still sitting up in bed, and with the help of a good deal of aspirin, Susie was able to translate Krutch's thesis into her own words.

Then it was time to get dressed and ready, and we all set off for school, Susie with her penciled pages in hand, the flush of fever still on her cheeks. . . .

By midafternoon there she stood on the stage of the school's multipurpose building, looking lovely and willowy and almost Grecian in her cap and gown as she delivered her speech. Unfortunately her throat was still so sore, she could hardly speak, and the microphone was broken, so only those of the audience in the first few rows could hear what she said, but to our proud parental ears it was a stunning speech, and at the end of it, one of the fathers, sitting just in front of us, turned to his wife and said, "Now, there's a speech that *says* something!"

I have no memory of even seeing, in the audience, the teacher who had phoned me, but her son had delivered a thoughtful and intelligent salutatory speech earlier in the ceremony. Then there'd been diplomas and awards, and after the band had struck up "Recessional" and the graduates had filed out the backstage exit for a celebration rendezvous with their parents in the school cafeteria that Susie was too sick to face, Hugo and I left quickly by the main exit to wait for her on the school's front steps to take her home and put her to bed.

There we came upon the typing teacher, another nice woman whom I knew only slightly but whose class both Mike and Susie had taken, as had most of the school's students at one time or another. Half concealed in the shadows of the building, she was crying quietly to herself. When she saw us, she tried to stop, embarrassed. "Isn't that awful?" she said, trying to make light of it and wiping her eyes. "I do this every year. I never get used to it."

The truth was, neither did we.

Chapter Twenty-seven

MORE OR LESS concurrently with Susie's belated growing up and our distress at her first suitor, Hugo had begun a new picture.

In spring of 1958, George Pepper had come on Peter Matthiessen's story *Travelin Man* in a back issue of *Harper's* magazine: the story of a black man who has broken out of jail and fled back to one of the Carolina islands he had known in his youth, where he is hunted by and in turn stalks a poaching gamekeeper. Hugo and Buñuel agreed it could be used as a springboard for a more elaborate story, George arranged for its purchase, and collaboration began on the script, which would be released under the title *The Young One*.

As a longtime member of the Writers Guild, I'm aware that writers have long deplored the director's claim to be the *"auteur"* of a film; how can anyone but the writer or writers claim initial authorship? But in the case of Buñuel and a few others Hugo had worked with (Renoir and Losey, for instance), the claim was justified: Buñuel *always* worked jointly with his writer on the screenplay from beginning to end, so the finished script was as much his creation as the writer's. In Hugo's experience, collaborating with Luis meant a several weeks' stay at a spa, often San José Purua in Michoacán, where there were no interruptions and the planning and writing of the script went on at a concentrated and intensive pace. It also meant, for Hugo, another heady period of time with one of the most offbeat, creative minds in the history of motion pictures, and he always came back from these stays fascinated and awed, both by the man and by the filmmaker.

This time he came home with his mind very much on certain

problems the script posed, which he didn't discuss. I would learn why as time went on.

In Buñuel's autobiography, *My Last Sigh*, published posthumously more than two decades later, Buñuel would speak of the picture as "anti-Manichean." In his personal life the kindest and most considerate husband, father, friend, he was the compleat iconoclast in both his conversation and his work, and apparently he considered it a triumph to dislodge Hugo from what he considered his "Manichean"—his too moralistic and therefore artistically limiting—attitudes.

But I also surmise (again, with hindsight) that other factors were at work with Hugo too: the stubborn hypertension, undoubtedly aggravated by the amphetamines he was taking; the continued irritations and frustrations of the blacklist; a growing sense of his own mortality (which I, with my talent for denial, dismissed as grossly premature)—or maybe, simply, life itself. In any event, when he gave me the completed script to read a few months later, I found it a strangely disturbing story of good and evil mixed, the black man neither good nor bad, and the redneck gamekeeper now the molester of a thirteen-year-old girl left unexpectedly in his care by the death of her handyman grandfather—but even this dreadful act was treated, in the script, with a touch of understanding and compassion.

I read the script with a nagging unease, an inexplicable anxiety. Why had Hugo and Buñuel written it this way? How could they empathize, even for a moment, with such a man—and expect the audience to feel for him too? Hugo's compassion, along with his wit, were the two qualities I had always found his most endearing, but his whole life long there had been an uprightness about him too, a profound sense of honor. Now, winding up my reading of the script and unsure how much of it was Hugo's and how much Buñuel's, I felt a curious fear that Hugo was moving off intellectually in a direction I was no longer able, or perhaps willing, to follow.

In fact, with our political beliefs still being sorely tested, and now with Hugo seeming to countenance (in the script) such a violation of his own sense of right and wrong, I had a sense that the very ground I stood on was shifting.

But at the time, these feelings were too vague, too inchoate, to put into words; my critical response to Hugo about the script was cautious and polite. What I couldn't explain to him was that the screenplay seemed somehow to represent some sort of threat to all I'd structured my life on, and I didn't know what to make of it or how to deal with it.

So I said as little as possible. And life went on.

George went up to New York to cast the picture, and we were pleased to hear from him that Zachary Scott, an actor we'd always respected, would play the gamekeeper. Now the other parts were cast, and preparations for production moved forward rapidly. About a week before the picture was to start shooting, Scott and his actress wife, Ruth Ford, arrived in Mexico, and at a small gathering to greet them, Hugo, afraid that Scott might withdraw from the picture if he learned it had been written by a blacklistee, was introduced as that convenient Canadian oilman and investor (first born on location for *Crusoe*), "Mr. Addis."

But a couple of days after this, when Hugo and I were having a courtesy lunch with the Scotts at their hotel, Ruth broke into an encomium on the script. "I was telling Zachary when I read it," she said, "that now he'll have made *two* pictures that were little masterpieces—this one and *The Southerner*."

Hugo's eyes met mine. Years ago, working with Jean Renoir, Hugo had written the adaptation and first draft screenplay of *The Southerner*, from George Sessions Perry's novel *Hold Autumn in Your Hand*. But then, discovering that Renoir, whom he idolized, had hired someone else to rewrite behind him, he had been so offended and so hurt that he had quit the job and taken his name off the script. Later, however, when the picture was previewed and he saw how much of his work had been retained, he had accepted an adaptation credit. (We did not find out, at the time, the name of the writer who worked with Renoir on the revisions, but years after, I discovered that it was a bona fide southerner named William Faulkner.) In any event, Ruth's praise was too sweet to ignore, and Hugo owned up to his work on both screenplays and our reason for being in Mexico.

Far from being upset at the revelation, the Scotts took us to their bosoms, and from that day on, the whole company became a warm, close-knit community.

—Fortunately, because though the interiors, shot on a local sound stage, went smoothly enough, the location shooting, on the verges of a lagoon in a jungle south of Acapulco (doubling as a Carolina swamp), proved fraught with problems: heat, union trouble(!), and logistics.

Finally, however, the camera work was finished, on time and on budget. As always, Buñuel had been so careful with his scheduling and so economic of footage that very little postshooting editing was needed, and it seemed only weeks between the company's wrap-up good-bye party in Mexico City (with, as always on such occasions, protestations of eternal friendship) and our first viewing of the finished cut in a local projection room.

Using Leon Bibb's recording of *Sinner Man* as its theme music over the credit titles, the completed picture had a strange, moody, almost hypnotic quality, and once again, watching it, I found myself reacting as I had to the reading of the script: I was far more disturbed by its amorality than I should be. It was as though I'd heard a far-off roll of thunder that might or might not presage a storm: too far away to worry about, but there was something, somewhere, that was trying to tell me all was not well.

By summer of 1960, *The Young One* was getting an art-house release in the States and a more general release in Mexico and abroad. And though it didn't make much money, it was sent as Mexico's entry to the Cannes Film Festival, where the jury unanimously voted it a special award for "extraordinary merit."

The screenwriting credit still listed, as Buñuel's cowriter, Hugo's pseudonymous alter ego, "H. B. Addis."

Poor Hugo. Even this award, which should have given him a lovely feeling of triumph, could only have served to remind him that the blacklist wasn't over yet. And we still didn't know when it would be.

Chapter Twenty-eight

SINCE BUÑUEL, unlike most directors, preferred to have his screenwriters available during shooting in case dialogue changes were needed, Hugo was still on the set of *The Young One* in January of 1960 when we learned that something astonishing was happening up in Hollywood.

Otto Preminger announced in *The New York Times* that he had hired Dalton Trumbo to write the screenplay of Leon Uris's enormously popular novel *Exodus* and that Trumbo would receive screen credit.

We were almost afraid to believe it. Far removed from the scene of the action and dependent mostly on the gossip that drifted down to us from California (though we could, and that day *did*, race downtown to buy a copy of *The New York Times*), we tried to be realistic. We warned ourselves that this one swallow did not a summer make, but nonetheless, like other blacklistees, we were jubilant.

Albert Maltz's enthusiasm, however, may have been more restrained. Expecting that *he* would be the one to break the blacklist at last, he had spent the last six months quietly researching and writing an adaptation of the book for Preminger, but his screenplay was an encyclopedic, and hence unshootable, four hundred pages. Preminger, with a production date looming, had reassigned the screenplay to Trumbo, who was known for his ability to write fast with no sacrifice of quality. Trumbo had put aside Albert's version and, with Preminger literally standing at his shoulder every day for a month (including Christmas), had restructured the material and written his own script. Preminger had met his deadline. It had been a triumphant race with time.

Soon after, Kirk Douglas, a bit indignant that Preminger had scooped him, announced that his produced but not yet released film of Howard Fast's novel *Spartacus* had also been written by Trumbo, and Trumbo's name was already *on* the film, which was due for release momentarily; Douglas had simply failed to make the announcement until now, that was all.

But what did it matter, we thought, who had been the first to hire a blacklistee openly? If Trumbo was now publicly acknowledged as the writer of two prestigious screenplays, it couldn't be long before the rest of us joined him with our names up there on the screen too, could it?

It could.

Late in March, Margaret Maltz came over to show us a full-page ad that had just appeared in the Hollywood trade papers that seemed to indicate a further thaw. A STATEMENT FROM FRANK SINATRA, it said, announcing that Sinatra, having bought William Bradford Huie's novel about the execution of Private Slovik, "the true story of the only execution of a soldier by the United States Army since the Civil War," had hired Albert Maltz to write the screenplay. Because, continued Sinatra, his conversations with Maltz had convinced him that Maltz's approach to the material would be thoroughly pro-American, and, moreover, "under the Bill of Rights, I was taught that no one may prescribe what shall be orthodox in politics, religion, or matters of opinion . . . As the producer of the film I and I alone will be responsible for it. I accept that responsibility. I ask only that judgment be deferred until the picture is seen."

A later paragraph gave a clue to the kind of pressure that had already been put on Sinatra to change his mind: "I would also like to comment on the attacks from certain quarters on Senator John Kennedy by connecting him with my decision on employing a screenwriter. . . . This type of partisan politics is hitting below the belt.

"I make movies. I do not ask the advice of Senator Kennedy on whom I should hire. Senator Kennedy does not ask me how he should vote in the Senate." (Sinatra was known at the time as a friend and supporter of the Kennedys.)

But this time, any celebrations were premature. Two weeks after Sinatra had flung down the gauntlet, he leaned down to pick it up again. The Maltzes brought us the clipping of another announcement, this time in *The New York Times,* signed by Sinatra and labeled simply STATEMENT.

"In view of the reaction of my family, my friends, and the American public," it said, "I have instructed my attorneys to make a settlement with Albert Maltz and to inform him that he will not write the screenplay for *The Execution of Private Slovik*.

"I had thought the major consideration was whether or not the resulting script would be in the best interests of the United States. Since my conversation with Mr. Maltz had indicated that he has an affirmative, pro-American approach to the story, and since I felt fully capable as producer of enforcing such standards, I have defended my hiring of Mr. Maltz.

"But the American public has indicated it feels the morality of hiring Albert Maltz is the more crucial matter, and I will accept this majority opinion."

So it seemed that though Trumbo no longer had to write under the table, the rest of us, including poor Albert, would have to continue doing so—for a while, at least.

Winding up his work with Buñuel and still seeking projects that could be shot inexpensively in Mexico, Hugo had now begun an adaptation of *Huckleberry Finn* on spec. He had followed his friend Waldo Salt on the Mickey Rooney version during his early days at Metro but now, in retrospect, felt he had missed the essence of the material and wanted another go at it.

That project too ended up on our shelves, but my novella about the father and his daughters during the Mexican revolution surprised us by selling almost by accident to the British magazine *Housewife*. I had sent it to a friend in London; without bothering to mention it to me, she had passed it on to an agent friend who had submitted and sold it. It would run as a three-part serial under the title *Shadows Under the Mexican Sun* and netted two hundred guineas, about $600. Not princely, but a good price for England. More important, it would carry my own name as author, and I was joyous.

Our lives, these first months of 1960, seemed on the surface to be marked only by the changes that time itself occasioned. Little Becky, who had just turned a soft and delicious two, was beginning to clown and to show signs of a wry wit. Debbie, turning seven and secure in the conviction that everyone in the world loved her (and vice versa), went off happily with her older sisters every morning on the school bus, a highly sociable hour-long journey the young passengers enjoyed thoroughly but that gave nervous breakdowns to a succession of teachers paid extra to ride herd on the rambunctious primarily gringo children of the Pedregal and San Angel. And Mary, now fourteen and an exemplary student, asked for and was given a permanent wave, and the round-cheeked, Dutch-bobbed child became an adolescent who went to school dances and bebopped with a look of concentration on her face as though she were solving an algebra problem.

In April there was a brief crisis when we learned that Mike, whose longtime romance with Nancy had ended a few weeks before, had once more become altogether miserable at Columbia, had cut too many classes, and was in danger of flunking out. Hugo flew up, conferred with deans and professors, made sure Mike would be allowed to take his finals, and, renting a two-room apartment, moved himself and Mike into it and sat with Mike while he studied for them. (In fact, Mike pulled a good enough average out of the wreckage so he could transfer to UCLA in the fall, where he changed his major to theater arts, recovered his self-esteem, and began laying the groundwork for a thriving future career in film and television.)

Susie's romance with Miguel, who would be going to Yale in the fall, continued contentedly, and another summer, with our customary influx of young guests from the States, began.

But it had become apparent that our dog Pablo had to go.

He was still a formidable watchdog, and hunter too. When the children were off at school, he spent much of the day in the enclosed lot adjacent to us, shoulder deep in tall grass, stalking rats or any other wild creature that had found its way there, and, when the children got home, came lolloping out to meet them with wildly waving collie tail and wide, dripping, cheerful St. Bernard grin. We still loved him as dearly as ever. But growing older had not improved his disposition; his territorial instincts now extended to the street outside the walls, and if we were not careful when we opened the gate, he would rush through it to attack any passing dog or poorly dressed workman. Emily, wrestling with him on the living-room floor one evening after he'd been in such a combat, happened to touch a wound we didn't know he had, and he whirled about and bit her savagely right through the upper lip. We had to rush her to a hospital for a plastic surgeon to repair the damage.

As for Pablo: at first we tried half measures. We took him to an animal shelter and paid his board for several weeks in advance, hoping that someone with a big yard and no children would adopt him.

But no one did; a month later we learned he was still there, now grieving and barely eating. So when two scoundrels vaulted the walls of the lot next door and invaded it, making their way "unobtrusively" toward our house (but were intercepted before they reached it), we figured we needed a watchdog, rethought Pablo's exile, and decided to give him another chance. But we took the precaution this time of having him neutered, on the theory that this would make him less aggressive.

It didn't work. After the surgery healed he came home, overjoyed to be back with the family again. But before long, when a friend of Debbie's came over to play, he took umbrage at some childish piece of roughhousing and grabbed her whole head in his jaws. He didn't break the skin, but marks of his teeth showed deep on her neck. We were aghast at what might have been.

Now there was no alternative. Though he'd been miserable in the shelter, he could no longer be trusted with children. He had to be put to sleep.

I snapped on his leash and walked him the few blocks in to San Angel, to the local vet. An assistant took him out to the office's courtyard, visible through a window in the rear; and as I paid the receptionist for the services to be rendered, Pablo sighted me through the window and came galloping over, where he stood with his nose pressed against the glass, waving his tail and grinning at me as though this separation were some sort of game we were playing and any moment he would discover what was expected of him. He was still standing there, full of bounce and energy, watching me through the window and waving his tail expectantly, when I left.

I cried all the way home.

* * * * *

The changes that would have a more profound effect on our lives, however, were subtler, seeming at this point of minor importance. But they were adding up.

More and more of our friends were moving away, some to Cuernavaca or Valle de Bravo, others back to the States. And we ourselves, without realizing it, may have begun to sense that an era was coming to a close for us too, that it was time to move on.

Hugo had written, on spec, two screen stories laid in Italy and in the process had developed an ardent interest in the country ("I was in love with Italy before I ever saw it," he told me later). And he was reading the French and Italian existentialists, although, as with *The Young One,* this was an area into which I didn't want to follow. To the extent that I understood it, it seemed a philosophy that conflicted with my need for a moral, orderly, predictable world, and I rejected it out of hand. However, I was reading Burckhardt on the Renaissance now, having broken ground on the subject with Ralph Roeder's book last year, and was growing eager to see some of the places I was reading about.

Then we *really* heard the sirens' call.

Life magazine ran an article on Italy's restaurants, with full-page color photos of tables laden with great piles of fruits and vegetables, crusty loaves of bread, joints of meat, and *fiascos* of wine, displayed against tantalizing views of Italian countrysides and wonderful cityscapes of Rome and Florence and Venice—a juxtaposition of food and landscape that we found achingly inviting.

Meanwhile questions were beginning to arise in our minds about the wisdom of staying on in Mexico. Problems we had turned a blind eye to earlier were now beginning to worry us. Some were cultural: the rampant male chauvinism (machismo), for instance. With the generalized acceptance of the all too common *"casa chica"* (the almost institutionalized household of "the other woman" in so many marriages here), the lot of the Mexican housewife was not one we wanted our girls to face any more than we wanted to see them in the role of "other woman." Too, Hugo was finding himself increasingly annoyed by the deep-seated resentment of the local film industry (indeed, of all Mexico) toward *"norteamericanos."* And though he understood it historically—stemming, he knew, from the States' conquest of Mexico in 1847 and Mexico's almost colonial dependence on stateside capital ever since—he was finding it hard to live and work with on a day-to-day basis.

And the physical changes in Mexico City were becoming almost palpable.

The long-dreamed-of industrialization of the valley of Mexico was proceeding apace: factory smokestacks thrust up on the skyline now, their fumes, imprisoned by the encircling mountains, visibly clouding the high, once clear air. On our trips back from Cuernavaca these days, as we came over the crest, we could see a substantial increase in that layer of smog hanging over the city; it had spread and now seemed to hang over much of the valley.

And as factories increased, traffic too was becoming heavy. Driving downtown now meant struggling through one continual traffic jam from San Angel all the way to the Zócalo, and Hugo was beginning to lose his temper at the aggressiveness of the other drivers on the road. One day he said to me grimly, "You know? I've either got to stop driving in this country or start carrying a gun!" (By this time I may have known about the amphetamines he was taking, though I still had no idea they might have anything to do with his own mounting irritability.)

In any event, though there was no single large reason for our growing restlessness with the country that had been so good to us for so long, there were a number of small ones, and when the wire from Rome arrived early in September, soon after Susie's departure for college (another connection severed), it seemed as though Fate itself had been reading our minds:

CAN YOU COME ITALY SIX WEEKS REWRITE BIBLICAL SUBJECT, it read, and was signed, ALDRICH.

PART THREE

Here is the ancient floor,
Footworn and hollowed and thin,
Here was the former door
Where the dead feet walked in.

She sat here in her chair,
Smiling into the fire;
He who played stood there,
Bowing it higher and higher.

Childlike, I danced in a dream;
Blessings emblazoned that day;
Everything glowed with a gleam;
Yet we were looking away!

—*Thomas Hardy*

Chapter Twenty-nine

ITALY!

Our heads spun with what-ifs. Bob was sending two first-class plane tickets, but what if the six weeks turned into a longer stay? Maybe we should trade the tickets in for tourist flights for the whole family. . . . We worked it out like a chess game. Hugo was due to leave the end of the month; since his mother, Margaret, wasn't well enough to travel at the moment, I could import his stepfather, Freddie, to oversee the household, and then I could follow Hugo to Rome. And if it looked as though the job might prove really substantial, the children could fly over when the school term ended in late November.

But beyond that?

We couldn't even guess how long Aldrich's "biblical rewrite" might take—or whether it might even lead to other jobs in Europe (we could dream, couldn't we?). What if we found we could stay in Italy? What then? We tried not to let our hopes get too high, but the thought of actually *living* in Rome made our hearts leap. Hugo took to wandering about the house making lists of possessions, with instructions for their disposal (SELL, STORE, SHIP) in case we had to deputize someone—Charles Small's wife, Bert, for instance, who by now was our most supportive friend—to close up the house in our absence and find another job for Ramona. I packed summer clothes, ours and the children's, in footlockers, to be shipped to us along with our books and manuscripts at some hoped-for future date; they could always be *un*packed if things didn't work out. We went down to the American Embassy to change our group passport for individual ones and to the department of *relaciones exteriores* to get notarized exit permissions for Debbie and Becky, who at this point had dual citizenship. We arranged for the sale of the dim-witted beagle puppy we had bought to replace (foolish thought) our beloved Pablo.

And there was one other possession to be disposed of.

Hugo broached the subject at table. School was over; the school bus had left the children off, and as always they had all come trooping in just in time for *comida*. Ramona had made tongue with *mole* for us, and partway through the meal, Hugo commented that we should try to sell Dandy before he left.

I glanced over at Emmie, worried that this prospect might upset her, but it didn't; the little horse's ill temper had long since exhausted any love Emmie felt for her. She simply nodded.

Hugo went on with his instructions: I should place an ad in the *Mexico City News* (the English-language paper) this afternoon. . . .

Foreseeing problems with the wording, I asked what it should say. Hugo shrugged. "'For sale, small Oaxacan pony, gentle with children,'" he said.

I stared at him, astonished. "We can't say that!"

He was irritated at the interruption. "Why not?"

"She isn't gentle with children!" I said. "She isn't gentle with anyone!"

"Do you want to sell her," he asked, increasingly annoyed, "or don't you?"

I was baffled at the amorality of his suggestion, which was totally unlike him. "We can't say she's gentle when she isn't," I said. "It just isn't true."

"What's the matter, are you afraid you'll get caught in a lie?" he asked icily—Hugo, who as far as I knew had never told an outright lie in his life.

"No!" I said, increasingly upset. "I'm afraid someone will buy Dandy for a small child, and Dandy will throw him and hurt him!"

"In other words," said Hugo, now coldly furious, "some child's going to get killed and it'll be my fault; is that it?"

"I didn't say that!" The whole scene was bewildering. In all the years I'd known him, he'd never done anything cynical or self-serving. And his anger was inexplicable; it had me so confused, I could hardly defend myself. Why was he acting like this?

"What you're implying," he went on savagely, "is that I'm some sort of monster. . . ."

By now I was crying in the face of his anger and unable to say anything at all. The children, who had never in their lives heard us quarrel, were aghast. Mary stared at us, fled the table, ran up to her room, and burst into huge sobs, which we could hear all the way downstairs. Emmie, with eyes brimming and lips pressed tight, ran outside to the yard, where she hid and cried. Debbie stayed at the table, silent, scared, looking from one of us to the other. It was a strange, new, frightening note in our lives and none of us understood it; for an hour or two the children thought it was the end of the world.

I don't remember how the quarrel ended or what wording the ad finally carried or even who placed it. And of course what none of us understood or would admit that day was that Hugo's outburst was another hint—not the first, certainly, but the most symptomatic—of slow, subtle, irreversible changes in the man we all idolized.

What we did feel was a desperate need to view the whole episode as a temporary aberration, to be put aside, covered over, *buried,* so we could get back to being a family again. By evening we were all (even Hugo) acting as though it had never happened.

Why?

I'm not sure. It must have had something to do with the way we saw ourselves as a family. Or, as with our refusal to discuss political changes with our fellow exiles, perhaps we felt there were too many hazards out there, too many unknowns; they could only be dealt with if we were united, a solid front, trusting and believing in each other no matter what.

As for Dandy—there was only one answer to the ad in subsequent days, from a man who wanted a pony for his little boy. But when Hugo took him out to the lot to see her, she behaved so badly the man left, and we ended up giving her back to the stable where we'd bought her.

In any event, the matter was banished from our minds almost immediately afterward by a dreadful little story that appeared in *U.S. News and World Report* and beside which everything else paled.

Triggered by the defection of two U.S. State Department employees who apparently passed through Mexico en route to Cuba and the Soviet Union, the story in a mid-September issue of the magazine stated that Mexico and Cuba had become "links in an 'underground rail-road'" that carried Communist sympathizers from the United States to Moscow, citing as evidence the departure three years earlier of Mexico City residents Alfred Stern and his wife, who, said the article, "fled behind the Iron Curtain while under indictment in the U.S. for espionage," and pointing out, as further substantiation, that from 1953 to 1957, Mexico was also the "hideaway" of economics professor Maurice Halperin, "who now works in Moscow but denies that he has defected."

Chairman Walter of HUAC, the story went on, had informed Congress that Halperin was once "a leader of the American Communist colony in Mexico." This colony consisted, said the congressman, of Frederick Vanderbilt Field, Hugo D. Butler, George Pepper, Mr. and Mrs. David Drucker, Albert Maltz, Bart and Edna van der Schelling, the Liebers, our former family doctor Jake Levine, a few other people we knew slightly or not at all, and, "until she fled to the Soviet Union, Mr. and Mrs. Alfred Stern—she is the former Martha Dodd."

It had begun all over again.

The implication, which was expanded to a categorical statement in a later issue published just after our departure, that our little band of refugees (enlarged in the later article to four hundred people) operated as an "underground railroad" for dissident U.S. officials was so outrageous, so infuriating, and so utterly without basis or even logic that for the moment our excited plans for Hugo's departure came to a dead halt. After ten years of minding our own business, of struggling to make a living and a reasonably happy life for our children, to be accused of such nonsense was really more than we could bear. I stopped sleeping at night, my mind instead going round and round in helpless anger, the adrenaline surging. Hugo, looking grim, was doing a good bit of pacing. And at school, our poor Mary became the target of taunts from the children of embassy officials. "Hi, Mary, I hear you're a Commie!" they accosted her, and, "Hey, Mary, how's your uncle Nikita (Khrushchev)?" Like their parents, they had never learned the difference between political dissent and disloyalty. At an age when acceptance by one's peers is more important than anything else in life, Mary was not allowed to forget the ugly story for a moment and carried the psychic scars for years after.

What were the facts—at least as far as we knew them?

Martha Dodd Stern was the daughter of a former U.S. ambassador to pre–World War II Germany. She had published a book (*Through Embassy Eyes*) describing her experiences there and another (*The Searching Light*) about her further political development, and she was known as a sponsor of left-wing causes. The Sterns' adopted son, Bobby, an attractive and appealing boy, was a classmate of Mary's at school, and she had a lively crush on him, but we had met the parents only three or four times during their four-year stay in Mexico. Actually, some months after their arrival, Mrs. Stern had phoned us, introduced herself, and invited us to a dinner party. We'd been somewhat taken aback by an invitation from someone we hadn't even met but decided that maybe the very rich could do things like that. So we'd accepted. At dinner we'd found ourselves sitting next to painter David Siqueiros and his wife, which impressed us no end, but we were still not fluent enough in the language to conduct a very profound conversation, I'm afraid.

(And here, apropos, a brief digression. In 1960, several years after this particular evening and soon after Mexico's new president Adolfo Lopez Mateos had been sworn into office, Siqueiros, visiting in Caracas, had made a speech about his country's newly elected leader in language so bitter that when he, Siqueiros, returned to Mexico, he was thrown in jail, where he remained for four years.

During this long incarceration, Fred Rinaldo, former comedy writer, husband of my oldest friend, and an indefatigable activist, had formed among his San Fernando Valley neighbors a committee of support for the jailed painter. When Siqueiros was released from jail in 1964, Fred had sent a wire congratulating him, on receipt of which Siquieros's wife, Angelica, sent back a wire of thanks on behalf of her husband. It was addressed to "Señor Fred Rinaldo and *the workers and peasants of Sherman Oaks, California*.")

But apart from meeting one of Mexico's most impressive painters at the Sterns' dinner party, we had found the atmosphere of the evening so oppressive—such an expanse of marble flooring, so many marble pillars, and a guest list of so many local luminaries, all so elegantly dressed—that we felt badly outclassed, if not downright shabby by comparison, and hadn't been anxious to pursue a closer friendship with our hosts.

On one of the few occasions when we met later (at someone else's dinner party, I think), I complimented Mr. Stern—Alfred—on his nice young son, and he in response gave me his own version of why they had left the States. In the wake of accusations of "spying" leveled against him by a disgruntled former partner in a music-publishing business, he told me, Bobby's natural mother had in effect begun to blackmail them by threatening to take the boy away from them. He said her demands had escalated, and rather than submit to further blackmail at the risk of losing Bobby, they had come down to Mexico.

I'd read almost nothing about the accusations against the Sterns, but our own experience with newspaper stories had taught me that where the Left is concerned, no journalistic holds were barred, so I found no particular reason to doubt Alfred's story. In addition, I couldn't figure out what kind of "spying" Alfred was supposed to have done; after all, someone in a music-publishing business is hardly likely to have access to key government secrets, and anyway, I'd never been able to understand the popular assumption that someone committing as grave an act as espionage would call attention to himself by openly advocating Marxism.

So I'd thought no more about the matter. But there had come a day in 1957 when Bobby was abruptly absent from school, and our telephone lines buzzed with gossip. The papers had reported that the Sterns, fearing extradition from Mexico to face U.S. grand jury questions about the business partner's allegations, had denounced the accusations as fantastic, renounced their American citizenship, obtained Paraguayan passports, and flown with Bobby to Czechoslovakia. Later it emerged that Maurice Halperin, who had moved to Mexico with his family a few years before, had bought the airline tickets for them.

The Halperins we knew even less well, though Mrs. Halperin had taught English (Mike had taken her class one year and liked it) and math at the American School. A year or so after the Sterns' abrupt departure, we learned that both Halperins, just ahead of another possible deportation order, had also left the country. (Gossip that reached us over the next several years would tell us they had traveled to Moscow and then to Cuba, where Maurice, a former economics professor, had outstayed his welcome by writing a book critical of Cuba's one-crop economy. He had then gone on to Canada, where he returned to teaching economics, this time at the British Columbia university Simon Frazier, where he would remain, teaching, until the end of his life.)

In any event, the hysteria caused by the two families' departures had, each time, been a nine days' wonder but had settled down and we thought we'd heard the last of it—till now. Now, however, all the old emotions, the old anxieties, came rushing back. We felt we'd been plunged back ten years, to the days in Hollywood during the HUAC hearings. It was truly never ending.

The approach of Hugo's actual departure for Italy galvanized us, finally, into action. Helping him pack served to get my mind at least partially off the magazine story, and on a day in late September or perhaps early October, I drove him to the airport, both of us assuming that if the Aldrich job went as we hoped, I'd meet him in Rome in a month.

The airport, as always, was crowded, jostling. As we said good-bye I could see that Hugo's thoughts were already a leap ahead of me, involved with the journey and the new assignment (which, apart from the fact that it was "biblical," we still knew nothing about, not even which Testament!). The news story, though annoying, had ceased to trouble him because he was moving away from it and, I guess he reasoned, the rest of us soon would be too. It was something we could all quickly forget.

Except that I couldn't forget. These last few weeks had raised anxieties in me that wouldn't diminish, though I'd have been hard put to define them. One mendacious piece of journalism shouldn't have loomed so important, but I felt as though our whole stay in Mexico had somehow been poisoned by it; all I wanted now was to follow Hugo as soon as I could, to leave the whole American continent behind me and get the children away too.

When Hugo moved on into the passengers' waiting room, I watched him through the wide glass window that separated us. He had his raincoat over his arm and was wearing the khaki fatigue cap with earflaps that he'd worn so much, it had almost grown to be part of his head. He saw me through the window, waved, and threw me a perfunctory kiss. Then, his mind on other things, he moved away and, with the rest of the passengers, began to crowd toward the door of the boarding area. In a moment, he had disappeared. I lingered a moment longer, then retraced my steps through the lobby of the terminal and out to the busy parking lot.

As I drove the familiar boulevards, which by now I could have navigated with my eyes closed (Avenida Viaducto, Diagonal San Antonio), I didn't think to wonder at Hugo's rapid disenchantment with Mexico, which had actually begun prior to the *U.S. News* story. The fact was, however, that of all of us, it was he who had been most nearly assimilated. He had loved everything Mexican, the food, the music, the bullfights, the countryside. It had been almost a passion with him. The possibility that it was not Mexico that had changed in so short a time, but Hugo himself, didn't cross my mind.

. . . And then the Diagonal gave onto the Avenida de los Insurgentes, and I was almost home, to get through my last month in Mexico without him.

Chapter Thirty

AND THEN, finally, it was almost time for me to go too.

I'd left a call with the cab stand in San Angel for a ten-thirty cab, to make a midnight flight. But a late storm—they should all have ended in September, but here was a *"norte"* hitting us with sudden ferocity the end of October—was in full cry, drenching the valley, hurling lightning at transformers and power lines and blacking out whole sections of the city, including ours.

Ramona had gotten dinner by candlelight, and after dinner the children had gone upstairs by candlelight to get ready for bed. A bit later I'd gone up too, still by candlelight, to put the last few items in my luggage, though I'd been packing and repacking for days and my bags were already overfull. In my carry-on (actually, a gaily embroidered shopping bag bought for a few pesos in the Toluca market), for reading on the journey, I'd already stowed a Holiday guidebook on Rome and Suetonius's *Lives of the Caesars,* and I'd been carrying my Italian phrase book around in my purse all week. Having arrived in Mexico with no Spanish, I would arrive in Italy able to say two whole sentences in Italian, *"Io vado su"* and *"Io vado giú"* ("I go up" and "I go down"). I might never find an occasion to use those phrases, but it was reassuring to know *some*thing.

My ticket was routed to Boston first, so I'd be able to have a fast visit with Susie at college. But there'd be no chance to say good-bye to Mike, who was now living happily with his grandmother and Freddie in Hollywood and going to UCLA (I discovered years later, when I sent for my FBI files under the Freedom of Information Act, that Mike's transfer to the West Coast had thrown the FBI into an uproar. They had somehow gotten the notion that it was *Hugo* who had moved back to Hollywood and enrolled at UCLA, and they'd sent an agent hot-footing it out to the university's enrollment files to find out what Hugo was up to there and what his "activities" were. It had taken them a frantic exchange of interoffice teletypes to get the whole matter straightened out.) There'd be a quick stopover in New York and then— dizzying thought—across the Atlantic to Italy.

I was to meet Hugo at the Hotel Inghilterra in Rome, which my guidebook told me was near something called the Piazza di Spagna. Hugo had stopped there only briefly since his arrival, I gathered, before he and Aldrich had begun to globe-hop, looking for locations (though he still hadn't identified the picture he was to write). I'd had one or two letters from him from Rome, then one from Israel, and then, when Israel's rate of exchange proved prohibitive for the film's budget, from Marrakesh, in Morocco. I'd found all those exotic postmarks intoxicating, and when I thought of actually *being* in Rome, I went almost faint with excitement.

All the arrangements for our step-by-step departure had fallen into place. Freddie would arrive day after tomorrow to look after the girls till school let out; I knew from his letters that he was as excited about coming to Mexico as I was about going to Italy. And if all things in Italy went as we hoped, he and Bert Small would put the girls on a plane when the school term ended and send them over to us, although the idea of having four of my children on a trans-Atlantic flight without me there to keep them safe from the elements was something I tried not to think about. We had even lined up a family to sublet Palmas 81, complete with Ramona, if we stayed away for any length of time.

But neither Mary nor I had found any tolerable way of living with the aftermath of the news magazine story. I had tried to avoid, as much as possible, any contact with the non-Left parents of the American School, but Mary was exposed to their children daily and was finding it more and more upsetting. If I had been less distracted by my travel plans, I might have been more aware of her unhappiness. As it was, all I could think of was counting the moments till it was time to leave.

And now, here it was.

Or almost. The memory of that night, the night that marked not only the end (or almost) of the decade but of a part of our lives too, should have been etched on my mind. Instead there are great gaps that, try as I may, I can't fill in. There I was, leaving this house, where against all odds we'd spent the happiest years we'd ever known, and I had not the least regret, not the slightest realization that it was, in its way, a flight from Eden. I should have treasured every moment of that leave-taking, but I've forgotten most of it.

I must have finished my packing in our candlelit bedroom (the ceramic storks long since gone from the bed tables), and I suppose it didn't occur to me to throw even a glance toward the now storm battered windows where for so many years I'd wakened every morning to the shape of the daylight outside, where the top branches of the big loquat tree in back, brushing against the iron window frame, had given access to that formidable scorpion when I was pregnant with Becky two and a half years ago. When my suitcase was squeezed shut, I must surely have gone into the children's room—strewn no doubt with clothing they hadn't picked up (a corollary of growing up in a society where there's always someone to pick up after you)—and kissed them good night and told them to "have a nice ride, dears," my talismanic phrase to keep them safe in transit, whether on the road while I was gone or during their possible flight to Italy. And I suppose I dragged my bulging suitcase out into the hall and down stairs that must have been perilously shadowy.

Since it was too dark in the living room to read, I have no idea how I spent the time until Ramona came in from her little house in back. But I do remember the storm, the flashes of light that lit up momentarily the outlines of this room, with its bare red-tiled floor—these chairs where we'd sat reading so many evenings and the daybed where the children had piled with Hugo to hear their Saturday night stories, the Coleman heater we'd had to buy that first cold winter when our electric radiators kept blowing the fuses, the portable gramophone with the children's dog-eared record albums, Bart's glowing boat picture over the fireplace, and Juan O'Gorman's mural on the wall of the dining alcove opposite—all illuminated in sudden bursts of blue-white light and then disappearing in shadows. This room had been the nerve center of our lives for most of our ten years in Mexico, but tonight I was almost unaware of it; there was too much else to think about.

And then—a memory that has remained with almost painful clarity, unlike most of that night—Ramona came in from outside in her nightclothes, with a rain-drenched *rebozo* covering her head, to make up the daybed in the living room so the children wouldn't be alone in the house when I left.

As we waited for the sound of the cab, she sat there in her flannel nightgown on the edge of the daybed, weaving her hair into a long braid. As the rain drummed against the windows and thunder shook the house, she looked at me, upset, and burst out, *"¡No se vaya, señora! No se vaya!"* ("Don't go, señora! Don't go!")

I know now it wasn't just my flying in such a storm that worried her. It was as though she was afraid that my leaving, *our* leaving, was the end of everything.

But I was unseeing, unthinking. Hugo and I had told her we'd send her a sizable severance paycheck if we stayed away—enough, finally, to pay off the mortgage on her little *"finca"* in Guadalajara. But we hadn't given a thought to what our lives would be like without her, nor hers without *us*. All I said, as the sound of rainwater gushed down the gutters and the raindrops beat on the windows, was that it was all arranged, the señor was expecting me, I had to go.

At last, through the storm sounds, we heard the honk of the cab's horn out on the street. I pulled on my raincoat, grabbed up my bags, gave Ramona a brief *abrazo,* and then, wrestling with bags, purse, umbrella, plunged out into the rain and the dark and headed by blind reckoning for the gates and the waiting cab beyond.

At some point during the drive to the airport, the streetlights came on, but I don't remember where, or whether it was still raining when we pulled up in front of the terminal. The lights were on again, I know, in the lobby of the terminal, but I have no specific recollection of being ticketed, or getting my *salida* (exit) papers, or even of walking out on the tarmac to board the plane; there had been other boardings and departures, and one memory disappears into all the rest. I'm sure I found my seat, and got rid of my wet raincoat, and buckled myself in, and I *think* I remember (but do I really?) looking out the rain-streaked window across the wet field, where puddles reflected the lights of the landing area, till our motors began to rev and we started to taxi.

By now, I guess, most of the storm had spent itself or swept away. I'm sure I was still looking out the windows as the plane lifted off. And as we pulled up over the valley, I'm sure I watched as I always did, arriving or departing, for the familiar pattern of lights in pinpricks about the city and the curve of lights edging the dark shape of Lake Texcoco. It couldn't have been more than a glimpse, though, before it all disappeared as we climbed into the rain clouds above. But it still didn't occur to me to feel a sense of loss or farewell; I was too excited about what lay ahead even to think of what I was leaving.

And then we were above the clouds, and the moon was shining.

Postscript

THE NIGHT of my arrival in Rome, a national election was in full swing.

As I might have known, it had been an eventful flight. Because the DC 10 I was traveling on had developed engine trouble halfway over the Atlantic, we'd had to put back to New York to get another one, which meant I missed my connection in Paris, and none of the wires I'd sent Hugo about the schedule changes reached him. So he had driven out to Rome's then airport at Ciampino three times to meet planes I wasn't on.

Meanwhile, by midafternoon, the plane I *was* on had come in low, finally, for a landing, and through the window I'd had my first glimpse of Roman ruins (Ostia Antica, probably) and was in a state of wild excitement. Finding no Hugo to meet me, I'd shared a cab into Rome with another passenger and had reached the Piazza di Spagna and the hotel to learn that Hugo had just left to meet yet another plane.

At last, though, he'd come back, altogether frazzled from all those trips to the airport, and we'd had time to catch up with my month's news about the family and his news about his job. It seemed the picture Bob Aldrich had called him over to rewrite was *Sodom and Gomorrah!*

And now it was evening and we were on our way to dinner in the little Austin Cooper Seven Hugo had bought with his first paychecks. My head was spinning with jet lag and culture shock. I was looking out the car window at Rome at its busiest hour: compacts and subcompacts whizzed by us, fairly gleaming with wax and tender loving care. And though at this hour many of the people who thronged the sidewalks must be home-going workingmen and women, to me, after all those years in Mexico, they all looked singularly well dressed—even chic. Hugo said Italy was in a period of enormous prosperity; business was booming. Fiats and Alfa Romeos were selling all over the world, as were Olivetti typewriters and Gucci bags and Ferragamo shoes and movies from Cinecittá. And as we turned off the bustling little street we were traveling along, he said he had something to show me.

We had turned onto an enormous piazza, all alight. This was Piazza di Popolo, he told me. There was a lovely fountain in its center, and churches and restaurants lined its periphery, and cars were darting past us every which way. Overhead, banners for the pending election, flood-lighted, were strung from one side of the piazza to the other. Hugo pointed out one of the banners. In huge letters it blazoned out, from one side of the piazza to the other, VOTA COMMUNISTA!

"Look at that," he said. "Isn't it great?" And then, "I sure as hell hope they don't win," he said. "But isn't it great to see it there?"

Author's Note

FASCINATING AS ROME was, and although during our almost three years there we both wrote pictures that put our names back on the screen, our marriage, which had survived such difficult years in Mexico, went sadly awry in Italy—in part because of Hugo's still undiagnosed but steadily worsening arteriosclerotic brain disease.

His dementia, finally diagnosed (wrongly) as Alzheimer's disease, became painfully apparent not long after we moved back to the States in late 1964. A bit more than three years later, at age fifty, he died of a massive heart attack.

Through most of this, Ramona was with us. She had joined us in Italy and later, on our final return to the States, had come with us as she'd always wanted to. She settled into her own tiny apartment here, joined a local branch of her church, and saw us through Hugo's last troubled years and death. The ensuing years were eventful for her: she married, was widowed, and married again. But we stayed close. And in the second half of the 1970s, she too died of a heart attack.

The children, one by one, all went off to college and now live in every corner (literally) of the States. There are seven grandchildren, two stepgrandchildren, and one great-grandchild with her parents in New Zealand.

As of this writing, our son, Mike, has been working in film and television for more than three decades. He's written movies (including *Gauntlet, Pale Rider*) and countless episodes of TV series, cocreating and serving as head writer of one of them (*Against the Law*), and has written a number of movies for cable television, including *Pronto, White*

Mile, and *Execution of Justice.* His earliest collaborator was Chris Trumbo, and he has remained close to all his high school friends. Three sons, a stepdaughter, a grandchild, and two former stepdaughters he's still in touch with.

Susie now teaches photography at Pine Manor, a women's college in Massachusetts, and in recent years she and her significant other (a painter) have built a house by hand in the Maine woods. Her book for older children, *The Hermit Thrush Sings,* has just been published. Two grown children.

After Radcliffe, Mary took an M.F.A. at UC Irvine and a Ph.D. in English literature at Stanford; published a number of poems in college literary magazines; was briefly married; is now a teacher. She is a devout Catholic.

Emily graduated Phi Beta Kappa from and took her M.L.S. at UC Berkeley; worked variously as children's and then head librarian, then county head of library programs, for about two and a half decades in various parts of the country. She's taken early retirement, is now trying life on a small farm and thinks she likes it. Married, no children.

Debbie took a degree in psychology at UCLA, with the only summa in the family. She is now a court reporter, a skill she has also taught. Widowed early, she has remarried. Two sons and a stepson.

Becky, who graduated from Radcliffe as a film major, worked for a time as an assistant producer of TV documentaries, took an L.C.S.W., is now a social worker in private practice, and consults at a facility for troubled teenagers. The second edition of her book on lesbian marriages, yclept *Ceremonies of the Heart,* is now on the stands.

The Butler grandchildren and stepgrandchildren include one designer of furniture and teacher of design; one cofounder, bass player, and music writer for a successful ska band; one philosophy student; one law student; one theater devotee working backstage; one pre-engineering student; one actor/drama student; one office receptionist; and one promising thirteen-year-old.

After Hugo's death I published several books, including young adult biographies of Pancho Villa and Benito Juárez and a gothic/suspense, wrote TV soap opera for ten years, published two editions of a how-to book on writing it, and taught soap-opera writing at local universities. I also eased my social conscience by serving on a variety of Writers Guild committees, on their board of directors, and for two decades as

stee on their pension and health funds and on an interguild credit
n. I've also spent a decade and a half on the documentary commit-
of the Motion Picture Academy. Nature abhors a vacuum.

As for our friends:

Cleo Trumbo lives in northern California near one of her daughters
and paints. Chris Trumbo writes for film and television (including *Pap-
illon* and *Ishi, Last of His Tribe*) and manages his wife's art-appraisal
office. He has also adapted and produced his father's book *Additional
Dialogue* for the stage. Nikola is a child psychologist, Melissa a still
photographer. Three grandchildren, three great-grandchildren.

After the Hunters' return to the States, Alice became an executive
with United Jewish Appeal, and in addition to his work with Ring, Ian
wrote a number of historical miniseries for television (including *The
Blue and the Gray*). Their son, Tim, who has four children, is a film
and television director whose work includes *Tex, River's Edge, Saint
of Fort Washington,* and episodes of *Twin Peaks*. He has also been,
since his boyhood, a film collector/anthologist.

Ring Lardner emerged from the blacklist to write several movies
(*Cincinnati Kid, The Greatest*) and to win his second Oscar for
M*A*S*H fifty years after his first one (*Woman of the Year*). He also
published a family memoir. Frances continued to act in theater, film,
and television. Ring's/their five children include two college professors, a writer/journalist, a teacher, and a research assistant. There are
seven grandchildren, four great-grandchildren.

After George Pepper's death in Mexico late in 1969, Jeanette returned to the States with their small daughter. Now remarried, she
volunteers with a women's political action group. Her recently wed
daughter is a teacher, writes poetry.

Berthe Small returned to New York after Charles's death in the late
1970s; there, she taught at a community college. Her sons include an
oncologist, a political activist, and a writer of poetry. She has two
grandchildren.

On their return from Mexico, the Hoffmans established a walk-in
counseling center in Los Angeles (which still provides services) and
then divorced. Hans and his second wife were killed in a car crash.
Anne did counseling until her retirement. Her older daughter, Erika,
married a teacher of film, works as a therapist, her younger daughter

as a children's nanny, and the two boys live and work in Spain. Six grandchildren, a great-grandchild.

George Oppen, who had begun again to write poetry late in the decade, returned to the States in 1960, gave occasional lectures or poetry readings at universities, and in 1969 a book of his poetry won the Pulitzer. He died in 1984 and Mary a few years later. Linda, after a divorce late in the 1990s, gave up a career training horses for dressage, came to the Bay Area to live and to mend old friendships and family relationships.

Albert Maltz left his wife, Margaret, returned to the States to marry another woman, was married to still another and working on an unsold novel at the time of his death. Margaret had died, brokenhearted, a few years after their divorce.

Nancy (now using the surname of her first husband, Rocha) is a simultaneous translator, lives in the United States but has built a house in Mexico. She and Mike were married for about a decade in the 1970s, then went their separate ways. Her two daughters (Mike's then stepdaughters), completely bilingual, teach and work helping mainstream immigrants into life and educational programs in the States. Diane Zykovsky has remained in Mexico, where she has married, raised two children, taught, edited the American School's newsletter, and is an occasional freelance writer of articles (dealing primarily with blacklist issues). And Mike's friend Rafael Buñuel is a playwright, has written game shows for TV, is a sculptor (and father of two).

* * * * *

Early in the 1990s, public attitudes about the blacklist began to change. Under relentless pressure from Paul Jarrico, the Motion Picture Academy took steps to restore the (till then) pseudonymous writing credits of some of their award-winning films, and in 1992 the Writers Guild of America, west, announced that at their annual awards event that year, they would restore Albert Maltz's screenplay credit on *Broken Arrow* and Trumbo's story credit on *Roman Holiday* (first sold under Ian Hunter's name before Ian's own blacklisting, though Ian had indeed been hired to write the screenplay, properly earning his own cocredit). The widows of both Maltz and Trumbo, the guild announced, would be present to receive the awards.

I'd brought Mike and Emily with me that evening. It was an elegant event in the grand ballroom of a Beverly Hills hotel, with perhaps a thousand guests: writers, producers, news people, a few actors, guild staff; dinner-jacketed waiters had served an elegant dinner. The regular writing awards had been presented when the giant monitor just beyond our table lit up with a scene from *Roman Holiday*. Actor Warren Beatty, fresh from playing radical John Reed in *Reds*, took the microphone and, for the benefit of those in the audience too young to have lived through it all, gave a brief history of the blacklist and Trumbo's part in it. Then he introduced Cleo Trumbo. And as she—shy as always—came onstage, the whole audience got to its feet and gave her a standing ovation.

It went on for ten minutes.

And as the yelling and the applause went on and on, the children and I could only stare at each other in silent wonder, thinking of the Mexico years, and of Hugo, and of the difference that time had wrought. When the tumult finally died down, and Cleo was given the Oscar and it was time for thanks on Trumbo's behalf, she was so close to tears, she could hardly form the words.

Index

(Page numbers referring to photographs are in italics.)

The Adventures of Robin Hood,
    203–4
Aldrich, Bob, 205
    and *Autumn Leaves* (Jean
        Rouverol), 85–86
    Hugo Butler working for, 51, 210
        in Italy, 246, 249
    in Italy, 262
Armas, Castillo, 128
Article 33 deportations, 185–87
Autumn Leaves, 85–86
Ayres, Agnes, 20

Baby Roo (Butlers' cat), 115,
    180–83
Baker, George Pierce, 167
Barzman, Ben, 207
Barzman, Norma, 207
Baseball, 45–47. *See also* Little
    League team
Beatty, Warren, 268

Bercovici, Leonardo, 207
Berdecio, Roberto, 209
Berkeley, Martin, 10
Bernstein, Walter, 206
Berry, John, 207
Bibb, Leon, 239
Biberman, Herbert, 208–10
Blasenheim, Bernard, 186–87
Brady, Alice, 167
The Brave One, 77–78, 204
Briehl, Walter, 221
Bright, John, 186
Bromberg, J. Edward, 129
Browder, Earl, 23, 25
Brown, Phil, 207
Brown v. Board of Education, 113
Bullfights, 73–77
Buñuel, Jeanne, 39, 153
Buñuel, Luis, 39–40, *139, 140*
    and *The Loved One,* 211
    and *Robinson Crusoe,* 47, 55

and *The Young One,* 236–38, 239

Buñuel, Rafael, 153–54, 267

Butler, Deborah (Debbie), 69, *196,* 199, 218–20, 242, 250–51, 265
  in Acapulco, 187–89
  birth of, 67
    registered with American Embassy, 221
  Diego Rivera visited by, 161
  on Susie's boyfriend, 227, 229

Butler, Emily, 41, 90, 100, 172, *195,* 197, 199, 215–17, 251, 265
  in Acapulco, 50, 187–89
  and Dandy, 217–19, 250
  Diego Rivera visited by, 161
  and grandparents, 4, 112
  and Kent Heller, 56
  and Pablo, 243
  with strep throat, 25
  at Writers Guild of America ceremony, 268

Butler, Ethel, 94–97, 220, 224–25

Butler, Frank, 10, 19–20, 20–21, 93–97, 134, 220, 224–25
  heart attack of, 4
  Oscars for, 93, 134

Butler, Hugo, *134, 135, 136, 139, 140,* 143–44, *191, 195,* 202
  and *Alacrán! (Scorpion!)/ Figuras de Arena (Sand Sculptures),* 54–55
  and *Autumn Leaves,* 86
  in baseball games, 45
  and *The Big Night,* 5
  at bullfight, 73, 76–77
  childhood of, 20–21
  as collector, 35–36
  and Communist party, 23–25, 252, 258
  on Dandy, 250–51
  death of, 264
  dinghy of *(El Traguito [The Little Drink]),* 108, 109–10, 114
  and *The Duel,* 124, 125
  and Eddie and Bea Huebsch, 15–16
  and Frank Butler, 93–95, 98, 220, 225
  friends of, 37–38, 75–76
  and HUAC subpoena, 2–4, 8, 10
  and *Huckleberry Finn,* 242
  in Italy, 246, 255–56, 262–63
  and Jean Rouverol
    introduced to, 21–22
    in Veracruz, 99–102
  on Linda Oppen, 177–78
  and Little League docudrama, 152, 154–55
  loans for, 64–67
  in Mexico, 9, 10–11
    deciding to go to, 6–7
    house hunting in, 27
    seeing HUAC witness in, 61–62
  in military, 22–23, 24
  pawned items of, 63–64, 84
  and pseudonym, 81–82
    of H. B. Addis, 54, 238, 239
    using name of Philip Ansel Roll as, 61
  on request from mother of salutatorian, 233–34
  and *Robinson Crusoe,* 33, 39, 47, 51
  on Rosenberg execution, 69–72
  and Sterns, 253
  telling stories to children, 171, 184
  and *Torero!,* 78–79
  writing, 30, 210–11, 213–14, 245
  and *The Young One,* 236–38

Butler, Jean Rouverol. *See* Rouverol, Jean

Butler, Mary, 18, *135, 138,* 172, *195,* 243, 251, 265
  in Acapulco, 50, 187
  and Baby Roo, 182–83

birth of, 24
friends of, 56
graduation of, 164
and grandparents, 4, 112
horse riding lessons for, 217
and literary contest, 170, 172
poem by, 151
taunted by schoolmates, 252,
   258
Butler, Mike, 34, 124, *136*, *138*,
   200
in Acapulco, 115, 153–54
anxiety of
   about parents, 84–85
as baby, 181
in baseball games, 45
capote for, 145–47
carpentry skills of, 176
and Columbia, 228–29
   acceptance to, 172
   leaving for, 178–79
   preparing for, 170
   return from, 220
and Diego Rivera, 44, 161–62
in earthquake, 150–51
in film and television, 264–65
and Frank Butler, 95–96, 98
friends of, 56, 141
graduation of, 172–73
and grandparents, 4
on Hugo Butler's dinghy
   (*El Traguito [The Little
   Drink]*), 114
illness of, 147–48, 213
and literary contest, 172
in Mexico
   trip to, 26
and Nancy Gast
   competition for, 142–44
   end of romance with, 243
   married to, 267
in New York, 206
reading, 170–71
with strep throat, 27
as teenager, 141–42

at UCLA, 257–58
at Writers Guild of America
   ceremony, 268
Butler, Rebecca (Becky), *169*, *196*,
   242, 265
birth of, 163–64, *165*
   registered with American
      Embassy, 221
exit permissions for, 250
Butler, Susie, *135*, *138*, 173–74,
   195, *198*, 200, 218, 257, 265
boyfriend of, 227–28, 229–30,
   243
and Erika Hoffman, 56
graduation of, 234–35
   as valedictorian, 232–33
and grandparents, 4
with Hoffmans, 184, 186
Hugo Butler telling stories to,
   171
and literary contest, 170, 172
in New York, 206
and Radcliffe College, 226, 230
with strep throat, 26
Butler family, *136*, *194*
in Acapulco, 50, 114–15, 187–89
   "agent" visiting, 184, 189–90
at bullfights, 73–74
children of, 22, 23–24, 180–81
at Christmas, 60–61
in Cuernavaca, 47–50
and Diego Rivera, 161
enlarging house, 99
in Ensenada, 12–13, 104–6, 108–9
grandchildren of, 264–65
and Little League team, 164–65
in Mexico
   house in, 30, 43–45
   trip to, 17–19, 25–29
and Oppens, 176–78
passports granted to, 220–21
sending Mike to college, 178–79
sightseeing, 27–29, 35
and Timmy Humboldt, 117–19
and Trumbos, 17

Cannes Film Festival, 40, 239
Carlos (son of Ramona), 222–23
Chambers, Whittaker, 212
Chaney, Frances, 37, 39, 266
Christian, Mady, 129
Churchill, Winston, 25
Civil rights, 129
Colbert, Claudette, 29
Cole, Lester, 2
Cole, Nat King, 86
Collier, John, 90
Collins, Richard, 10
Colman, Paula, 205
Colman, Ronald, 205
Cooper, Gary, 164
Corey, Hope, 108, 164, 223–24
Corey, Jeff, 108, 164, 223
Crawford, Joan, 86
Croves, Hal, 117, 121
Cuba, 251–52
Cummings, Bob, 4

Dalí, Salvador, 40
Dandy (horse), 218–19, 250–51
Danny (friend of Mike Butler), 148,
    174, 177
Dassin, Jules, 207
Davy (boyfriend of Susie), 227–28
Denton, Crahan, 140
Día de los Muertos (Day of the
    Dead), 59–60
Dmytryk, Edward, 7
Dodd (Stern), Martha, 252–54
Don José (mason), 99
Don Ramon (gardener), 183
Douglas, Kirk, 240–41
Douglas, William O., 221
Drucker, David, 45–46
Drucker, Esther, 45, 46
Druckers, 45, 89–90, 186, 252
The Duel (Chekhov), 124

Earthquake, 150–51
Eden, Anthony, 129

Endore, Guy, 212

Fast, Howard, 241
Faulkner, William, 238
Faz, César, 155–57, 165
Fernandez, Jaime, 54
Field, Frederick Vanderbilt, 116,
    252
Field, W. C., 133
Fles, Barthold, 212–13
Flores (postman), 65–66, 230
Ford, Ruth, 238
Foreman, Carl, 206, 208
Foster, Norman, 29–30, 132
Francis, Anne, 51
Freddie (stepfather of Hugo Butler),
    20, 104, 224, 249, 258
The Front, 206

Garfield, John, 129
Gast, Nancy, 142–45, 172, 178–79,
    220, 243, 267
Gilman, Page, 135
Gold, Lee, 207
Gordon, Bernard, 207
Guzmán, Jacobo Arbenz, 128

Hale, Barbara, 4
Halevy, Julian (Julian Zimmer), 207
Halperin, Maurice, 252, 254
Haskins, "Lucky," 155–57
Heller, Jeanne, 41
Heller, Kent, 41, 56
Hellers, 56
Henreid, Paul, 51
Hess, Harriet, 90
Hoffman, Anne, 46, 266–67
Hoffman, Erika, 56, 266–67
Hoffman, Hans, 46, 119–22, 124,
    148, 266–67
Hoffmans, 60, 165, 176, 186,
    266–67
"Hollywood Ten," 2, 7, 25
Hope, Bob, 135

House of Representatives' Un-American Activities Committee (HUAC), 1–3, 9–10, 129, 252
Hovey, Tamara, 207
Howard, Kathleen, *133*
HUAC hearings, 1–3, 9–10, 129, 252
Huebsch, Bea, 15–16
Huebsch, Eddie, 15–16, 164–65, 205
Huie, William Bradford, 241
Humboldt, Charles, 117, 122, 124
Humboldt, Timmy, 117–21, 122, 124
Hunter, Alice, 37, 266
Hunter, Ian, 203–4, 205, 266, 267–68
    in baseball games, 45
    friends of, 36, 37–38
    in New York, 56
Hunter, Tim, 37, 56, 266
Hunters, 203–4
    grandchildren of, 266
    to Mexico, 36
    and Mexico art, 39
    return to America of, 56
Huston, John, 210–11

Isabel (housekeeper), 34, 183, 187, 230–31

Jackson, Anne, 51
Jackson, Donald, 66–67
Jamie (grandchild of Ethel Butler), 224–25
Jarrico, Paul, 8, 9–10, 208, 267
Jevne, Jack, 85–86
Juárez, Benito, 185

Kahlo, Frida, 161
Kahn, Gordon, 90
Kanga (cat), 180, 181
Kapoian, Harry, *140*
Kennedy, John, 241
Kent, Rockwell, 221

Kilian, Crawford, 45, 56, 144–45, 148, 150–51, 170, 172
Kilian, Lincoln, 45, 56, 144–45, 148, 150–51
Kilian, Michael, 205
Kinch (Oppens' dog), 58
King, John, *132*
King brothers, 77–78, 90, 204
Kramer, Stanley, 206
Krushchev, Nikita, 127

L'Age d'Or, 40
Lardner, Jr., Ring, 203–4, 205
    and *The Ecstasy of Owen Muir,* 39
    friends of, 36, 37–38
    and HUAC subpoena, 1–2
    in jail, 7, 36–37
    in New York, 56
    Oscar for, 266
Lardner, Katie, *195*
Lardners, 36, 55–56, 203–4, 266
Lazy T
    (Trumbo ranch), 6
Le Chien Andalou, 40
Lees, Robert, 8
Levi, Primo, 207
Levine, Jake, 118–22, 124, 147, 252
Levitt, Al, 205
Levitt, Helen, 205
Lieber, Butchy, 121
Lieber, Max, 87, 252
Lieber, Minna, 87, 120–21, 252
Little League team, *199, 191*
    at Butlers' house, 164–65
    docudrama on, 154–55
    in World Series, 151–52, 156–57
"Little Smith Act," 116
Loeb, Phil, 129
Losey, Joseph, 5, 207, 236
Los Olvidados (The Young and the Damned), 40
Los Pequeños Gigantes (How Tall Is a Giant?), 154–55, *191,* 199

Macbeth, 53
Macías, Angel, 151, 156–57
Madison, Julian, *133*
Maltz, Albert, 126–27, 210, 240
    and "American Communist
        colony," 252
    credits restored to, 267–68
    and Frank Sinatra, 241–42
    and "Hollywood Ten," 48–49
Maltz, Margaret, 48–49, 267
    in plane crash, 87–88
    using pseudonym
        of Margaret Larkin, 212
Maltzes
    in Mexico, 48–49, 87–88
    and Timmy Humboldt, 117, 121
    visited by immigration agents,
        186
Mañanitas, 15, 110–11, vii–viii
Manoff, Arnold, 206
Manzanar, 7–8
Margaret (mother of Hugo Butler),
        4, 10, 20, 180, 220
    on birth of Rebecca, 163, 165
    Butler family visiting, 224
    in Ensenada, 104–7
    health of, 249
Mariquita (housekeeper of Diego
        Rivera), 160, 162
Mateos, Adolfo Lopez, 253
Matthiessen, Peter, 236
McCarran Act, 7–8
McCarthy, Joseph, 1
McIntire, Jeanette Nolan, 53
Mexico
    Cannes Film Festival awards for,
        40, 239
    changes in, 245–46
    industrialization of, 123–24
        and labor problems, 185, 186
    as "underground railroad" for
        Communists, 251–52
Minnie (owner of Minnie's Place),
        104–7

Minnie's Place, 104–8
The Miracle, 93–98, 108
Monte de Piedad, 64, 74, 84
Moore, Roger, 96
Moreno, Rita, 51
Motion Picture Academy, 78, 169

Neustaedter, Peter, 189–90

O'Gorman, Juan, 43–44, 99, 201
O'Herlihy, Dan, 53–55
One Man's Family, 5, *135*
Oppen, George, 57–59, 114, 175,
        176, 177, 267
Oppen, Linda, 56, 58, 144–45, 172,
        176, 267
    in baseball games, 46
    boyfriends of, 174–75
    and Jean Rouverol, 177–78
Oppen, Mary, 57–58, 176, 267
Oppens, 56–60
    friendships of, 176–77, 178
    and Linda, 174–75
    on Russian trials, 125–26
    and Timmy Humboldt, 118
Ornitz, Sam, 7

Pablo (Butlers' dog), 115, 182,
        243–44
Pepper, George, 33, 126–27, 221
    and "American Communist
        colony," 252
    death of, 266
    Fidel Ruíz with, 232
    and Hugo Butler, 210
    and Little League docudrama,
        152, 154–55
    and *The Loved One,* 211
    and pseudonym
        of George P. Werker, 54
    and *Robinson Crusoe,* 33, 40
    and *Torero!,* 78–79
    and *The Young One,* 236, 238
Pepper, Jeanette, 33, 182, 232, 266

Perry, George Sessions, 238
Pete (friend of Danny), 174
Polonsky, Abraham, 206
Preminger, Ingo, 61, 63, 85, 211
Preminger, Otto, 240
Procuna, Luis, 76–77, 145–47
Pruenza, Teresa, 159–60

Ramirez, Ignacio, 160
Ramona (housekeeper), 13–15, 34,
    43, 196, 249, 258, 264
  in Acapulco, 153–54
  cooking
      for Little League team,
        164–65
      for the musicians, 110–11
      for wedding lunch, 90
  death of, 264
  on Diego Rivera, 160, 162
  in Ensenada, 104–8
  in Guadalajara, 16, 27
  and Jean Rouverol, 52, 259–60
  passport for, 221–22
  son (Carlos) of, 222–23
Reinhardt, Max, 93–94
Renoir, Jean, 236, 238
Reuther, Walter, 191, 229
Revueltas, Rosaura, 208–9
Rinaldo, Fred, 8, 108, 253
Rinaldo, Marie, 108
Rivera, Diego, 41, 44, 150, 159–61
Robert Redford's Sundance Institute,
    205
Robertson, Cliff, 86
Robinson, David, 205
Robinson, Earl, 205
Robinson Crusoe, 7, 33, 192
  filming of, 54–55
  in post production, 61
  preparations for, 40, 47, 53
Rocha, Nancy. See Gast, Nancy
Roeder, Ralph, 185, 217
Roll, Philip Ansel, 61
Rooney, Mickey, 10, 242

Rosenbergs, 69–71
Rouverol, Bill, 167–68, 224
Rouverol, Jean, 2–4, 39, 82–83,
    131, 132, 136, 196, 202,
    265–66
  in Acapulco, 153–54
  and agent, 211–13
  children of, 51–52, 152–53, 163,
      180–81
  and Communist party, 23–25
  in Ensenada, 104
  father of, 166–68
  and hepatitis, 158–59
  and Hugo Butler
      introduced to, 21–22
      in Veracruz, 99–102
  in Italy, 257, 260–63
  leaving Hollywood, 11
  and Linda Oppen, 177–78
  Mañanitas for, 110–11
  in Mexico
      house in, 41
      leaving, 249, 258–60
      seeing HUAC witness in,
        61–62
      seeing Norman Foster in,
        29–30
  and The Miracle, 95–98, 108
  mother of, 10, 103, 166–67
      death of, 111–12
      health of, 95, 100, 109
  novella by
      made into movie (Autumn
        Leaves), 85–86
      from Margaret's childhood,
        125
  selling Shadows Under the
      Mexican Sun, 242
  on One Man's Family, 5, 135
  and pseudonym, 81–82
  and Rosenberg execution, 69–72
  So Young, So Bad by, 51, 63
  and Sterns, 253
  and Susie, 174–75, 233–34

at Trumbo ranch, 6
at Writers Guild of America
ceremony, 268
Ruíz, Fidel, 157, *191*, 200, 231–32
Rushkin, Shiman, 108

Salk vaccine, 113
Salt, Waldo, 2, 21–22, 23–24, 205,
242
Salt of the Earth, 208–10
Scott, Adrian, 7, 208
Scott, Zachary, *140*, 238
Seeger, Pete, 129
Sinatra, Frank, 241–42
Siqueiros, Angelica, 253
Siqueiros, David, 253
Small, Berthe ("Bert"), 116–17, 249,
258, 266
Small, Charles, 116–17, 266
"Smolny Institute," 206
The Southerner, 238
Stalin, Joseph, 127–28, 129–30
Stern, Alfred, 252–54, *254*
Stern, Bobby, 253
Stern, Martha Dodd, 252–54
Stevenson, Phil, 212
Stone, Lewis, 10

Tarloff, Frank, 206–7
Thomas, J. Parnell, 37
Torero!, 78–79, 81, 84, *193*
Townsend, Leo, 61–62
Traven, B., 117, 121
Trumbo, Chris, 56, *136*, *138*, 170,
195, 265–66
and Columbia, 172
in Mexico
traveling to, 26
return to America of, 91
with strep throat, 27
visiting Butler family, 144–45
Trumbo, Cleo, 6, *198*, 204, 266
in baseball games, 45

as photographer, 19, 25, 38–39,
136–37
return to America of, 91
visiting Butler family, 108
at Writers Guild of America
ceremony, 268
Trumbo, Dalton, 39, *137*, 204, 208,
240–41, 266
answering HUAC queries, 2
The Brave One by, 77–78, 204
as collector, 35–36, 91–92
credits restored to, 267–68
friends of, 36, 37–38, 75–76
in jail, 5, 7
in Mexico
decision to go to, 6–7
house hunting, 27
pawned items of, 64
Trumbo, Melissa (Mitzi), 18, 56,
137, *138*, 266
return to America of, 91
visiting Butler family, 144–45
Trumbo, Nikola, *138*, 176, *195*,
266
in Mexico
traveling to, 26
return to America of, 91
with strep throat, 17
Trumbos, *136*
at bullfights, 75–76
grandchildren of, 266
in Mexico
preparing for move to, 16
traveling to, 17–19, 25–29
return to America of, 88–92
sightseeing, 27–29, 35

Under the Volcano (Malcolm
Lowry), 48
Uribe, Ramona (housekeeper). *See*
Ramona (housekeeper)
Uris, Leon, 240
Uris, Mickey, 4

USSR
    anti-Semitism in, 125–28

van der Schelling, Bart, 87, 115–16,
    252
van der Schelling, Edna, 87, 252
Vorhaus, Bernard, 51, 207

Waldeen (dance instructor), 120–21
Walter (chairman of HUAC), 252
Weinstein, Hannah, 204
Wexley, John, 10–11

Wilson, Michael, 208
Writers Guild of America, 86,
    267–68

Yordan, Phil, 207
Young, Ned, 208
The Young One, 236–39

Zimmer, Julian (Julian Halevy),
    207
Zykofsky, Diana, 115, 144–45, 187,
    267